Practical Intelligence in Everyday Life

This path-breaking book reviews psychological research on practical intelligence and describes its importance in everyday life. The authors reveal the importance of tacit knowledge – what we have learned from our own experience through action. Although it has been seen as an indispensable element of expertise, intelligence researchers have found it difficult to quantify. Based on years of research, Dr. Sternberg and his colleagues have found that tacit knowledge can be quantified and can be taught.

The data show that practical intelligence is psychologically and statistically distinct from academic intelligence and is distinct as well from personality and styles of thought. The data also indicate that practical intelligence predicts job performance and even aspects of school performance as well as or better than does academic intelligence. This volume thoroughly examines studies of practical intelligence in the United States, as well as in many other parts of the world, and for varied occupations, such as management, military leadership, teaching, research, and sales.

Robert J. Sternberg is IBM Professor of Psychology and Education at Yale University.

George B. Forsythe is Professor and Vice Dean of Education at the United States Military Academy, West Point, New York.

Jennifer Hedlund is Associate Research Scientist in the Department of Psychology, Yale University.

Joseph A. Horvath is Senior Consultant at the IBM Institute for Knowledge Management.

Richard K. Wagner is Professsor of Psychology at Florida State University.

Wendy M. Williams is Associate Professor in the Department of Human Development, Cornell University.

Scott A. Snook is Academy Professor in the Department of Behavioral Sciences and Leadership, United States Military Academy.

Elena L. Grigorenko is Research Scientist at Yale University and Associate Professor in the Psychology Department, Moscow State University.

PRACTICAL INTELLIGENCE IN EVERYDAY LIFE

Robert J. Sternberg

George B. Forsythe

Jennifer Hedlund

Joseph A. Horvath

Richard K. Wagner

Wendy M. Williams

Scott A. Snook

Elena L. Grigorenko

CAMBRIDGE
UNIVERSITY PRESS

PUBLISHED BY THE PRESS SYNDICATE OF THE UNIVERSITY OF CAMBRIDGE
The Pitt Building, Trumpington Street, Cambridge, United Kingdom

CAMBRIDGE UNIVERSITY PRESS
The Edinburgh Building, Cambridge CB2 2RU, UK   http: //www.cup.cam.ac.uk
40 West 20th Street, New York, NY 10011-4211, USA   http: //www.cup.org
10 Stamford Road, Oakleigh, Melbourne 3166, Australia
Ruiz de Alarcón 13, 28014 Madrid, Spain

First published 2000

Printed in the United States of America

Typeface Palatino 10/13pt.   *System* QuarkXPress™   [HT]

A catalog record for this book is available from the British Library

Library of Congress Cataloging-in-Publication Data is available

ISBN 0 521 65056 9 hardback
ISBN 0 521 65958 2 paperback

This book is dedicated to the memory of
David C. McClelland, the modern-day father of
research on practical intelligence.

Contents

Preface

Practical intelligence is what most people call common sense. It is the ability to adapt to, shape, and select everyday environments. Intelligence as conventionally defined may be useful in everyday life, but practical intelligence is indispensable. Without some measure of it, one cannot survive in a cultural milieu or even in the natural environment. In our work, we have studied many aspects of practical intelligence, although we have concentrated on one particularly important aspect of it, *tacit knowledge,* namely the procedural knowledge one learns in everyday life that usually is not taught and often is not even verbalized. Tacit knowledge includes things like knowing what to say to whom, knowing when to say it, and knowing how to say it for maximum effect. In our work, we have studied tacit knowledge in populations as diverse as business managers, military leaders, university professors, elementary school teachers, janitors, secretaries, salespeople, and American and rural Kenyan children. But when most people think of intelligence, they think neither of tacit knowledge in particular nor of practical intelligence as a whole.

An enormous literature has emerged in the field of intelligence that is compatible with the notion that intelligence is a single entity, sometimes called g, or the general factor. Indeed, two books have been written recently, both with the same title of *The General Factor* (Brand, 1996; Jensen, 1998). The authors of these books review a multitude of studies that purport to demonstrate a general factor of intelligence. An earlier volume by Carroll (1993) did much the same.

We challenge this view in the present book. In particular, we argue that practical intelligence is a construct that is distinct from general intelligence and that general intelligence is not even general but rather applies largely, although not exclusively, to academic kinds of tasks. Moreover, practical intelligence is at least as good a predictor of future success as is the academic form of intelligence that is commonly assessed by tests of so-called general intelligence. Arguably, practical intelligence is a better predictor of success than is the academic form of intelligence. We believe that previous investigators have failed to find the importance of practical intelligence simply because they have never adequately measured it or, in most cases, made any attempt to measure it. By confining their efforts to a narrow band of tests, they failed to find a class of tests that would enhance not only their predictions but their theoretical models.

Of course, there are other theorists and researchers who have made claims similar to ours. We believe that our research program is unique in several regards, however.

First, we have gone beyond armchair theorizing actually to collect data testing our theories. Some theorists arguing against general ability have gone little beyond "just so stories," in the sense that they have not collected empirical data of their own that have been published in refereed scientific journals but rather have reviewed past data that are available and that can be interpreted in terms of their arguments. The problem is that their intellectual opponents in favor of g have an equal number of just-so stories to tell, plus empirical scientific data collected specifically to test their claims. In contrast, we have collected data testing our theories from many studies in many parts of the world with many different populations and have published most of these data (some are too recent to have been published) in refereed scientific journals.

Second, we have gone beyond demonstration studies that show that "context matters" but that provide little basis for the development of a rigorous program of measurement and research into the construct of practical intelligence. In our research we have constructed measures that we assess by the usual psychometric criteria, such as reliability, convergent validity, and discriminant validity, and show that our measures work by these customary criteria.

Third, we try to avoid contentious verbal arguments based on ideological position rather than scientific data. Opponents of g theory have a tendency to be dismissive of masses of data in support of g in much the same way that supporters of g have a tendency to be dismissive of data that tend to question g. We believe that the scientific evidence in favor of what is called the g factor is overwhelming but that this factor is not, in fact, general. Rather, it appears because of a restricted range of participants, tasks, and situations in which testing is conducted.

Practical Intelligence presents the data on practical intelligence collected during more than 15 years of research by the Sternberg Research Group and collaborative research groups around the world, as well as by other research groups with whom the Sternberg group has not collaborated. The studies presented herein were, for the most part, specifically designed to address the question of whether practical intelligence is psychologically distinct from academic intelligence. Our conclusion is that practical intelligence is indeed a distinct entity. We present a number of studies showing dissociations between academic and practical intelligence and even describe a study we have done (Sternberg et al., 1999) in which the correlations between a test of practical intelligence and tests of academic intelligence were significantly negative.

Our goal is not to denigrate the importance of academic intelligence. There is an overwhelming array of evidence of different types that academic intelligence, as conventionally defined, predicts a large number of criteria, both inside schools and outside them. Rather, our argument is that academic intelligence is not enough and that successful prediction and, more importantly, understanding of performance in the everyday world requires assessment of practical as well as academic intelligence.

Our book is written primarily for a scholarly audience but addresses concerns of anyone interested in practical intelligence. We believe our results will be of special interest to industrial and organizational, educational, cognitive, school, developmental, military, and social and personality psychologists. It should also be of interest to educators, anthropologists, managers, and military officers.

A book such as this one depends on the efforts of many people. Hedlund, Horvath, Wagner, Williams, and Grigorenko all are, or have been at one time or another, members of the Sternberg Research Group. Forsythe and Snook are members of a research group at the United States Military Academy at West Point, with whom the members of the Sternberg Research Group have collaborated successfully for roughly 7 years. Other members of the Sternberg research group who have worked on practical intelligence include Cynthia Berg, David Caruso, Alice Jackson, Lynn Okagaki, and Shih-ying Yang. Other members of the West Point team working on practical intelligence have included John Wattendorf, Jeff McNally (deceased), Pat Sweeney, and Craig

Bullis. Many others have collaborated with us as well, and they are cited in the book. The members of the Sternberg Research Group are especially grateful to Sai Durvasula, our administrator, and Melissa Droller for editorial assistance. We also thank Howard Gardner and his group at Harvard for their collaborations over 6 years on the Practical Intelligence for Schools studies. Although we have not collaborated with him directly, we thank Ulric Neisser, whose conceptualizations of academic and practical intelligence have provided much of the intellectual stimulation for our work. Finally, we are grateful to Julia Hough for contracting the project and shepherding it through the publication process.

Funding for our research on practical intelligence has been provided primarily by the U.S. Army Research Institute (ARI, Contract MDA903–92–K). Our contract monitors at ARI have included Judith Orasanu, Trueman Tremble, Rex Michel, and Joseph Psotka, all of whom have made valuable contributions to our work. Other organizations that have funded some of this work include the Office of Educational Research and Improvement, U.S. Office of Education (Grant N206R950001), with Patricia O'Connell-Ross as our scientific monitor; U.S. Office of Naval Research, with Marshall Farr and then Susan Chipman as our contract monitors; the Partnership for Child Development; the James S. McDonnell Foundation; the National Center for Educational Statistics; and Statistics Canada. The views presented in this book are our own, however, and no endorsement on the part of any of these funding agencies should be inferred.

CHAPTER 1

What Is Practical Intelligence?

To do well in any everyday endeavor, whether the endeavor pertains to school, work, or play, requires practical intelligence. Although intelligence as conventionally defined may be useful in everyday life, practical intelligence is indispensable. It is the ability to adapt to, shape, and select everyday environments. Practical intelligence, like most abilities, can be viewed as a form of developing expertise (Sternberg, 1998a). Individuals who have developed the knowledge, skills, and abilities needed to succeed in a particular domain generally are characterized as experts. Therefore, understanding expertise and how it develops provides a method of insight into practical intelligence.

So how do we come to characterize practical intelligence as a form of developing expertise? We begin with a distinction between viewing *entity /* abilities as relatively stable attributes and viewing them as developing *incremental* expertise.

CONCEPTIONS OF INTELLIGENCE

The conventional view of intelligence is that it is some relatively stable *entity* attribute of individuals, which develops as an interaction between heredity and environment (Sternberg & Grigorenko, 1997b). Conventional tests of intelligence and related abilities measure achievement that individuals should have mastered several years before (Anastasi & Urbina, 1997). Tests such as those of vocabulary, reading comprehension, verbal analogies, arithmetic problem solving, and the like are, in part, all tests of achievement. Even abstract reasoning tests measure achievement in dealing with geometric symbols, which are skills taught in Western schools (Laboratory of Comparative Human Cognition, 1982).

/ incremental

An alternative view is that of intelligence as *developing expertise* and intelligence tests as measuring an aspect, typically a limited aspect, of developing expertise (Sternberg, 1998a, in press-b). Developing expertise is defined here as the ongoing process of the acquisition and consolidation of a set of skills needed for a high level of mastery in one or more domains of life performance. We believe that the problem regarding the traditional model is not in its statement of a correlation between ability tests and other forms of achievement but in its proposal of a causal relation whereby the tests reflect a construct that is somehow causal of, rather than merely temporally antecedent to, later success. The developing expertise view in no way rules out the contribution of genetic factors as a source of individual differences in the ability to develop a given amount of expertise. Many human attributes, including intelligence, reflect the covariation and interaction of genetic and environmental factors. However, the contribution of genes to an individual's intelligence cannot be directly measured or even directly estimated; rather, what is measured is a portion of what is expressed, namely, manifestations of developing expertise.

According to this view, measures of intelligence should be correlated with later success, because both measures of intelligence and various measures of success require developing expertise of related types. For example, performance both on tests of intelligence and on indices of success typically require what Sternberg (1985a) has referred to as *metacomponents* of thinking: recognition of problems, definition of problems, formulation of strategies to solve problems, representation of information, allocation of resources, and monitoring and evaluation of problem solutions. These skills develop as results of gene–environment covariation and interaction. If we consider these skills to reflect intelligence, then we should recognize that what we are calling intelligence is a form of developing expertise.

The developing expertise point of view presented here integrates the study of intelligence and related abilities (Sternberg, 1990a, 1994a, in press-b) with the study of expertise (Chi, Glaser, & Farr, 1988; Ericsson, 1996; Ericsson & Smith, 1991; Hoffman, 1992). These studies, typically viewed as distinct, here are viewed as ultimately involved with the same psychological mechanisms. We review here briefly some of the perspectives and theories on expertise and its development. Then we discuss how the developing expertise view provides a framework for understanding the role of practical intelligence in everyday life.

CONCEPTIONS OF EXPERTISE

Researchers have conceptualized expertise in different ways (Sternberg, 1994a, 1995a). One conception is knowledge-based, defining an expert as someone who knows a lot about a given area of endeavor. It seems likely that knowledge is a necessary condition for expertise; no one would want to go to doctors, lawyers, or psychotherapists who lacked knowledge of their fields. Another conception is that expertise is not just the possession of knowledge, but the flexible application of the knowledge base.

The application of knowledge depends on analytical, creative, and practical skills (Sternberg, 1994a). Experts need to analyze problems that are presented to them. Doctors analyze reports of symptoms and themselves look for diagnostic signs of various illnesses. Musicians need to analyze the pieces they play in order to meet the technical requirements of these pieces. Most kinds of expertise also require the application of some kind of creative skill. Lawyers devise creative legal strategies to free their clients from legal jeopardy. Scientists create new theories and experiments to chart the unknown. Finally, expertise requires practical skills. The successful doctor needs patient skills, that is, ways to reach out to patients, comfort them, and reassure them that they are getting care in which they can have confidence. Lawyers need to convince their clients to tell them the truth so that they can adequately represent these clients. Scientists need to convince a frequently skeptical public, scientific or otherwise, that their ideas are not just some hare-brained concoction of fact and fiction but rather a good representation of scientific facts. Musicians and artists need to reach out to potential audiences so that these audiences will pay attention to their performances or art works.

Expertise may be viewed as an attribute not just of a person but of the way the person is perceived by other persons – as an interaction between a person and a situation. In this case, expertise can be seen as in part a labeling phenomenon whereby some group of people declares a person an expert (Sternberg, 1994a). Without that declaration, the person may have difficulty in exercising expertise. For example, an individual trained in medicine cannot practice without a license; an individual trained in the law cannot represent clients without having passed the bar. A scientist can engage in science without academic credentials but may have difficulty obtaining an academic job or research funding without those credentials. In chess, expertise is often recognized in terms of a person's numerical rating according to a system of evaluation of how well the person plays chess. Becoming labeled as an expert may require practical skills in the sense that others need to be convinced of one's expert status.

Theories of Expertise

Theories of expertise focus primarily on either the mental processes underlying performance or the knowledge resulting from those processes and its organization. These factors are studied in trying to distinguish individuals with more from those with less expertise. We shall now briefly characterize these theories, which have been reviewed by Ericsson and Smith (1991), Sternberg & Ben Zeev (in press), and Sternberg, Grigorenko, and Ferrari (in press).

THEORIES FOCUSING ON MENTAL PROCESSES. Some theories of expertise emphasize the role of planning, problem solving, and reasoning processes (Charness, 1981, 1991; Charness, Krampe, & Mayr, 1996). Other theories emphasize information processing (Lesgold et al., 1985; Patel & Groen, 1991; Sternberg, 1985b). Sternberg identified metacomponential processes, such as planning, monitoring, and evaluating one's problem solving and decision making, as distinguishing experts from novices. Experts and novices represent information differently, and experts engage in more sophisticated strategies and performance monitoring than do novices.

Experts also spend relatively more time than do novices in *global planning*, or strategic planning for solving a problem as a whole. Novices, in contrast, are more likely to begin problem solution relatively quickly but with the result that later on during problem solving they are more likely to have to restart their work. The dividends of more time spent in global planning are later paid in less time that needs to be devoted to *local planning*, the tactical planning that needs to be done as one proceeds through the steps of problem solving. In the long run, local planning likely will drain more time from the problem solving process when global planning was incomplete or inadequate (Sternberg, 1981).

Because experts can recognize the deep structure of the problem they are able to solve problems by working forward, whereas novices are much more likely to solve problems working backward. In other words, experts look at the terms of the problem and then proceed forward from the problem statement to a conclusion. Novices are more likely to start with the known or intended solution and then to work backward to try to figure out how they could get to the terms of the problem, given where they are trying to go.

The persistent difference in representation of problems (Chi et al., 1988) is crucial for understanding an important aspect of the difference between experts and novices. Although the apparent problem being solved by the expert and the novice is the same, the psychological problem being solved, or at least the representation of it, is different. The problem that an expert physicist sees as being about a principle of physics might be seen by a novice physicist as being about a mechanical device. The problem a layperson might see as being about a person's mood swings might be seen by a psychiatrist as being about a manic–depressive personality. The differences in representation show how difficult it is to separate knowledge from information processing; the representations that experts construct typically would not be possible without very extensive and well organized knowledge bases.

THEORIES FOCUSING ON KNOWLEDGE. Theories focusing on the role of the knowledge base and its organization often stress the role of stored information in long-term memory as a key to understanding expertise. These theories generally have their origins in the work of de Groot (1978) and of Chase and Simon (1973).

De Groot (1978) asked chess players of differing levels of expertise to think aloud while they contemplated the next moves they would make from several different presented chess positions. In most cases, grand masters and chess experts not at the grand master level evaluated moves similarly. There was no difference in the number of moves considered by the groups of differing levels of expertise, but grand masters arrived at the best move earlier in their consideration of moves than did the more typical experts. De Groot concluded that the grand masters rely on a more extensive knowledge base than do the more typical chess experts. They recognized the presented position as similar or identical to one they had seen before and hence were able to zero in rapidly on the optimal move. Knowledge acquired through experience rather than any special kind of information processing seemed to be what distinguished the chess grand master from the other experts.

Chase and Simon (1973) suggested that the grand masters simply may have better memories than do the more common experts. They tested this hypothesis by presenting grand masters and experts with chess configurations for 5 sec and then asking the two groups to recall them. They included both configurations of pieces from real games and random configurations of pieces. If the grand masters simply had better memories for pieces than the experts, their recall should have been better for all chess board configurations, regardless of whether they were real or not. However, the level of chess expertise influenced recall only of sensible (real game) configurations of chess pieces; it had no influence on recall for random chess positions. In other words, what distinguished the experts from the novices and the grand masters from the experts was not overall superior recall abilities but rather the extent and organization of their knowledge base.

Chase and Simon (1973) found also that the more expert players were able to use their knowledge base to retrieve large amounts of information in each recall of chess pieces. Simon and Gilmartin (1973) confirmed via computer simulation that chess experts draw on huge knowledge bases unavailable to novices in doing the chess-related tasks. These knowledge bases may be organized into *problem schemas,* or organized bodies of knowledge on which people can draw to help them represent and then solve a problem.

The same basic finding regarding the role of the knowledge base has been replicated in a number of other domains, such as the game of Go (Reitman, 1976), electronic circuit diagrams (Egan & Schwartz, 1979), and bridge (Charness, 1979; Engle & Bukstel, 1978). Thus, a vast and organized knowledge base and the problem schemas that come with it seem to be of fundamental importance to many different kinds of expertise. Such schemas and the information within them are not rapidly acquired. Simon and Chase (1973) estimated that it would take about 3,000 hours of play to become a chess expert and 30,000 hours to become a chess master. But how does the acquisition of expertise take place?

The Acquisition of Expertise

A number of theories have been proposed of how people may become experts, whether in music, athletics, art, or whatever (Anderson, 1987, 1993; Newell, 1990; Sternberg & Ben Zeev, in press). We consider two primary approaches to understanding the acquisition of expertise. One approach addresses the stages involved in acquiring expertise, and the other considers the contributing factors in developing expertise.

THE ACT* THEORY OF SKILL ACQUISITION. Anderson's theory, which is embedded within his ACT* theory of cognition, represents a stage model. (ACT stands for "A Cognitive Theory.") According to Anderson

(1987, 1993), skill acquisition proceeds through three main stages, which represent successive levels in the development of expertise.

In the first stage, the kind of situation that evokes the skill and the method for solving problems in that situation are encoded as declarative knowledge. Usually, this declarative knowledge derives from explicit instruction, which may include an abstract presentation of the type of problem situation and how to solve it as well as examples of problem solving in action. In this stage of development, problem solving is relatively slow and deliberate. The more a given problem departs from the exact way in which its solution was taught, the harder is the problem, to the point that even minor levels of transfer may fail to occur.

In the second stage, knowledge comes to be represented procedurally, in the form of *productions,* or condition–action statements, that can be used in the performance of a task. For example, one such production might be, "If you see a dot over a note, play that note in staccato (short and punctuated) fashion."

In the third stage, the productions are combined into successively more elaborated production systems, or sequences of condition–action statements that can be used to execute a complex series of task requirements. Now, performance of the task becomes more highly automated and requires less conscious effort on the part of the individual doing the task.

Although these stages may characterize the development of expertise, there are individual differences in terms of the progression through the stages. In other words, some individuals are more likely to acquire expert skill level than others. We next consider the factors that contribute to this distinction.

THE ROLE OF DELIBERATE PRACTICE AND INNATE ABILITIES. Opinions differ regarding whether expertise is a function of deliberate practice, innate abilities, or some combination of the two. We consider two views, one emphasizing the role of deliberate practice and the other emphasizing the joint roles of deliberate practice and talent.

One view of the development of expertise is that it requires deliberate practice. Deliberate practice is not just any old practice, but rather practice in which the task is at an appropriate level of difficulty for the individual, it provides informative feedback to the individual, it provides opportunities for repetition, and it allows correction of errors (Ericsson, 1996).

Ericsson (1996) argues that deliberate practice is not just a necessary condition for the development of expertise but a sufficient condition as well. In other words, engaging in sufficient deliberate practice will, under normal conditions, produce an expert. Ericsson and his colleagues (Chase & Ericsson, 1982; Ericsson, Krampe, & Tesch-Römer, 1993) have pointed to studies with musicians and students to support their claim. They found, for example, that top violinists spend more hours in deliberate practice than do their less expert cohorts. Chase and Ericsson (1982) showed that individuals can develop exceptional memory through extensive training.

Many theorists believe that talent, or innate ability, plays an important role in the development of expertise, not just deliberate practice (Bloom, 1985; Shiffrin, 1996; Simonton, 1996; Sternberg, 1996; Winner, 1996a, 1996b). They argue that although deliberate practice is likely to be a necessary condition for the development of expertise, it is not likely to be a sufficient one.

First, behavior–genetic studies show a role for genetic factors in interaction with environmental ones in the development of various kinds of expertise (Plomin & McClearn, 1993). Many different types of abilities seem to have at least some heritable component as a source of individual differences, and the kinds of expertise studied by psychologists seem to be no exception.

Second, advocates of the talent plus practice position argue that the deliberate practice view is just not plausible. Is one to believe that anyone could become a Mozart only by putting in the time? Or that anyone could reach the level of skill shown by Michael Jordan in basketball just by working hard enough at it? Although this argument is one of plausibility rather than data, on its face it is not a simple matter to refute. Many people have tried to reach the exceptional levels of accomplishment shown by the top people in a given field and most have given up in disappointment.

Third, the advocates of the mixed position argue that the demonstrations of deliberate practice lack control groups or contain inadequate ones. They speculate that other people who do not become experts may put in the same hours of deliberate practice as the experts, but because these nonexperts disappear from view, they may never make it into studies of expertise.

Fourth, the advocates of the mixed position argue that deliberate practice is itself a confounded measure, representing talent as well as practice. How could deliberate practice be a function of talent? The idea (Sternberg, 1996; Winner, 1996b) is that only those with high levels of talent continue to put in the deliberate practice it takes to reach high levels of expertise. Their talent motivates them to try harder and thus rack up more hours of deliberate practice. Consider music lessons, for example. Many millions of children over the years take music lessons, but many of those quit. Why? Perhaps because they discover that they lack the talent to become professional or even skilled musicians. So they never put in many hours of practice over the course of their lifetime. The result is that the correlation between deliberate practice and expertise may in part be affected by levels of talent.

Having considered some of the different views of expertise and how it is acquired, we now discuss a view of intelligence and in particular, practical intelligence, as a form of developing expertise.

PRACTICAL INTELLIGENCE AS A FORM OF DEVELOPING EXPERTISE

Some intelligence theorists point to the stability of the alleged general factor of human intelligence as evidence for the existence of some kind of stable and overriding structure of human intelligence. But the existence of a g factor may reflect little more than an interaction between whatever latent (and not directly measurable) abilities individuals may have and the kinds of expertise that are developed in school. With different forms of schooling, g could be made either stronger or weaker. In effect, Western and related forms of schooling may, in part, create the g phenomenon by providing a kind of schooling that teaches in conjunction the various kinds of skills measured by tests of intellectual abilities.

Thus, conventional tests may unduly favor a small segment of the population by virtue of the narrow kind of developing expertise they measure. When one measures a broader range of developing expertise, the results look quite different. Moreover, the broader range of expertise includes kinds of skills that will be important in the world of work and in the world of the family.

Analytical, creative, and practical abilities, as measured by our tests or anyone else's, can be viewed as forms of developing expertise (Sternberg, 1998a). All are useful in various kinds of life tasks. However, conventional tests may unfairly disadvantage those students who do not do well in a fairly narrow range of kinds of expertise. By expanding the range of developing expertise that we measure, we discover that many children not now identified as able have, in fact, developed important kinds of expertise. The abilities that conventional tests measure are important for school and life performance, but they are not the only abilities that are important.

We have conducted studies in which we have measured informal, procedural knowledge in children and adults. We have found in studies with business managers, college professors, elementary school students, salespeople, college students, and general populations that this important aspect of practical intelligence is generally uncorrelated with academic intelligence as measured by conventional tests (Sternberg, Wagner, Williams, & Horvath, 1995). Moreover, the tests predict performance as well as or better than do tests of intelligence quotients. The lack of correlation between the two kinds of ability tests suggests that the best prediction of job performance will result when both academic and practical intelligence tests are used as predictors. Most recently, we have developed a test of common sense for the workplace (e.g., how to handle oneself in a job interview) that predicts self-ratings of common sense but not self-ratings of various kinds of academic abilities.

Both conventional academic tests and our tests of practical intelligence measure forms of developing expertise that matter in school and on the job. The reason the correlations are often null is that the kinds of developing expertise they measure are quite different. The people who are good at abstract, academic kinds of expertise are often people who have not emphasized learning practical, everyday kinds of expertise, and vice versa.

In this volume, we address the practical kind of expertise that contributes to successful performance in school, work, and any life endeavor. In the first half of the book, we consider the diverse views on intelligence and the increasing recognition in both research and practice that practical abilities are important to success. In the second half of the book, we describe a program of research that seeks to understand practical intelligence from the perspective of the knowledge acquired and used by experts (i.e., successful individuals) in a given domain.

CHAPTER 2

The Nature of Intelligence

Intelligence generally is defined as the ability to adapt flexibly and effectively to the environment (Sternberg, in press-a; Sternberg & Detterman, 1986). Although theorists of intelligence might disagree as to the exact details of this definition, most would accept the general idea that intelligence serves the purpose of adaptation. The origins of the contemporary study of intelligence were largely based in school settings (e.g., Binet & Simon, 1905; Spearman, 1904). The field has stayed, for the most part, school-based. Our goal, however, is to understand intelligence as it relates to performing everyday, real world tasks. We begin by reviewing various theories of and approaches to studying intelligence (Sternberg, 1990a, 1994b).

HISTORY OF INTELLIGENCE TESTING

Certainly one of the most influential books of all time has been Charles Darwin's (1859) *Origin of Species*. In it, Darwin proposed that the evolution of species and the development of humans could be traced to an evolutionary process of natural selection. The book profoundly affected many different kinds of scientific endeavors, one of which was the investigation of human intelligence and how it develops. Darwin suggested that the capabilities of humans were in some sense continuous with those of lower animals.

Darwin's cousin Sir Francis Galton was probably the first to explore the implications of Darwin's book for the study of human intelligence. Galton (1883) suggested that two general qualities distinguish people who are more intelligent from those who are less so. The first is energy, or the capacity for labor. Galton suggested that intellectually able people in a variety of fields are characterized by remarkable levels of energy. The second quality is sensitivity. According to Galton, the smarter we are, the more sensitive we are to the stimuli around us.

For seven years, between 1884 and 1890, Galton ran a service at the South Kensington Museum in London where, for a small fee, people could have their intelligence tested. The tests consisted of a hodge-podge of measures, such as a whistle to measure the highest pitch a person could perceive and a gun cartridge filled with different materials to determine if the person could detect different weights. Most of us would question the idea that our ability to detect high-pitched sounds or varying weights is an indicator of our intelligence. At the time, however, people took these tests seriously, including a psychologist named James McKeen Cattell, who brought Galton's ideas to the United States. Cattell (1890) devised a similar test that included squeezing an instrument and inflicting pressure until the person experienced pain. A student of Cattell's, Wissler (1901), found that scores on this test were unrelated to each other and to college grades, which raised questions about the validity of intelligence tests of the Galton and Cattell variety.

From an evolutionary perspective, Galton's ideas made sense. At one time, animals and humans with acute sensory abilities likely had a selective advantage over those who did not, but in our time, sensory acuity is no longer a major factor leading either to human reproductive advantage or to survival in general. The tests that followed approached intelligence from a different perspective.

In 1904, the minister of public instruction in Paris created a commission to find a way to distinguish truly mentally "defective" children from those who were not succeeding in school for other reasons. The goal of the commission was to ensure that children would be placed in classes for the mentally retarded only if they were "unable to profit, in an average measure, from the instruction given in the ordinary schools." Alfred Binet and his colleague Theodore Simon devised tests to meet this placement need.

Binet and Simon's (1916) concept of intelligence and of how to measure it differed quite a bit from Galton's and Cattell's. Referring to the others' tests as "wasted time," Binet and Simon spoke of the core of intelligence as "judgment, otherwise called good sense, practical sense, initiative, the faculty of adapting one's self to circumstances. To judge well, to comprehend well, to reason well, these are the essential activities of intelligence."

Most people recognize Binet only for his test, but he also had a theory of intelligence. He suggested that intelligent thought has three distinct elements, which he called direction, adaptation, and criticism. Direction involves knowing what has to be done and how to do it. Adaptation refers to customizing a strategy for performing a task and then keeping track of that strategy and adapting while implementing it. Criticism is the ability to critique your own thoughts and actions.

Binet's ideas, like Galton's, were imported to the United States. Lewis Terman, a professor of psychology at Stanford University, created an Americanized test based on Binet's theory and tests (Terman, 1916). The most recent version of the Stanford-Binet test is still a leading competitor in the intelligence testing business (Thorndike, Hagen, & Sattler, 1986). The Stanford-Binet Intelligence Scale, Fourth Edition (SB IV), is only the most recent in a series of scales that dates back to 1905. The first revision (i.e., the second edition) of the Stanford-Binet appeared in 1937 (Terman & Merrill, 1937) and a third edition in 1960 (Terman & Merrill, 1960). The test can be given to children as young as 2 years and to individuals up to any age, although the actual standardization of the test was conducted only on people up to 23 years of age. There are 15 subtests in all, only 6 of which are given throughout the entire age range of the test. The subtests break down into four categories: verbal reasoning, quantitative reasoning, figural and abstract reasoning, and short-term memory.

The Wechsler scales represent an alternative to the Stanford-Binet and are the most widely used intelligence scales. They are based on the same kinds of notions about intelligence as the Stanford-Binet. There are three levels of the Wechsler: the third edition of the Wechsler Adult Intelligence Scale – III (WAIS-III) (Wechsler, 1997), the third edition of the Wechsler Intelligence Scale for Children (WISC-III) (Wechsler, 1991), and the second edition of the Wechsler Preschool and Primary Scale of Intelligence (WPPSI-R) (Wechsler, 1989).

The Wechsler tests yield three main scores: a verbal, a performance, and an overall score. The verbal score is based on tests such as vocabulary and verbal similarities, in which the test taker has to say how two things are similar. The performance score is based on tests such as picture completion, which requires identification of a missing part in a picture of an object, and picture arrangement, which requires rearrangement of a scrambled set of cartoonlike pictures into an order that tells a coherent story. The overall score combines the verbal and the performance scores.

The movement in intelligence testing over the past few decades has been toward more theory-based approaches. Several tests have been developed based on the theory of *fluid* and *crystallized* intelligence (Cattell, 1971; Horn, 1994). Fluid intelligence is involved in flexible thinking and the ability to solve novel problems. Crystallized intelligence represents accumulated knowledge. Tests designed specifically to assess fluid and crystallized intelligence include the Kaufman Adolescent and Adult Intelligence Test (KAIT) (Kaufman & Kaufman, 1993) and the Woodcock-Johnson Tests of Cognitive Ability–Revised (Woodcock & Johnson, 1989). Another theory-based test is the Das-Naglieri Cognitive Assessment System (Das & Naglieri, 1997). This test is based on the theory of Luria (1973, 1976), discussed in the section on biological theories, according to which the brain comprises three units: a unit of arousal, a sensory-input unit, and an organization and planning unit. The Das-Naglieri test yields scores on attention, planning, simultaneous processing, and successive processing.

Another direction in intelligence testing is the increased attention to typical rather than maximal performance and dynamic assessment. Traditional tests of intelligence emphasize maximal performance, that is, exerting extensive intellectual effort to maximize one's score. Typical-performance tests (Ackerman, 1994; Ackerman & Heggestad, 1997) are intended to supplement traditional intelligence tests by measuring interest and preference for intellectual activities, in other words, the level of intellectual effort that is more typical of one's performance in everyday tasks. These tests have the advantage of reducing stress and of measuring intelligence in the kind of situation in which it typically is displayed. At the same time, the validity of such tests with respect both to other tests and to external criteria remains to be shown. To date, correlations with other measures have been modest.

Finally, dynamic testing is an approach that assesses one's potential ability. The idea of dynamic testing originated with Vygotsky (1978) and was developed by Feuerstein (1979) and Feuerstein, Rand, Haywood, Hoffman, and Jensen (1985). It is based on the notion that there is a difference between one's latent capacity and actually developed ability, which Vygotsky refers to as the zone of proximal development. Dynamic tests attempt to measure this zone by assessing learning at the time of the test. There are potential limitations in terms of standardizing and validating dynamic tests, which raise questions as to the tests' general applicability to intelligence testing (Grigorenko & Sternberg, 1998). Measurement operations are also difficult in terms of defining a score that precisely captures the notion of the zone of proximal development. Yet we have found in our own work that dynamic tests can provide incremental prediction of school and other performances over and above what is provided by static tests (Grigorenko, Sternberg, & Ehrman, 1999; Sternberg et al., 1999). We thus believe these tests have great potential, but that this potential has yet to be fully realized.

Although there have been changes in the way intelligence is tested, many questions remain as to what conventional intelligence tests actually measure (Sternberg, 1990a). There is also some question as to what the companies that produce most of the tests are interested in finding out (Sternberg & Kaufman, 1996). Tests are used in numerous settings (e.g., schools, the military, corporations) and for a variety of purposes (e.g., placement, selection). Given the reliance by some societies on intelligence tests and their relatives, it is important to consider the various ways in which intelligence is defined, both by laypersons and scientists. We now review the various theories of intelligence that are recognized today.

THEORIES OF INTELLIGENCE

Intelligence theorists do not agree about much, and strangely enough, they probably agree least as to what intelligence is, beyond the ability to adapt flexibly to the environment. We consider here some of the alternative views, based on the framework of Sternberg (1990a) and Sternberg and Kaufman (1998).

Implicit Theories

In implicit theorizing about intelligence, one asks people what they believe intelligence to be in order to discover an "ordinary-language" definition. This approach was suggested by Neisser (1979) and was implemented by Sternberg, Conway, Ketron, and Bernstein (1981) and Sternberg (1985b). Sternberg et al. (1981) asked samples of laypeople in a supermarket, a library, and a train station, as well as samples of academic researchers who study intelligence, to provide and rate the importance and frequency of characteristics of intelligent individuals. Factor analyses of the frequency ratings showed three major aspects of people's conceptions of intelligence: the ability to solve practical problems (e.g., balancing a checkbook), verbal ability (e.g., writing and speaking well), and social competence (e.g., getting along with other people).

There are limitations, however, with this ordinary-language view of intelligence. One is with respect to age. Siegler and Richards (1982) asked adults to characterize intelligence as it applies to people of different ages. They found that adults tended to view intelligence as increasingly less perceptual–motor and as increasingly more cognitive with increasing age. Thus, coordination of hand and eye was seen as more important to the intelligence of an infant, whereas reasoning ability was more important to the intelligence of an adult. When children are asked to characterize intelligence, their answers differ from those of adults. Yussen and Kane (1985) asked children at roughly 6–7, 8–9, and 11–12 years of age what their conceptions of intelligence are. They found that older children's conceptions of intelligence included more aspects than younger children's and that older children were less likely than younger children to think that certain kinds of overt behavior signal intelligence.

Another limitation of implicit theories of intelligence is related to culture. Different cultures perceive intelligence in different ways, and a view held in one culture may be diametrically opposed to that held in another culture. Western notions of intelligence, for example, differ in many ways from those of other cultures. In contrast to Sternberg et al.'s (1981) findings, Yang and Sternberg (1997) found that Taiwanese Chinese conceptions of intelligence included five factors: a general cognitive factor, interpersonal intelligence, intrapersonal intelligence, intellectual self-assertion, and intellectual self-effacement. Chen (1994) found three factors underlying Chinese concepts of intelligence: nonverbal reasoning ability, verbal reasoning ability, and rote memory. Chen's methodology was different from and perhaps less sensitive than Yang and Sternberg's, which may account for the difference in results. In addition, Gill and Keats (1980) noted differences between Australian university students, who viewed academic skills and the ability to adapt to new events as intelligence, and Malay students, who considered practical skills, speed, and creativity to be indicators of intelligence.

Studies conducted in Africa also provide a useful contrast to Western societies. Serpell (1982) found that Chewa adults in Zambia emphasize social responsibility, cooperativeness, and obedience. Kenyan parents view responsible participation in family and social life as important aspects of intelligence (Super & Harkness, 1982). In Zimbabwe, the word for intelligence, *ngware*, means to be prudent and cautious (Dasen, 1984). The emphasis on social aspects of intelligence seems to be a part of both Asian and African cultures, to a much greater extent than in the conventional Western view, although there is variability in conceptions of intelligence within the latter (Okagaki & Sternberg, 1993).

Although there is greater emphasis in African and Asian cultures on social aspects of intelligence than in the United States, these cultures still recognize the importance of cognitive aspects. In a rural village in Kenya, Sternberg and Grigorenko (1997a), working with Wenzel Geissler from the Bilharziasis Laboratory of Copenhagen, Catherine Nokes, Donald Bundy, and Ruth Prince from Oxford, and Frederick Okatcha from Kenyatta University in Nairobi, found that children who learned how to apply natural herbal medicines to their various ailments were viewed as more adaptive and intelligent than those who have not acquired this knowledge (Sternberg, Nokes et al., in press). Moreover, their knowledge of these natural herbal medicines was negatively correlated both with school achievement in English and with scores on conventional tests of crystallized abilities, which suggests that those who display higher levels of intelligence relevant to a particular contextualized situation actually may do worse on standardized measures of intelligence. The authors suggested that the reason for the negative correlations lay in the lack of value placed on school-based skills by many children and their parents in rural Kenya. Virtually all of the children drop out of school and do not finish high school. From an economic point of view, their best course is to learn a trade. Learning school-based material is not particularly helpful to their future economic position or status. Thus, children who spend a great deal of time on school-based learning may be viewed as rather foolish because they are taking away from the time they might be using to learn a trade and become economically self-sufficient. These results suggest that scores on ability or achievement tests always have to be understood in the cultural context in which they are obtained.

The research also suggested that the villagers in rural Kenya have variegated conceptions of intelligence (Grigorenko et al., in press). Four different terms could be viewed as pertaining to intelligence. One of these terms, *rieko*, has a meaning that is very similar to the Western view of intelligence, but the other three terms are quite different. Moreover, parents and their children seem more to value *luoro*, a kind of social-practical intelligence, than they do *rieko*, at least as it pertains to school.

Whether or not intelligence actually is the same across and even within cultures, it is certainly not perceived as the same (Berry, 1984).

Most theorists of abilities, however, have argued that whatever the differences may be across cultures, there are at least some aspects of intelligence that are the same. For reviews of some of these issues, see Laboratory of Comparative Human Cognition (1982) or Sternberg and Kaufman (1998). We consider next some of the major explicit theories of intelligence.

Explicit Theories

Explicit theories of intelligence are those proposed by psychologists or other scientists and tested by comparing the theories' predictions with data collected from human participants. Explicit theories involve various approaches to studying intelligence. We organize these approaches into psychometric, cognitive, biological, contextual or cultural, and systems theories.

PSYCHOMETRIC. One of the earliest views of intelligence, going back to the beginning of the century, is that intelligence can be understood in terms of hypothetical mental entities called *factors*. These factors are alleged to be the sources of the individual differences we observe in people's performance in school, on the job, and even in their social interactions. Psychometric theories are so called because they are based on the measurement (-metric) of psychological (psycho-) properties. Usually, such theories are tested by the measurement of individual differences in people's psychological functioning. The individual-differences approach has people perform a large number of tasks that seem to predict intelligent performance (in school or on the job), including recognizing meanings of words, seeing verbal or figural analogies, classifying which of several words does not belong, solving simple arithmetic problems, completing series of numbers, or visualizing spatial relationships between abstract forms. The psychologist uses data from these and similar tasks to analyze patterns of individual differences in task performance. These data are analyzed by factor analysis in order to identify the basic underlying factors of human intelligence.

The earliest factorial theory of the nature of human intelligence was formulated by Spearman (1904), who also invented factor analysis. His theory is called the two-factor theory. Spearman (1927) suggested that intelligence comprises two kinds of factors, a general factor and specific factors. General ability, or g, is required for performance on mental tests of all kinds. Each specific ability, as measured by each specific factor, is required for performance on just one kind of mental test.

Thus, there are as many specific factors as there are tests but only a single general factor (Jensen, 1998). Spearman suggested that the ability underlying the general factor could best be understood as a kind of mental energy.

Thomson (1939) suggested an alternative interpretation. He disputed Spearman's claim that the general factor represented a single underlying source of individual differences. Instead, he proposed that the appearance of a general factor was due to the working of a multitude of mental bonds, including reflexes, learned associations between stimuli, and the like. Performance of any particular task activates large numbers of these bonds. Some bonds will be required for the performance of virtually any task requiring mental effort, and these bonds in combination will give rise to the appearance of a general factor.

Thurstone (1938), like Thomson, accepted Spearman's hypothesis of a general factor, but he disputed its value. He argued that it is a second-order factor or phenomenon, one of little importance. What are really important are factors that Thurstone called primary mental abilities. Thurstone suggested that these abilities include verbal comprehension, measured by tests such as knowledge of vocabulary; word fluency, measured by tests requiring rapid word production (e.g., a listing of as many words as possible with c as their third letter); number skill, measured by tests of arithmetic reasoning and computation; spatial visualization, measured by tests requiring mental manipulation of geometric forms; perceptual speed, measured by tests requiring rapid visual scanning (e.g., skimming a page looking only for instances of the letter a); memory, measured by tests of recall and recognition of previously presented information; and reasoning, measured by tests such as completing a number series.

Guilford (1967) parted company from the majority of factorial theorists by refusing to acknowledge the existence of any general factor at all. Instead, he proposed that intelligence comprises 120 elementary abilities, a number that he later increased to 150 (Guilford, 1982), each of which involves the action of a mental operation on some sort of content (e.g., figural, symbolic, verbal) to produce an intellectual product. An example of an ability in Guilford's structure-of-intellect model is cognition of verbal relations. This ability involves recognition (mental operation) of a conceptual connection, that is, a relation (product) between two words (verbal content)—for example, recognition that a peach is a kind of fruit.

Probably the most widely accepted factorial description of intelligence is a hierarchical one. A good example of this class of description was proposed by Vernon (1971), who suggested that intelligence can be described as comprising abilities at varying levels of generality. At the top of the hierarchy is general ability as identified by Spearman. At the second level are major group factors, such as verbal-educational ability, needed for successful performance in courses such as English or history, and practical-mechanical ability, needed for successful performance in courses such as craftsmanship and car mechanics. At the next level are minor group factors, which are obtained by subdividing the major group factors, and at the bottom of the hierarchy are the specific factors as proposed by Spearman. This description of intelligence may be viewed as filling the gaps between the two extreme kinds of factors proposed by Spearman. Between the general and specific factors are group factors of intermediate levels of generality.

Other well-known hierarchical models have been proposed by Gustafsson (1988), Horn (1994), and Carroll (1993). For example, Carroll proposed his hierarchical model of intelligence, based on the factor analysis of more than 460 data sets obtained between 1927 and 1987. His analysis encompasses more than 130,000 people from diverse walks of life and even different countries of origin (although non-English-speaking countries are poorly represented among his data sets). The model Carroll proposed, based on his monumental undertaking, is a hierarchy comprising three strata: Stratum I, which includes many narrow, specific abilities (e.g., spelling ability, speed of reasoning); Stratum II, which includes various group-factor abilities (e.g., fluid intelligence, involved in flexible thinking and seeing things in novel ways, and crystallized intelligence, the accumulated knowledge base); and Stratum III, which is a single general intelligence, much like Spearman's (1904) general intelligence factor. Of these strata, the most interesting is perhaps the middle stratum, which includes, in addition to fluid and crystallized abilities, learning and memory processes, visual perception, auditory perception, facile production of ideas (similar to verbal fluency), and speed (which includes both sheer speed of response and speed of accurate responding).

BIOLOGICAL. Whereas the psychometric approach seeks to identify the ways in which individuals differ in terms of various mental abilities, the biological approach seeks to understand the internal locus of abilities, whether in terms of current functioning (the brain and central nervous system) or of the transmission of functioning (the genes). Various biological theories of intelligence have been proposed.

Earlier biological theories of intelligence tended to be global in nature. One of the most influential of these theories was that of Hebb (1949), who distinguished between two basic types of intelligence, intelligence A and intelligence B. Intelligence A is innate potential, is biologically determined, and represents the capacity for development. Hebb described it as "the possession of a good brain and a good neural metabolism." Intelligence B is the functioning of a brain in which development has occurred. It represents an average level of performance by a person who has matured. Although some inference is necessary in determining either intelligence, Hebb suggested that inferences about intelligence A are far less direct than inferences about intelligence B. Hebb argued that most disagreements about intelligence are over intelligence A, or innate potential, rather than over intelligence B, which is the estimated mature level of functioning. Hebb also distinguished an intelligence C, which is the score one obtains on an intelligence test. It is the basis for inferring either of the other intelligences.

Hebb's main interest was in intelligence A, and his theory, the neuropsychological theory of the organization of behavior, can be seen in large part as an attempt to understand what intelligence A is. The core of Hebb's theory is the concept of the cell assembly. Hebb proposed that repeated stimulation of specific receptors slowly leads to the formation of an assembly of cells in the brain. More intelligent people have more elaborate sequences of cell assemblies.

Another biologically based theory that has had an influence on intelligence research and testing is that of Luria (1980). Luria suggested that the brain is a highly differentiated system whose parts are responsible for different aspects of a unified whole. In other words, separate cortical regions act together to produce thought and action of various kinds. Luria suggested that the brain comprises three main units. The first unit consists of the brainstem and midbrain structures and is responsible for arousal. The second unit of the brain is responsible for sensory input functions. The third unit includes the frontal cortex and is involved in organization and planning.

Some biological theories focus on the relation between hemispheric specialization and intelligence. Theories of hemispheric specialization can be traced back to a country doctor in France, Marc Dax, who in 1836 noted a connection between loss of speech, now known as aphasia, and damage to the left hemisphere of the brain. His claim was expanded upon by Broca (1861).

This finding by Dax has been followed up by many researchers, most notably Sperry (1961). Sperry argued that each hemisphere of the brain behaves in many respects like a separate brain. He concluded from his research that visual and spatial functions are primarily localized in the right hemisphere, whereas linguistic functions are primarily localized in the left hemisphere. However, there is some debate as to whether language is completely localized in the left hemisphere (Farah, 1988; Gazzaniga, 1985). Levy (1974) further applied Sperry's theory to information processing, suggesting that the left hemisphere tends to process stimuli analytically, whereas the right tends to process it holistically. Continuing with this line of reasoning, Bogen (1975) suggested that the difference in processing of stimuli in the two hemispheres can be characterized in terms of what he refers to as *propositional* versus *appositional* information processing. Propositional applies to speaking, writing, and other verbal activities that are dominated by the left hemisphere, whereas appositional emphasizes the figural, spatial, nonverbal processing of the right hemisphere. The right hemisphere, in his view, understands patterns and relationships that are not susceptible to propositional analysis and that may not even be logical.

Gazzaniga (1985) has taken a different position and argues that the right hemisphere of the brain is organized modularly into relatively independent functioning units that work in parallel. Many of these modules operate at a level that is not even conscious but that parallels our conscious thought and contributes to conscious processing. The left hemisphere tries to assign interpretations to the processing of these modules. Thus, the left hemisphere may perceive the individual operating in a way that does not make any particular sense or that is not particularly understandable. In other words, our thoughts are relatively distinct from our understanding of them.

Some biological theorists have pursued the notion that intelligent people act and think faster than less intelligent people. They attribute this difference to the speed of neural functioning, or nerve conduction velocity.

This perspective on intelligence was originally supported by reaction time studies (Jensen, 1982). These studies showed that greater variability in response rate to a stimulus (e.g., a light) was associated with lower scores on ability tests. More recent studies have attempted to measure conduction velocities more directly. Reed and Jensen (1992) used performance during a pattern reversal task (e.g., using a modified checkerboard in which the black squares changed to white and the white squares to black) to measure two medium-latency evoked potentials, N70 and P100. The correlations between the latency measures and IQ were small (in the range of −.1 to −.2) but significant in some cases. Correlations were negative because longer latencies corresponded to lower IQs. Vernon and Mori (1992) measured nerve conduction velocity in the median nerve of the arm using electrodes. They found significant correlations between conduction velocity and IQ (around .4). However, they were unable to replicate these findings in later studies (Wickett & Vernon, 1994).

One of the more popular biological approaches is to examine the relation between brain activity and intelligence. Most research in this area uses evoked potentials to measure brain activity. Evoked potentials are electrical responses of the brain during neural transmission. McCarthy and Donchin (1981) found that one evoked potential, P300, seems to reflect the allocation of cognitive resources to a given task; P300 is so named because it is a positively charged response occurring roughly 300 milliseconds after the stimulus is presented.

Schafer (1982) has suggested that the tendency to show a large P300 response to surprising stimuli may reflect individual differences. More intelligent individuals should show greater P300 responses to unfamiliar stimuli, as well as smaller P300 responses to expected stimuli, than would less intelligent ones because they do not need to devote as much attention to familiar stimuli. Schafer reported a correlation of .82 between individual differences in evoked potentials and IQ. This level of correlation appears not to be generally replicable.

Hendrickson and Hendrickson (1980) have suggested that errors can occur in the passage of information through the cerebral cortex. These errors, which probably occur at synapses, are alleged to be responsible for variability in evoked potentials. Thus, it would follow that individuals with normal neural circuitry that conveys information accurately will form correct and accessible memories more quickly than individuals whose circuitry is "noisy" and hence makes errors in transmission. They have shown a strong level of correlation between complexity of an evoked potential measure and IQ. The meaning of this correlation, however, is unclear, and it has not been replicated.

One of the most interesting areas of biological research on intelligence involves examining the rate of cortical glucose metabolism. In two studies, Richard Haier and his colleagues have studied cortical glucose metabolic rates using positron emission tomography (PET) scan analysis while subjects solved Raven Matrix problems or played the computer game Tetris (Haier et al., 1988; Haier, Siegel, Tang, Abel, & Buchsbaum, 1992). In both studies they found that more intelligent subjects showed lower metabolic rates, which suggests that more intelligent individuals expend less effort when working on these tasks. The direction of this relationship, however, remains to be shown. It is not clear whether smarter people expend less glucose, or lower glucose metabolism contributes to higher intelligence.

Finally, researchers have explored the role of genetics in determining intelligence, a subject that has been reviewed in depth by Sternberg and Grigorenko (1997b). Based on the existing research, it appears that approximately half the total variance in IQ scores is accounted for by genetic factors (Loehlin, 1989; Plomin, 1997). The percentages vary with age, however, with heritability of IQ generally increasing with age. It is also important to note that many researchers argue that the effects of heredity and the environment cannot be separated clearly (Bronfenbrenner & Ceci 1994; Wahlsten & Gottlieb, 1997) and that research attention should be devoted to understanding how heredity and environment work together to determine or influence intelligence (Jensen, 1997; Scarr, 1997). In any case, heritability can vary with population and environmental circumstances, so that any values of the heritability coefficient have to be considered in the context of the circumstances under which they are obtained.

There are many different biological approaches to studying intelligence. These approaches have yielded interesting insights about the relation between abilities and the brain. Researchers have been exploring both quantitative (Vernon & Mori, 1992) and qualitative (Levy, 1974) differences between people. Although the above studies have been characterized as strictly biological, it is important to point out that not everyone who takes a biological perspective considers it to be the only way to understand human abilities. Biological measures can help to elucidate cognitive processing, just as cognitive processing can help to elucidate biological functioning. We discuss some cognitive views of intelligence next.

COGNITIVE. Cognitive approaches to intelligence complement rather than contradict biological ones. According to the cognitive perspective, as people think, they execute a set of mental operations, and these operations plus the system that generates them constitute the bases of intelligence.

The cognitive approach, as well as the psychometric approach, has its origins in the work of Spearman (1923). Spearman proposed three fundamental qualitative principles of cognition. *Apprehension of experience* is the perception of a stimulus and the relation of it to the contents of long-term memory, which we today call *encoding; eduction of relations* is the interrelation of two stimuli so as to understand their similarities and differences, which we now refer to as inference; and *eduction of correlates* is the application of an inferred relation to a new domain. Spearman suggested that the analogy problem is an ideal test for studying these cognitive principles, because in an analogy such as "LAWYER is to CLIENT as DOCTOR is to _____?," a subject has to encode each term of the analogy, infer the relation between the LAWYER and CLIENT, and apply this relation to DOCTOR to compete the analogy using PATIENT.

The cognitive approach proposed by Spearman lay dormant until Cronbach (1957) called for the merging of the correlational and experimental disciplines of psychology. It was not until the 1970s that research stemming from this call for unification began to emerge.

One cognitive approach uses a very simple task. This task is called the inspection-time task (Deary & Stough, 1996; Nettlebeck, 1982). In this task, two adjacent vertical lines are presented tachistoscopically or by computer, followed by a visual mask (to destroy the image in visual iconic memory). The two lines differ in length, as do the lengths of time for which the two lines are presented. The participant's task is to say which line is longer. Instead of using raw response time as the dependent variable, however, investigators typically use measures derived from a psychophysical function estimated after many trials. For example, the measure might be the mean duration of a single inspection trial at which 50% accuracy is achieved. Correlations between this task and measures of IQ appear to be about .4, a bit higher than is typical in psychometric tasks. There are differing theories about why such correlations are obtained, but such theories generally attempt to relate the cognitive function of visual inspection time to some kind of biological function, such as speed of neuronal conduction. Let us consider as well some other cognitive approaches.

Research by Hunt, Frost, and Lunneborg (1973) and Hunt, Lunneborg, and Lewis (1975) showed that tasks that formerly had been studied by cognitive psychologists also were applicable for understanding human intelligence. These authors suggested that verbal ability could be understood in large part in terms of speed of access to lexical information stored in long-term memory, and to test their claim, they used a task proposed earlier by Posner and Mitchell (1967).

Hunt, Lunneborg, and Lewis (1975) used a letter comparison task in which subjects are shown a pair of letters, such as "A A," "A a," or "A B," and are asked to indicate, as quickly as possible, if the two letters are identical in appearance or if the two letters are identical in letter name. The difference in response time between the two tasks is viewed as the speed of access to lexical information in long-term memory. The difference score is used to subtract out sheer speed of accessing the visual information inherent in the letters. Hunt et al. considered this difference to be a measure of verbal ability. They showed a correlation of about –.3 between scores on these information processing tasks and scores on psychometric tests of intelligence, with faster response times associated with higher intelligence.

An alternative approach, called the cognitive components approach, focuses on the time it takes to perform individual mental processes in more complex tasks, such as analogies and series completions. Sternberg (1977, 1983) proposed a method of studying intelligence called componential analysis. The first part of this method involved isolating the information processing components and strategies used to solve a cognitive task hypothesized to relate to intelligence. Using problems such as Spearman's verbal analogy, Sternberg determined whether or not each participant used the processes of encoding, inference, and application, how long each took, and how susceptible each process was to error. The second part of Sternberg's method involved correlating component scores with psychometric test scores hypothesized to correlate and not correlate with the target cognitive processes. For example, one might expect components of analogical reasoning to correlate with scores on psychometric tests of inductive reasoning but not with scores on psychometric tests of perceptual speed. Using this method, Sternberg (1983) showed that the same cognitive processes are involved in a wide variety of intellectual tasks, and he suggested that these and other related processes underlie scores on intelligence. The limitation of this approach is that more complex tasks do not lend themselves to this type of decomposition because subjects do not solve the problems in a linear way.

Alternative cognitive approaches have been used to study more complex tasks. The most prominent of these is the study of artificial intelligence. Artificial intelligence approaches use the computer as a metaphor for understanding human intelligence.

For example, Newell and Simon (1972) used a computer program, called the General Problem Solver, to model problem solving that involves a series of clearly defined steps to problem solution. At the same time, other researchers (Minsky, 1968; Winograd, 1972) were developing programs of semantic information processing. Schank (1972) proposed a model of *conceptual dependency* to understand how concepts could be related to one another. This model served as the basis for *script theory* (Schank & Abelson, 1977), which attempts to account for how we know what to do in certain situations. A script is a schema that consists of a set of actions that we typically follow in a given situation.

Perhaps the most influential of the artificial intelligence approaches has been the development of expert systems. The general characteristics of expert systems include a language processor facilitating communication between user and system; a knowledge base, which is subdivided into knowledge of facts and rules; an interpreter, which applies these rules; a scheduler, which controls the sequence of application; a consistency enforcer, which modifies conclusions when new data contradict old data; and a justifier, which can explain the system's line of reasoning (Hayes-Roth, Waterman, & Lenat, 1983). These approaches typically do not simulate human cognitive processing but rather attempt to create the most effective and efficient processor. Some theorists, however, have tried to create programs that simulate human intelligence. Most notable among these is Anderson's (1983, 1986) ACT model. Anderson has used his model to compare human information processing to a computer program. All of the traditional artificial intelligence theories are based on the assumption that human intelligence is at its core a serial symbolic processing system and therefore that computers can provide a good model for what is unique about human intelligence. However, more recent connectionist models assume massive parallel processing (McClelland & Rumelhart, 1988).

CONTEXTUAL. Although cognitive approaches have provided insight about the relation between mental processes and representations and human abilities, many scientists argue that they are too narrow to capture the broad nature of intelligence. Contextual approaches to intelligence attempt to take into account the complexity of the construct. As is consistent with the difference found in implicit theories of intelligence, they take the position that intelligence cannot be understood outside of a cultural context.

The most extreme position is that of radical cultural relativism (Berry, 1974). This view rejects the assumption that there are psychological universals across cultural systems. Intelligence should be studied within each culture separately, within the system in which its meaning was created. According to this approach, it is inappropriate to translate a standardized test from one culture to another.

Less extreme contextual views recognize both the differences and similarities in conceptions of intelligence. The Laboratory of Comparative Human Cognition (1982) proposed a kind of conditional comparativism by which comparisons between cultures are possible as long as tasks are made equivalent for members of the different cultures. For example, Luria (1976) found that when he asked Russian peasants, "From Shakhimardan to Vuadil it is three hours on foot, while to Fergana it is six hours. How much time does it take to go on foot from Vuadil to Fergana?" they responded with answers such as "You're wrong ... it's far and you wouldn't get there in three hours." Simply changing the names of locations does not make the task equivalent. In a similar vein, cross-cultural studies of memory (Wagner, 1978) have shown that whether people do well on memory tasks depends very heavily on the familiarity of the content. People tend to do better with more familiar content, so that the relative scores of two cultural groups will depend in part on what kinds of materials are used in testing.

The contextual approach has been criticized for not making clear what is meant by *context*. Berry and Irvine (1986) have proposed a four-level model of context that specifies, at least in part, what context means. At the highest level is ecological context, which is the natural cultural habitat in which one lives. The second level is the experiential level, or the pattern of recurrent experiences that provide the basis for learning. The third level is the performance context, comprising the limited set of environmental circumstances that account for particular behaviors at specific points in space and time. And the lowest level is the experimental context, which refers to the context in which research or testing occurs.

Varied contexts at any of these levels can have an effect on the outcomes of a task, including intelligence tests. Ceci and Bronfenbrenner (1985), for example, found that the pattern of performance on a time estimation task varied for children who were studied in a laboratory or in their home environment. They concluded that data obtained in a laboratory do not necessarily transfer to a home environment, or vice versa. Other investigators have found that performance on traditional ability tests as given in school settings (e.g., IQ tests, arithmetic tests) correlates poorly with performance on everyday, practical tasks, for example, handicapping horses (Ceci & Liker, 1986), comparative grocery shopping (Lave, 1988), and street vending (Nuñes, Schliemann, & Carraher, 1993). We discuss this research further in chapter 3 on practical intelligence. Sternberg and Wagner (1986) obtained similar findings with business executives, salespersons, and college professors, as reviewed in chapter 8.

Contextual approaches clearly show that context is important to the study of intelligence. Contextual differences emerge at various levels, from broad cultural differences to differences in the specific setting in which a task is performed. In measuring intelligence, we need to be sensitive to the potential differences that may artificially produce different scores for different groups or for the same individuals in different environments. However, understanding the contextual influences alone does not answer all our questions about intelligence. Ideally, theories should take into account both cognition and context. Development of a more integrative approach to studying intelligence is the objective of systems theories.

SYSTEMS. System theorists view intelligence as a complex system. Their theories attempt to incorporate diverse elements from various approaches that we have considered so far. Two such theories are Gardner's (1983, 1993, 1999) theory of multiple intelligences and Sternberg's (1985a, 1997a, 1998c, in press c) triarchic theory of successful intelligence.

Gardner (1983) proposed that intelligence is not a unitary construct but rather that there are distinct and independent multiple intelligences. His theory of multiple intelligences (MI theory) originally posited seven multiple intelligences. The first, linguistic intelligence, is involved in reading and writing, listening and talking. The second, logical-mathematical intelligence, is involved in numerical computations, deriving proofs, solving logical puzzles, and most scientific thinking. The third, spatial intelligence, is used in marine navigation, as well as in piloting a plane or driving a car. The fourth, musical intelligence, is used in singing, playing an instrument, conducting an orchestra, composing, and to some extent, appreciating music. The fifth, bodily–kinesthetic intelligence, involves the ability to use one's body or various portions of it in the solution of problems, in the construction of products, or in athletics. The sixth, interpersonal intelligence, is involved in understanding and acting on one's understanding of others. Finally, the seventh, intrapersonal intelligence, is the ability to understand one-self – to know how one feels about things, to understand one's range of emotions, to have insights about why one acts the way one does, and to behave in ways that are appropriate to one's needs, goals, and abilities. More recently, Gardner (1998) proposed an additional intelligence, that of naturalistic intelligence, which is the ability to discern patterns in nature. He also has suggested existential and spiritual "candidate" intelligences. There have been no empirical validations of Gardner's theory as a whole since it was first proposed, and so its status as a scientific theory is uncertain at this time.

Sternberg (1997a) argues that most conventional conceptions of intelligence are too narrow and thus deal with only a small portion of intelligence as a whole. They fail to address what he refers to as successful intelligence, or the ability to adapt to, shape, and select environments to accomplish one's goals within the context of one's society and culture. The theory attempts to link cognition to context through three parts or subtheories.

The componential subtheory addresses the relation of intelligence to the internal world (Sternberg, 1985a). It specifies the components that people use to process information. For example, metacomponents are used to plan, monitor, and evaluate an activity, performance components are involved in the actual execution of activities, and knowledge acquisition components help individuals to learn how to do things in the first place. The three kinds of components interact and provide feedback to one another. For example, if one travels to a foreign country, metacomponents plan and supervise the trip, whereas performance components coordinate day-to-day actual needs, and knowledge acquisition components are used to learn about the country, both in preparation for and during the trip.

The experiential subtheory postulates that the above components are applied to tasks with which we have varying levels of experience (Sternberg, 1985a). At one extreme we have tasks that are extremely novel and that we have never encountered before. At the other extreme we have tasks that are so familiar we can accomplish them with little intellectual effort. According to the subtheory, tasks that are relatively unfamiliar are relevant to measuring intelligence. Tasks that are totally novel (e.g., giving calculus problems to first-grade children) are poor measures of intelligence because the individual simply has no experience to bring to bear. Well learned or automated tasks (e.g., reading, driving) are also important for understanding intelligence because they are part of everyday functioning, but they tell us little about how people function in the face of new challenges. Intelligence involves a balance between coping with relative novelty and eventually rendering tasks automatic so that they can be done with little conscious effort. Take, for example, the very practical skill of driving. Initially, when one learns how to drive, one needs to focus intensely and avoid distractions. One may be able to do just one thing at a time. Eventually, when one has automatized performance, one may be able to drive, carry on a conversation, listen to the radio, and let one's mind wander, all at the same time.

The contextual subtheory states that the information processing components are applied to experience in order to serve one of three functions in real world contexts (Sternberg, 1985a). The first, adaptation to environments, refers to changing oneself to suit the environment in which one lives; the second, shaping of environments, refers to changing the environment to suit oneself; and the third, selection of environments, refers to choosing a new environment when one is unable to make the environment work through adaptation or shaping. The successfully intelligent person is able to perform all three of these functions as necessary.

Underlying this theory is the notion that intelligent people are those who recognize their strengths and weaknesses and who capitalize on their strengths while at the same time they compensate for or correct their weaknesses. People attain success, in part, by finding out how to exploit their own patterns of strengths and weaknesses. These strengths and weaknesses can be related to three broad kinds of abilities that are important to successful intelligence: analytic, creative, and practical (Sternberg, 1988, 1997a).

Analytic ability involves critical thinking; it is the ability to analyze and evaluate ideas, solve problems, and make decisions. Creative ability involves going beyond what is given to generate novel and interesting ideas. Practical ability involves implementing ideas; it is the ability involved when intelligence is applied to real world contexts. In the next chapter and in the remainder of this book, we focus on the practical aspect of intelligence. We consider in more detail what practical intelligence is and what role it serves in understanding successful performance in everyday life, which conventional approaches to understanding intelligence fail to accomplish.

CHAPTER 3

The Specificity of Practical Intelligence

Its Nature and Development

Practical, or everyday, intelligence is different from the kind of intelligence associated with academic success (Neisser, 1976, 1979). There are any number of ways in which we see this difference in our everyday lives. We see people who succeed in school and fail in work or who fail in school but succeed in work. We meet people with high scores on intelligence tests who seem inept in their social interactions. And we meet people with low test scores who can get along effectively with practically anyone. Laypersons have long recognized a distinction between academic intelligence (book smarts) and practical intelligence (street smarts or common sense). This distinction is confirmed by research on the implicit theories of intelligence held by both laypersons and researchers (Sternberg, 1985b; Sternberg et al., 1981).

ACADEMIC VERSUS PRACTICAL INTELLIGENCE

There may be any number of reasons for the apparent difference between academic and practical intelligence. We argue that a major source of this difference is the sheer disparity in the kinds of problems one faces in academic versus practical situations. The problems faced in everyday life often have little relation to the knowledge or skills acquired through formal education or the abilities used in classroom activities. Consider the following example of an observation made of a garbage collector in Tallahassee, Florida.

> Tallahassee, priding itself on the service it provides to its citizens, requires garbage collectors to retrieve trash containers from the backyards of residents. Each resident fills a large trash container in the backyard rather than placing standard-sized garbage cans on the

curbside to be picked up. Trash collectors must locate and retrieve each full container from the backyard, heave it into the truck, and then drag the empty container back to each yard. Many of the garbage collectors are young high school dropouts, who because of their lack of education might be expected to score poorly on intelligence tests. On the surface, the job appears to be more physically than intellectually demanding. Each stop requires two trips to the backyard, one to retrieve the full can, and another to return it when it is empty.

One summer it was noticed that the collection routine had changed after a new, older employee joined the crew. This change involved relaxing the constraint that each household retain the same container. Because the trash bins were issued by the city and not purchased with personal funds, they were identical. The new routine consisted of wheeling the previous house's empty container to the current house's backyard, leaving it to replace the full can, which was in turn wheeled to the truck to be emptied. Once emptied, this can was wheeled to the backyard of the next house to replace its full can, and so on. The new routine required only one trip to each house, whereas the previous one required two trips. The new employee's insights cut the work nearly in half. This solution had eluded other garbage collectors and the managers who trained them.

Everyone encounters problems to which solutions are neither readily available nor readily derivable from acquired knowledge. This type of problem solving, frequently experienced in daily life, is referred to as *practical problem solving*. Such problems can be experienced in the workplace or in school, the household, stores, movie theaters, or anywhere. There is no consensus on how to define practical problems encountered in life, but building on a distinction made by Neisser (1976), Sternberg (1985a, 1997a) and Wagner and Sternberg (1986) have classified problems as academic or practical in nature. Academic problems tend to be formulated by others; well-defined; complete in the information they provide; characterized by having only one correct answer; characterized by having only one method of obtaining the correct answer; outside of ordinary experience; and of little or no intrinsic interest.

Practical problems, in contrast to academic problems, tend to be unformulated or in need of reformulation; of personal interest; lacking in information necessary for solution; related to everyday experience; poorly defined; characterized by multiple appropriate solutions, each with liabilities as well as assets; and characterized by multiple methods for picking a problem solution. Given the differences in the nature of academic and practical problems, it is no surprise that people who are adept at solving one kind of problem may well not be adept at solving problems of the other kind.

The intellectual skills that individuals exhibit in finding solutions to practical problems may be referred to as *practical intellectual skills* (Baltes, Dittman-Kohli, & Dixon, 1984; Berg, in press; Berg & Sternberg, 1985; Rogoff, 1982; Sternberg, 1985a, 1997a; Wagner, in press). When combined, these skills are often referred to as practical intelligence, which is defined as intelligence that serves to find a more optimal fit between the individual and the demands of the individual's environment, whether by adapting to the environment, changing (or shaping) the environment, or selecting a different environment (Sternberg, 1985a; Sternberg, 1997a). The concept of practical intelligence takes into account the distinction presented above between academic and practical tasks. The abilities emphasized in formal schooling have limited value if they cannot be used to address practical, everyday problems.

Research on Practical Problem Solving Ability

The research on practical ability is becoming more and more central to mainstream psychology (Berg & Klaczynski, 1996). Initially, the examination of practical intelligence issued from a concern that the intelligence of adults functioning largely outside the academic environment from the moment they obtained their academic credentials and virtually for the rest of their lives was evaluated primarily by traditional tests of intelligence constructed to predict academic success.

Various aspects of the concept of practical intelligence are expressed in a number of diverse constructs. Some researchers define everyday intelligence as a specific expression of conventional abilities that permit adaptive behavior within a distinct class of everyday situations (Willis & Schaie, 1986), whereas others stress the unique nature of practical abilities (Neisser, 1976; Wagner, 1987). Most psychological studies of practical abilities focus on solving problems that are ill-structured in their goals and solutions and are frequently encountered in daily life at home, at work, and in dealing with people (Cornelius & Caspi, 1987; Denney, 1989).

A number of studies have addressed the relation between practical and academic intelligence. These studies have been carried out in a wide range of settings, using a variety of tasks, and with diverse populations. We review some examples of research on problem solving and reasoning. Other reviews are those by Ceci and Roazzi (1994), Rogoff and Lave (1984), Scribner and Cole (1981), Sternberg and Wagner (1986, 1994), Voss, Perkins, and Segal (1991), and Wagner (in press). Taken together, these studies show that ability measured in one setting (e.g., school) does not necessarily transfer to another setting (e.g., real-world task).

Several studies compared performance on mathematical types of problems across different contexts. Scribner (1984, 1986) studied the strategies used by milk processing plant workers to fill orders. Workers who assemble orders for cases of various quantities (e.g., gallons, quarts, or pints) and products (e.g., whole milk, 2% milk, or buttermilk) are called assemblers. Rather than employing typical mathematical algorithms learned in the classroom, Scribner found that experienced assemblers used complex strategies for combining partially filled cases in a manner that minimized the number of moves required to complete an order. Although the assemblers were the least educated workers in the plant, they were able to calculate in their heads quantities expressed in different base number systems, and they routinely outperformed the more highly educated white collar workers who substituted when assemblers were absent. Scribner found that the order-filling performance of the assemblers was unrelated to measures of school performance, including intelligence test scores, arithmetic test scores, and grades.

Another series of studies of everyday mathematics involved shoppers in California grocery stores who sought to buy at the cheapest cost when the same products were available in different-sized containers (Lave, Murtaugh, & de la Roche, 1984; Murtaugh, 1985). (These studies were performed before cost per unit quantity information was routinely posted.) For example, oatmeal may come in two sizes, 10 ounces for $0.98 or 24 ounces for $2.29. One might adopt the strategy of always buying the largest size, assuming that the larger size is always the most economical. However, the researchers (and savvy shoppers) learned that the larger size did not represent the least cost per unit quantity for about one third of the items purchased. The findings of these studies were that effective shoppers used mental shortcuts to get an easily obtained answer, accurate enough to determine which size to buy. A common strategy, for example, was mentally to change the size and price of an item to make it more comparable with the other size available. For example, one might mentally double the smaller size, thereby comparing 20 ounces at $1.96 versus 24 ounces at $2.29. The difference of 4 ounces for about 35 cents, or about 9 cents per ounce, seems to favor the 24-ounce size, given that the smaller size of 10 ounces for

$0.98 is about 10 cents per ounce. These mathematical shortcuts yield approximations that are as useful as the actual values of 9.80 and 9.33 cents per ounce for the smaller and larger sizes, respectively, and are much more easily computed in the absence of a calculator. When the shoppers were given a mental arithmetic test, no relation was found between test performance and accuracy in picking the best values (Lave et al., 1984; Murtaugh, 1985).

Ceci and Liker (1986, 1988) and Ceci and Ruiz (1991) studied expert racetrack handicappers. Ceci and Liker (1986) found that expert handicappers used a highly complex algorithm for predicting post time odds that involved interactions among seven kinds of information. By applying the complex algorithm, handicappers adjusted times posted for each quarter mile on a previous outing by factors such as whether the horse was attempting to pass other horses and if so, the speed of the other horses passed and where the attempted passes took place. By adjusting posted times for these factors, a better measure of a horse's speed is obtained. It could be argued that the use of complex interactions to predict a horse's speed would require considerable cognitive ability (at least as it is traditionally measured). However, Ceci and Liker reported that the successful use of these interactions by handicappers was unrelated to their IQ.

A subsequent study attempted to relate performance at the racetrack to making stock market predictions in which the same algorithm was involved. Ceci and Ruiz (1991) asked racetrack handicappers to solve a stock market prediction task that was structured similarly to the racetrack problem. After 611 trials on the stock market task, the handicappers performed no better than chance, and there was no difference in performance as a function of IQ. Ceci and Roazzi (1994) attribute this lack of transfer to the low correlation between performance on problems and their isomorphs (problem isomorphs are two or more problems that involve the same cognitive processes but use different terminology or take place in different contexts).

The same principle that applies to adults appears also to apply to children. Carraher, Carraher, and Schliemann (1985) studied Brazilian children who, for economic reasons, often worked as street vendors (Nuñes, 1994). Most of these children had very little formal schooling. Carraher et al. compared the performance of these children on mathematical problems that were embedded in a real-life situation (i.e., vending) with their performance on problems presented in an academic context (e.g., 2 + 4 = ?). The children correctly solved significantly more questions that related to vending than mathematical problems that were academic in nature. When the academic problems were presented as word problems (e.g., "If an orange costs 76 cruzeiros and a passion fruit costs 50, how much do the two cost together?"), the rate of correct responses was substantially better, but still not as high as when the problems were presented in the context of vending.

This lack of transfer also appears to work in the reverse direction. For example, Perret-Clermont (1980) found that many schoolchildren had no problem solving paper-and-pencil arithmetic questions but could not solve the same type of problem in a different context (e.g., counting bunches of flowers). That is, schoolchildren may fail to transfer academic knowledge to everyday problems.

Roazzi (1987) found similar results when comparing the performance of street vendor children and middle-class schoolchildren on a class inclusion task. To assess the performance of the street vendor children, the researcher posed as a customer and asked questions about the items to find out if the children understood the relationship among classes and subclasses of food (e.g., mint and strawberry chewing gum as part of the class chewing gum). At a later time, the same children were given a formal test that had the same logical structure but was irrelevant to their street vending jobs. The middle-class children were given the same two tests. Street vendor children performed significantly better on the class inclusion task in the natural than in the formal context, whereas middle-class children were more successful on the formal version of the task.

Additional research has shown that the use of complex reasoning strategies does not necessarily correlate with IQ. Dörner and Kreuzig (1983) and Dörner, Kreuzig, Reither, and Staudel (1983) studied individuals who were asked to play the role of city managers for the computer-simulated city of Lohhausen. A variety of problems were presented to these individuals, such as how best to raise revenue to build roads. The simulation involved more than 1,000 variables. Performance was quantified in terms of a hierarchy of strategies, ranging from the simplest (trial and error) to the most complex (hypothesis testing with multiple feedback loops). No relation was found between IQ and complexity of strategies used. A second problem was created to cross-validate these results. This problem, called the Sahara problem, required participants to determine the number of camels that could be kept alive by a small oasis. Once again, no relation was found between IQ and complexity of strategies employed.

The above studies indicate that demonstrated abilities do not necessarily correspond between everyday tasks (e.g. price comparison shopping) and traditional academic tasks (e.g., mathematics achievement tests). In other words, some people are able to solve concrete, ill-defined problems better than well-defined, abstract problems that have little relevance to their personal lives, and vice versa. Few of these researchers would claim, however, that IQ is totally irrelevant to performance in these various contexts. There is evidence that conventional tests of intelligence predict both school performance and job performance (Barrett & Depinet, 1991; Schmidt & Hunter, 1998; Wigdor & Garner, 1982). What these studies do suggest is that there are other aspects of intelligence that may be independent of IQ and that are important to performance but have largely been neglected in the measurement of intelligence. We also observe this incongruity between conventional notions of ability and real-world abilities in research on age-related changes in intellectual ability.

The Fun of Growing Older: Do Age-related Patterns in Practical Intelligence Resemble Those in Conventional Intelligence?

Throughout the century of existence of cognitive psychology, many cognitive variables, mostly those contributing to the g factor (Berg, in press; Sternberg & Berg, 1992) have been found to be associated with age across the life-span. Most of these associations are rather complex and represented by a curvilinear function reflecting rapid growth during the years of formal schooling and slow decline thereafter (Salthouse, 1998). However, the results of research also suggest somewhat different developmental functions for changes in performance on various kinds of intellectual tasks across the adult life span. In particular, data show that older adults commonly report growth in practical abilities over the years, even though their academic abilities decline (Williams, Denney, & Schadler, 1983).

As for specific cognitive functions, cognition during adulthood is characterized on one hand by losses in the speed of mental processes, abstract reasoning, and specific characteristics of memory performance (Salthouse, 1991) and on the other hand by gains in the metacognitive ability to integrate cognitive, interpersonal, and emotional thinking in a synthetic understanding of the world, self, and others (Labouvie-Vief, 1992).

The most commonly used theoretical framework adapted for the interpretation of findings on age-related changes in intellectual performance is that of fluid and crystallized abilities (Cattell, 1971; Horn, 1994; Horn & Cattell, 1966). *Fluid* abilities are those required to deal with novelty, as in the immediate testing situation (e.g., discovering the pattern in a figure sequence). *Crystallized* abilities are based on accumulated knowledge (e.g., finding a synonym of a low-frequency word). Using this distinction, many researchers have demonstrated that fluid abilities are relatively susceptible to age-related decline, whereas crystallized abilities are relatively resistant to aging (Dixon & Baltes, 1986; Horn, 1982; Labouvie-Vief, 1982; Schaie, 1977/1978), except near the end of life.

In addition, Willis and Schaie (1986) studied the relationships in the elderly between fluid and crystallized abilities and everyday intelligence (the latter being defined as the ability to perform core activities of independent life, such as cooking, managing finances, or using the telephone, and measured by a variant of the ETS Basic Skills Test). The researchers reported substantial correlations between performance on the Basic Skills Test and a measure of fluid ($r = .83$) and crystallized ($r = .78$) abilities.

The majority of these findings, however, were obtained in the framework of cross-sectional methodologies – that is, by comparing different groups of individuals of various ages. When the same individuals are followed across time in the framework of longitudinal design, the findings show that, with respect to fluid intelligence, decline does not generally begin until the 60s and loss of crystallized intelligence occurs almost a decade later, in the 70s (Schaie, 1996).

In addition, even when there are age-based group differences in intellectual performance, there is extensive interindividual variability for specific cognitive abilities within age groups. For instance, Schaie (1996), although consistently reporting mean cross-sectional differences in overall intellectual performance, pointed out impressive variability within age groups. To quantify this variability, Schaie (1988) investigated the overlap in distributions of intellectual performance among young adults and the elderly. Even in the group 80 years old and over, the overlap was such that about 53% scored well above the mean of their age group. In other words, half or more than half of individuals in the late age groups perform comparably to a group of young adults on measures of both crystallized and fluid intelligence.

Moreover, there is also a considerable amount of interindividual variability in the longitudinal patterns of decline, maintenance, and improvement. Specifically, Schaie and Willis (1986) categorized older individuals of mean age 72 years into those who declined and those who remained stable in their performances on the Primary Mental Abilities Test (using the space and reasoning subtests) over a period of 14 years. Of the sample population studied, 47% remained stable on both measures, whereas only 21% declined on both measures. Some of these individuals were followed into their 80s, and virtually none of them showed universal decline across all five subtests of the Primary Mental Abilities Test (Schaie, 1989). It is thought that those who show age-related maintenance and improvement in intellectual development differ from those showing decline with respect to a constellation of factors, including educational background, occupational pursuits, health history, life habits, and such personality styles as rigidity and flexibility (Schaie, 1996).

The trend of intellectual development across the life-span, however, appears to be yet somewhat different for practical abilities. Williams et al. (1983) interviewed men and women over the age of 65. The questions posed to these adults had to do with their perception of age-related changes in their ability to think, reason, and solve problems. Surprisingly enough, the responses obtained from these adults were largely contradictory to the view that late development of intelligence consists of decline (Berg, in press). In the study by Williams et al. (1983), 76% of the elderly adults believed that their ability to think, reason, and solve problems had actually increased over the years, with 20% reporting no change and only 4% reporting that their abilities had declined with age. The researchers confronted the participants with the overwhelming evidence of decline in conventional test performance on completion of formal schooling, but the explanation of the elderly people was that they were talking about solving kinds of problems different from those found on psychometric tests. The problems they had in mind when answering the interviewer's questions were those of an everyday or financial nature. Of course, these responses might be simply discounted as self-deceiving and self-reassuring, but a number of formal psychological studies within the last decade have provided significant support for the claim made by the elderly in the study by Williams et al. (1983).

In particular, the idea that practical and academic abilities might have different developmental trajectories was supported in a number of studies (Berg & Klaczynski, 1996). Denney and Palmer (1981) were one of the first research teams to demonstrate this discrepancy. They compared the performance of adults aged 20 through 79 on traditional analytical reasoning problems (e.g., a "20 questions" task) and a problem solving task involving real-life situations (e.g., "If you were traveling by car and got stranded out on an interstate highway during a blizzard, what would you do?"). One of the many interesting results obtained in this study was a difference in the shape of the developmental function for performance on the two types of problems. Performance on the traditional problem solving task or cognitive measure declined almost linearly from age 20, onward. Performance on the practical problem solving task increased to a peak in the 40- and 50-year-old groups, declining thereafter. Expanding on this line of research, Smith, Staudinger, and Baltes (1994) compared responses to life-planning dilemmas in a group of younger (mean age 32) and older (mean age 70) adults. Unlike the results of studies on aging and academic abilities, which demonstrated the superior performance of younger adults over the elderly, in this study younger and older adults did not differ. In addition, each age cohort group received the highest ratings when responding to a dilemma matched to their own life phase.

Similar results were obtained in a study by Cornelius and Caspi (1987), who studied adults between the ages of 20 and 78. These researchers examined relationships between performance on tasks measuring fluid intelligence (letter series), crystallized intelligence (verbal meanings), and everyday problem solving (e.g., dealing with a landlord who won't make repairs, filling out a complicated form, responding to criticism from a parent or child). Performance on the measure of fluid ability increased from age 20 to 30, remained stable from age 30 to 50, and then declined. Performance on the everyday problem solving task and the measures of crystallized ability increased through age 70.

Likewise, the neofunctionalist position, advanced by Baltes (1987), Baltes et al. (1984), Baltes, Smith, and Staudinger (1992), and Dittmann-Kohli and Baltes (1990) acknowledges that although some aspects of intellectual functioning estimated via traditional tests may decline with age, stability and growth also exist, if to a lesser extent. The approach of Baltes and colleagues also operates within the constructs of fluid and crystallized intelligence, although a different emphasis is placed on the relative roles and meanings of these two kinds of intelligence. Here, both aspects of intelligence are considered as coequals in defining the developmental course of intelligence. In general, Baltes argues that crystallized intelligence has been too narrowly defined, and that its importance increases as one moves into adulthood and old age. In this sense, it may be inappropriate to associate a decrease in fluid intelligence with an average decline in intellectual competence.

Baltes and associates see adult cognitive competence in terms of a dual-process model. The first process, called the *mechanics* of intelligence, is concerned with developmental change in basic information processing, which is genetically driven and assumed to be knowledge-free. With aging, there is a biologically based reduction in reserve capacity (Baltes, 1987; Baltes et al., 1992). The second process, the *pragmatics* of intelligence, relates the basic cognitive skills and resources of the first process to everyday cognitive performance and adaptation. Measures of pragmatic intelligence within select domains are viewed as tapping abilities more characteristic of adult intellectual life than are traditional psychometric measures of cognitive abilities. Baltes, Sowarka, and Kliegl (1989) showed that similarly to empirical findings on the distinction between fluid and crystallized intelligence, the mechanics of intelligence tend to decline with age almost linearly, whereas the pragmatics of intelligence tend to maintain relative stability throughout adulthood. For example, whereas linear declines were found in the speed of comparing information in short-term memory (i.e., aspects of intellectual mechanics), no age differences were registered for measures of reasoning about life planning (i.e., aspects of intellectual pragmatics).

Cognitive abilities are assumed to operate on content domains involving factual and procedural knowledge; they are regulated by higher-level, transsituational, procedural skills and by higher-order reflective thinking (metacognition), all of which define the *action space* in which problem solving occurs within a given individual. According to this approach, successful aging entails limiting one's tasks and avoiding excessive demands. Baltes and Baltes (1990) use the concept of selection to refer to a self-imposed restriction in one's life to fewer domains of functioning as a means to adapt to age-related losses. It is assumed that by concentrating on high-priority domains and devising new operational strategies, individuals can optimize their general reserves (Baltes, 1993). By relating adult intelligence to successful cognitive performance in one's environment, this position acknowledges that not all tasks are equally relevant for measuring intelligence at different ages (Baltes et al., 1984; Baltes et al., 1992).

Specific manifestations of pragmatic intelligence are said to differ from person to person as people proceed through selection, optimization, or compensation (Dittmann-Kohli & Baltes, 1990). Selection refers simply to restricting the scope of one's activities to things that one is still able to accomplish well despite a diminution in reserve capacity. Thus, research shows that elderly people tend to leave jobs that require quick sensorimotor responses (Barrett, Mihal, Panek, Sterns, & Alexander, 1977). Optimization refers to the fact that older people can maintain high levels of performance in some domains by practice, greater effort, and the development of new bodies of knowledge. Compensation comes into play when a level of capacity beyond remaining performance potential is required. For example, Salthouse (1984) was able to show that older typists, although slower on several simple speeded reaction time tasks, were able to compensate for this deficit and maintain their speed by reading further ahead in the text and planning ahead. According to Salthouse and Somberg (1982), age-related decrements at the "molecular" level (e.g., in speed of execution of the elementary components of typing skill) produce no observable effects at the "molar" level (i.e., the speed and accuracy with which work is completed).

Charness (1981) showed similar effects with older chess players, who exhibited poorer recall in general but were better able to plan ahead than younger, less experienced players. In related studies, older adults have been found to compensate for declines in memory by relying more on external memory aids than do younger adults (Loewen, Shaw, & Craik, 1990). Older adults must often transfer the emphasis of a particular task to abilities that have not declined in order to compensate for those that have (Bäckman & Dixon, 1992). In other words, when a task depends heavily on knowledge and speed of processing is not a significant constraint, peak performance may not be constrained in early to middle adulthood (Charness & Bieman-Copland, 1994). As an example, consider chess competitions by correspondence. In these competitions, players are permitted 3 days to deliberate each move. The mean age of the first-time winners of one postal world championship is 46. In contrast, the peak age for tournament chess, where deliberation averages 3 min per move, is about 30 (Charness & Bosman, 1995).

A series of studies on the relationship between aging and cognitive efficiency in skilled performers attests to the compensatory and stabilizing role of practical intelligence (Baltes & Smith, 1990; Charness & Bosman, 1990; Colonia-Willner, 1998; Hartley, 1989; Willis, 1989). Sternberg and colleagues' studies of tacit knowledge in the domains of business management, sales, and academic psychology showed increases in tacit knowledge with age and experience across groups of under-graduates, graduate students, and professionals (Sternberg, Wagner, & Okagaki, 1993; Wagner, 1987; Wagner, Rashotte, & Sternberg, 1994; Wagner & Sternberg, 1985). Colonia-Willner (1998) found evidence that older managers who performed at the highest levels on average had high levels of tacit knowledge, even though on average they had rela-tively low scores on psychometric reasoning measures. In addition, Colonia-Willner pointed out an interesting detail: Even though tacit knowledge of managerial skills was shown to be related to some indi-cators of job success for the total sample of bank managers, the relative weight of this knowledge was higher for the highest success group (that group rewarded most highly). It might be that job-related tacit knowledge is especially important for detecting superachievers among a fairly restricted, high-achieving, conventional population of man-agers engaged in heterogeneous activities.

Moreover, training studies conducted in Germany (Baltes et al., 1984; Baltes et al., 1992) and in the United States (Schaie, 1986; Schaie & Willis, 1986; Willis & Schaie, 1994) have shown that older individuals still have a great deal of potential plasticity, or reserve capacity for development. The results demonstrated that intervention can lead to significant gains in abilities such as problem solving (Denney, 1979), perceptual speed (Hoyer, Labouvie, & Baltes, 1973), and fluid intelli-gence (Baltes & Lindenberger, 1988; Willis, 1987). In general, interven-tion research has targeted those abilities that have been shown to decline the most, namely, fluid intelligence and processes representa-tive of the mechanisms of intelligence.

In general, results from intervention studies have convincingly demonstrated the remarkable plasticity of human intelligence in the elderly (Willis, 1987). In the German studies, better performance was demonstrated for target training (Baltes & Willis, 1982; Willis, Blieszner, & Baltes, 1981), for independent self-practice (Baltes et al., 1989; Hayslip, 1989a, 1989b), and for removed time constraints (Hofland, Willis, & Baltes, 1981). Willis and Schaie (1986), Schaie and Willis (1986), and Willis and Schaie (1994) obtained similar findings within a longitudinal design.

These results were replicated in a further follow-up study con-ducted in 1991 with both new participants and participants from the original training study. Specifically, results from the Seattle Training Study, a component of the Seattle Longitudinal Study (Schaie, 1996), indicated that the performance of the elderly can be successfully restored to the level of more than a decade before. The Seattle researchers set up five 1-hour sessions aimed at training the elderly adults' spatial and reasoning abilities. The training had differential impact on certain subgroups of the study population. For those who had shown decline on either of the Primary Mental Ability Test subtests over the preceding 14 years, training was effective in returning performance nearly to the original level. For those who had remained stable over the preceding 14 years, training raised performance beyond the level at which they had performed 14 years earlier. In addition, the training has been found to be effective not only in the short run, but over 7 years (Neely & Backman, 1993; Willis & Nesselroade, 1990).

One of the outcomes of these studies is the realization that longer and more structured training seems to be necessary for remediation in the very old (Schaie, 1994; Willis, 1989). The importance of these studies is that they suggest that cognitive decline in many individuals may be due to disuse of certain cognitive abilities and that remediation is possible for a significant number of participants, especially the young old (Schaie, 1994; Willis, 1990; Willis & Schaie, 1994).

The developmental trajectory of everyday intelligence has been examined by a number of researchers (Berg, in press; Berg & Klaczynski, 1996). The summary of the field today is that the pattern of age differences in everyday intelligence differs dramatically depending on how problems to be solved are defined and on what criteria are used for optimal problem solving. For example, Berg, Klaczynski, Calderone, and Strough (1994), studying participants' own ratings of how effective they were in solving their own everyday problems, did not find any age differences. Denney and Palmer (1981) and Denney and Pearce (1989) used the number of "safe and effective solutions" as the criterion of optimal problem solving and found that the highest number of such solutions was generated by middle-aged adults, with both younger and older adults offering fewer solutions. Cornelius and Caspi (1987), using the closeness between participants' ratings of strategy effectiveness and a "prototype" of the optimal everyday problem solver as the criteria, found an increase in everyday problem solving ability with adult age.

A number of studies have examined everyday problem solving with a neo-Piagetian approach to intellectual development in adulthood (Labouvie-Vief, 1992). According to this paradigm, in middle and late adulthood, the formal operational reasoning of late adolescence and young adulthood, with its focus on logic, is replaced by more sophisticated mental structures distinguished by relativistic reasoning based on synthesizing the irrational, emotive, and personal. Specifically, Blanchard-Fields (1986, 1994) and Blanchard-Fields and Norris (1994) state that when dealing with social dilemmas, older adults are superior to younger adults in their integrative attributional reasoning (i.e., reasoning based on the integration of dispositional and situational components).

To conclude, there is reason to believe that the developmental trajectories of abilities used to solve strictly academic problems do not coincide with the trajectories of abilities used to solve problems of a practical nature.

WHAT DEVELOPS IN PRACTICAL INTELLIGENCE?

The evidence supporting the supposition that practical intelligence has a different developmental trajectory than academic intelligence supports the etiological independence (not necessarily complete) of practical and academic abilities but is only one of many research advances revealing the developmental mechanisms of practical intelligence. Developmental research on practical abilities is still in its early stages. However, data available at this point shed some light on what Sinnott (1989) has called the chaotically complex reality of practical problem solving; evidence supports the existence of different developmental trajectories (maintenance, improvement, and decline) across the lifespan without a pronounced preference for any single trajectory.

There is no formal theory of the stages of the development of practical intelligence (Berg, 1992). Some results, however, suggest that the difference in performance on practical and analytical tasks is observed rather early. Freeman, Lewis, and Doherty (1991) have shown that the performance of preschoolers on the false belief tasks (tasks involving formation of false beliefs and determination and overcoming of their false nature) is better if they are asked to act out answers rather than to give them verbally. These researchers suggest that the reason for this discrepancy is that early implementation of a theory of intentionality is "only" practical. In other words, preschool children are able to distinguish between true and false expectations and true and false causes but do it by carrying out practical actions (e.g., acting with the right object) rather than by explaining why those particular objects should be chosen. These and other findings contribute to the hypothesis that reflective awareness and verbalization emerge gradually from the implicit practical intelligence schemas that are their necessary precursors (e.g., Bickhard, 1978; Karmiloff-Smith, 1988).

Developmental research on practical intelligence is moving in a number of directions, each of which may help us to detect the internal mechanisms of its development. Most of the work is centered on specific characteristics of practical tasks. The assumption here is that if we understand the differences in the ways these tasks are formulated and solved at different stages of development, we will be closer to understanding the developmental dynamics of practical intelligence. Drawing on the distinction made earlier between academic and practical tasks suggests five main directions of research: (1) studies of developmentally variable contexts of practical problem solving; (2) studies of developmental changes in the content of practical problems encountered at different stages of development; (3) studies of the developmental diversity of the goals of practical problem solving; (4) studies of differential strategies used in practical problem solving at different periods of development; and (5) studies on developmental variation in problem interpretation and definition.

Context of Practical Problem Solving

There is virtually unanimous agreement on the centrality of context for understanding practical problem solving. This view, which holds that practical problem solving cannot be separated from the context in which it unfolds, is referred to as the contextual perspective (Dixon, 1994; Wertsch & Kanner, 1994). In general, the metaphor used to describe the contextual approach is that of trying to follow constantly changing events (i.e., the life course is represented as being a series of changing events, activities, and contexts). When applied to studies of practical problem solving, this perspective assumes that (1) the demands posed by these contexts vary across development; (2) strategies accomplishing adaptation differ across contexts; (3) these strategies also differ across individuals; and, finally, (4) the effectiveness of everyday problem solving is determined by the interaction of individual and context (Berg & Calderone, 1994). Several studies have found that the context in which the problem occurs (e.g., family, work, or school) impacts everyday problem solving in all its components (content, goal, and strategy).

Consider the following examples. Ceci and Bronfenbrenner (1985) and Ceci (1990), employing a dual context paradigm, have conducted a series of studies concerning the impact of physical and social contexts on cognition. The dual context paradigm proposes that children be made to perform the same task in two or more contexts. The assumption here is that some settings elicit more effective forms of cognition than do others by stimulating or activating different strategies. The view of Ceci and Bronfenbrenner is that a task perceived in a modified form might recruit a set of strategies acquired previously but not elicited by the original, unmodified task. (For example, a video game task, which is a modification of a simple task requiring a participant to follow the movements of dots, might recruit strategies that the dot task alone would not.) Cohen (1996) studied the mathematically oriented activity of 3- and 4-year-olds and found that when mathematical operations were embedded in the broader context of a "play store" setting, children were able to solve problems that exceeded an age-appropriate level of difficulty. In addition, the children satisfied the demands of the task in using a variety of solution strategies.

One of the most interesting developments in studies on context and practical problem solving concerns the effect of compensation, the phenomenon in which gains in (mostly) practical intelligence balance out age-related decrements in others. Researchers argue that compensation – considered in terms of the dynamic relationship between the individual's changing cognitive skills and expectations of performance on the one hand and shifting contextual demands on the other hand – should be viewed as central to cognitive aging (Dixon, 1994). One example of practical intelligence compensating for declines in g-based intellectual performance is older adults' effective use of external aids. One common source of external cognitive aid is other people. For example, Dixon (1994) explored the extent to which older and younger adults use same-age collaborators in solving memory problems and found that older adults use previously unknown collaborators to boost their performance levels to a much greater extent than do younger adults.

Two other important characteristics of the context in which practical problem solving occurs, which might explain some aspects of the observed development variability in practical intelligence, are the complexity and familiarity of the context.

As for the complexity of the environment in which practical intelligence unfolds, one variable that has been pointed out as extremely important for shaping the development of practical abilities in adulthood is that of the immediate conditions and demands of work

(Schooler, in press). For example, Kohn and Schooler (1983), in a group of men between the ages of 24 and 64, longitudinally studied the link between the extent to which work-related activities involve independent thought and judgment and workers' flexibility in dealing with complex intellectual demands. They found that the more the substantive complexity of the job, the greater the incremental gains in intellectual performance over a 10-year period. Even more astounding, a similar relationship between job complexity and intellectual performance was revealed for women doing complex housework (Schooler, 1984). Moreover, Miller and Kohn (1983) found that individuals with higher flexibility in dealing with complex intellectual activities tended to engage in more stimulating and demanding intellectual activities (e.g., reading books versus watching television). The major criticism of this nonexperimental evidence of the intellectual effects of doing complex work (whether in the workplace or the household) is that these designs are unable to rule out the possibility that individuals who maintain their intellectual functioning are more capable of pursuing and staying in challenging work environments. Yet, even though the causal path is difficult to infer among individuals, the evidence that among individuals more intellectually complex work leads to enriched intellectual functioning deserves attention and more thorough investigation.

Regarding familiarity or experience with the domain in which practical problem solving is carried out, studies have demonstrated that intellectual performance is greater for both younger and older adults when individuals are given either familiar materials (Smith & Baltes, 1990) or a chance to practice prior to assessment (Berg, Hertzog, & Hunt, 1982). Yet, results are ambiguous as to whether differential familiarity is a factor that can help to explain age differences in practical problem solving (Denney & Pearce, 1989).

Researchers reported, for example, that older adults perceived traditional intelligence tests as less familiar than did young adults (Cornelius, 1984). Therefore, when younger and older adults are compared on conventional intelligence tests, older adults might look worse because these tests are less familiar to them and they may have forgotten how to evoke specific strategies relevant to situations of intellectual assessment.

To explore the importance of the familiarity factor, several studies have been carried out in which younger and older adults were asked to solve problems that were constructed to be more familiar or more normative for one age group or the other. For example, Denney, Pearce, and Plamer (1982) showed that, in adults, the more normative everyday problems are for their age group, the better their performance is. Similarly, Smith and Baltes (1990) found that adults perform best when the problems are more normative for their age group. As Berg (in press) points out, memory research using tasks with familiar materials (e.g., remembering words that were in frequent use during their adult years versus contemporary equivalents) is consistent in showing that older adults tend to perform better with materials more familiar to them (Barrett & Watkins, 1986; Worden & Sherman-Brown, 1983).

Content of Practical Problem Solving

The main hypothesis underlying this line of research is that the content of practical problem solving differs at different stages of development. The literature published to verify this hypothesis contains heterogeneous evidence; some is supportive (Aldwin, Sutton, Chiara, & Spiro, 1996) and some is not supportive (Folkman, Lazarus, Pimley, & Novacek, 1987) of the assertion that individuals of different ages experience different everyday problems.

Berg and Calderone (1994) and Sansone and Berg (1993) asked preschoolers, teenagers, college students, and older adults to describe a recent problem (hassle, conflict, challenge, and so on) that they had experienced and to describe the problem in as much detail as possible. The intent was to investigate whether the types of domains of problems remain constant across development or whether different types of problems would appear for different age groups. The researchers found significant variation in the content of everyday problems across development. The everyday problem solving content for 5- to 6-year-olds consisted predominantly of problems dealing with family (e.g., disagreements with family members) and assigned responsibilities (e.g., home chores). For 11- to 12-year-olds, everyday life problems centered on school and after-school activities and environments. No single content area dominated the everyday life of college students, and their salient problems had to do with free time, work, friends, family, and romantic relationships. Finally, the everyday problem solving of the older adults centered on the family context and health.

Barker (1978) suggested that the content of practical problem solving is determined by the ecological characteristics of a given developmental period. Researchers carried out detailed observations of settings inhabited and experienced by elementary school children on a daily basis and found that children most frequently occupy settings embedded in schooling and family life. This piece of work is unique in terms of its thoroughness and attention to details; however, based on sporadic evidence accumulated in research on developmental life tasks, the general assumption in the field is that the content of the practical problem solving of adults differs in a variety of ways across the life-span. In other words, it might be impossible to carry out studies such as those of Barker (1978) in all ecological settings encountered in adulthood, but it might be possible to target the few that appear to be crucial at specific developmental periods. Specifically, it has been shown that college students' tasks are primarily aimed at succeeding academically, forming social networks, developing an identity, and separating from family (Cantor, Norem, Neidenthal, Langston, & Brower, 1987), whereas adults focus on a variety of tasks, ranging from starting a family and a career in young adulthood through the pragmatic tasks of middle adulthood to adapting to impairments of health and adjusting to retirement during old and advanced old age (Baltes et al., 1984; Havinghurst, 1972; Neugarten Moore, & Lowe, 1968).

Goals of Practical Problem Solving

The goal directedness (e.g., Goodnow, 1986; Scribner, 1986; Wertsch, 1985) of practical problem solving is one of the most often cited characteristics of practical intelligence in application. Therefore, another line of research concerns the developmental trajectories of goals of practical problem solving.

Strough, Berg, and Sansone (1996) showed that there is developmental variation in the types of goals underlying everyday problem solving. The profile of this developmental variation reflects developmental life tasks (Cantor, 1990). Specifically, preadolescents reported more goals for task improvement, and a large portion of their problems involved the school context. Interpersonal goals appeared to be more salient to middle-aged adults than to preadolescents. Preadolescents, however, reported more other-focused assistance recruiting goals than did adults. Older and middle-aged adults reported more physical goals than did younger individuals, and the adult group as a whole reported more affective goals than did preadolescents.

Klaczynski, Laipple, and Jurden (1992) studied practical intelligence among adolescents in college preparatory or vocational training tracks. Depending on the chosen developmental life track, adolescents in the two groups differed in their interpretation of practical problem situations. In particular, vocational students were concerned primarily with goals involving the acquisition of adult status, such as marriage, steady employment, and independence. College preparatory students, on the other hand, reported more achievement-oriented goals, such as doing well in school, gaining admission to quality colleges, and scoring well on entrance examinations.

Belief in the plasticity and fluidity of human developmental goals throughout the life span also is reflected by the notion that there is no single outcome or end point to intellectual development in general or to the development of practical intelligence in particular (Rogoff, 1982). The implication of this line of reasoning is that the individual and his or her context form a complex systemic unit; changes in the unit shape the content, dynamics, and adaptability of the individual's intellectual functioning in specific contexts. Thus, there is no ideal trajectory of intellectual development, and there is no optimal instrument assessing intellectual functioning equally well at all periods of the life span.

Practical Problem Solving Strategies

One of the main research trajectories in the field of practical intelligence focuses on strategies used in problem solving. Among the central characteristics of strategies discussed in the research literature of the past 20 years (Belmont & Butterfield, 1969; Berg, 1989; Brown, 1975; Flavell, 1970; Naus & Ornstein, 1983; Pressley, Forest-Pressley, Elliot, Faust & Miller, 1985) are selectivity, goal directedness, and intentionality. Many developmental researchers have been especially interested in strategy selection as both an individual and a developmental indicator of everyday problem solving performance (Frederiksen, 1986; Frederiksen, Jensen, & Beaton, 1972; Lazarus & Folkman, 1984).

Most of the early developmental work on everyday problem solving has been carried out under the assumption that individuals' chosen strategies can be compared irrespective of the developmental variation in the goals motivating these strategies (Band & Weisz, 1988; Berg, 1989; Cornelius & Caspi, 1987; Folkman, Lazarus, Pimley, & Novacek, 1987). The major theoretical hypothesis dominating the field is that greater experience with everyday problems leads to better problem solving (Baltes et al., 1984; Denney, 1982). This claim assumes that a particular type of strategy – for example, primary control reflected in independent coping and problem-focused action – is a more effective way of dealing with various problems than is some other strategy – for example, secondary control reflected in reliance on others and emotion-focused action (Denney, 1989; Folkman et al., 1987). For example, self-action was the strategy most frequently mentioned across all ages in a study of reported everyday problems (Berg, Strough, Calderone, Sansone, & Weir, 1998). Problem-focused action was most frequently mentioned for hypothetical problems (Blanchard-Fields, Jahnke, & Camp, 1995). Developmental differences have been encountered, which suggests that secondary control strategies, emotion-focused strategies, and dependence on others increases across early childhood (Band & Weisz, 1988), with further elevation in later adulthood (Brandtstaedter & Greve, 1994; Denney & Palmer, 1981; Folkman et al., 1987; Heckhausen & Schultz, 1995). For instance, Band and Weisz (1988) found that older children were more likely to use secondary control strategies, such as efforts to modify the subjective psychological state of the self to better suit the present conditions of the problem, whereas younger children were more likely to use primary control strategies, such as efforts to influence the problem so that it meets the problem solver's expectations.

The empirical literature, however, does not uniformly support the claim that "more experience equals better problem solving" (Baltes, 1997; Berg, 1989; Cornelius & Caspi, 1987). Recent research suggests that strategies are differentially effective depending on the context of the everyday problem (Berg, 1989; Ceci & Bronfenbrenner, 1985; Cornelius & Caspi, 1987; Scribner, 1986). Thus, Cornelius and Caspi (1987) showed that different types of strategies (problem-focused action, cognitive problem analysis, passive-dependent behavior, and avoidant thinking and denial) were viewed as differentially effective in different contexts.

Findings regarding the localization of age differences are also somewhat contradictory. The often cited trend in the literature is that older adults tend to use more secondary control (Heckhausen & Schulz, 1995) and less problem-focused action or primary control (Folkman et al., 1987) as compared with younger adults. Blanchard-Fields, Jahnke, and Camp (1995) found minimal age differences in problem-focused action. Furthemore, Berg, Strough, Calderone, Sanson, and Wier (1998) reported age differences for older adults only, with older people using relatively less cognitive regulation and more self-action than either college students or middle-aged adults. The situation has become even less transparent, with Aldwin, Sutton, Chiara, and Spiro (1996) showing that for the most part, age differences existed among adults only when individuals' strategies were assessed through a checklist; these distinctions were greatly reduced when individuals' strategies were elicited through open-ended interviews.

One of the possible explanations for the heterogeneity of these findings is that what develops over time is sensitivity to specific contexts.
In other words, the repertoire of approaches to everyday problems is
rather broad, and different modules of problem solving are used in different situations; in many ways, consistency across situations may be
maladaptive (Mischel, 1984). Some researchers argue that successful
everyday problem solving will involve carefully fitting strategies to the
specific demands of a problem and modifying these strategies in
response to changes in the problem (Berg & Sternberg, 1985; Rogoff,
Gauvain, & Gardner, 1987; Scribner, 1986). Furthermore, sensitivity to
the contextual features of a problem is characteristic of a developmental factor (Mischel, 1984; Rogoff et al., 1987). Other authors, on the contrary, suggest that these strategies become less context-dependent with
age (Kreitler & Kreitler, 1987).

Yet another, although not contradictory, possibility is that the lesson
derived from experience with everyday problems is how to avoid the
everyday problems in the first place (Berg, 1989). Thus, it is plausible
that no simple relation between kind of experience and everyday problem solving ability is likely to exist. Moreover, researchers have presented evidence demonstrating that so-called "effective across all
contexts (e.g., primary) strategies" fail in situations in which so-called
ineffective strategies (e.g., relinquishing) work (Berg, Calderone, &
Gunderson, 1990, as cited in Berg & Calderone, 1994). Certain kinds of
experience may be differentially related to success at solving particular
kinds of everyday problems, and development might better be con-
strued as improved ability to modify strategies or to avoid potentially
problematic situations (Berg, 1989; Rogoff et al., 1987).

Another line of research focuses on studying individual differences
that appear to lead to more optimal problem solving performance (Ceci
& Liker, 1986; Denney, 1989; Willis & Schaie, 1986). Many factors (e.g.,
conventional intellectual abilities, personality traits, social skills,
achievement motivation) have been shown to influence the utilization
of strategies in everyday problem solving (Ceci & Liker, 1986;
Charness, 1981; Kuhn, Pennington, & Leadbeater, 1983), but no specific
constellations of these factors were found to be better predictors of
effective problem solving.

Problem Interpretation (Definition)

In an attempt to systematize the literature on the development of
everyday problem solving, Berg and colleagues have introduced the

concept of *problem interpretation* (Berg & Calderone, 1994; Sansone & Berg, 1993) or *problem definition* (Berg et al., 1998). The problem interpretation arises at the edge of the context and the individual and is essentially the transaction between the individual and the context. The interpretation derives from features of both the individual and the context, but it might selectively engage all or only some features. Berg and her colleagues argue that such individual and contextual features may have different weights and may be differentially combined at different stages of development; thus, the search for developmental variation in everyday problem solving should focus on the development of problem interpretation (Berg & Calderone, 1994).

As it is interactive in nature, problem definition reflects those aspects of the self and context that are activated with respect to a specific problem unfolding at a specific moment in time. Problem definition is a complex, psychological, subjective reality, which, according to Berg et al. (1998), reflects the individual's goals and expectations (Bandura, 1986), determines the strategies to be used to meet these expectations and accomplish subjective goals (Vallacher & Wegner, 1987), affects the outcome attribution and meaning interpretation (Dodge, Pettit, McClaskey, & Brown, 1986), and induces the affective representation of the problem (Fleeson & Cantor, 1995).

A number of studies provide supportive evidence for the transactional approach to everyday problem solving. Sinnott (1989) showed that older adults' interpretation of Piagetian logical combination problems, especially those encountered in real life (e.g., assigning relatives to sleeping locations), vary to a greater degree than do the interpretations of younger adults. Specifically, older adults tend to be more sensitive to social and interpersonal facets of the problem when compared with younger adults, who concentrate on the problem's logical aspects. Similarly, Laipple (1992) showed that older adults were less likely to interpret the logical problem–solving situation as intended by the experimenter; older adults tended to leave the logical confines of the problem and inject into the experimental situation more personal experience than did the younger adults. Chi and Ceci (1987) suggested that many types of problem solving appear to be directly influenced by the mental context a child brings to the task.

In their own work, Berg and Calderone (1994) registered a number of developmental characteristics of problem definition. First, they showed that with age, there was a decrease in the frequency of task-oriented interpretations of problems and an increase in interpersonal, self, and mixed (e.g., task and self) interpretations. Researchers have suggested that these findings correspond to the literature on the development of the self system, according to which changes of the self system involve movement away from a concrete and specific system to one that incorporates more abstract and interrelated psychological constructs (Harter, 1983). Berg et al. (1998) further studied the link between the problem definition and the selection of strategies for problem solving. In general, problem definition appears to be a more precise predictor of strategy selection than does problem context. Specifically, individuals who defined a problem in terms of interpersonal concerns alone were more likely to report using strategies that involved regulating or including others. On the contrary, individuals who defined a problem solely in terms of competence concerns were more likely to use strategies based on independent action and less likely to engage others. Finally, the links between problem definition and strategy selection were not found to vary as a function of age.

Problem definition is very important to practical intelligence. For example, a key difference between the results of Berg et al. (1998) and those of previous research is the importance that individuals placed on the social aspects of practical problem solving. Berg and colleagues found that the majority of individual problem definitions in any age group (preadolescents, college students, and adults) involved interpersonal concerns. These problem definitions, in turn, determined the selection of strategies that involved regulating or including others. Note that this interpretation differs significantly from the argument used in previous research. Earlier work typically assumed that reliance on others reflected ineffective problem solving because individuals exhibited dependence on others (e.g., Cornelius & Caspi, 1987; Denney & Palmer, 1981; Folkman et al., 1987). However, the reinterpretation of the role of social-dependent strategies suggests that using others to deal with everyday problems is a strategy rather well suited to particular problems (Baltes, 1997; Meacham & Emont, 1989).

PROTOTYPIC FORMS OF DEVELOPED PRACTICAL INTELLIGENCE

During the last few years there has been a new and interesting trend in developmental studies of practical intelligence. A number of researchers have proposed that along with dissecting practical problem solving into its components, we need to study higher-level structures developing in the context of, based on, or functioning as components or prototypic forms of practical intelligence. We consider two such constructs here, intuition and wisdom.

Intuition

A conventional definition of intuition describes this metaconstruct as "...knowing without being able to explain how we know" (Vaughan, 1979). The examination of intuition, despite its apparent importance from anecdotal accounts (Bastick, 1982; Cosier & Aplin, 1982; Goldberg, 1983), is performed somewhat reluctantly. Yet, the very nature of today's society stresses the importance of intuition, which we rely on heavily in day-to-day life as we increasingly have more alternatives and less time to screen them. The importance of intuition has been praised in the arena of professional decisions (Ray & Meyers, 1989; Rockenstein, 1988), in the context of discovery (Bowers, Regehr, Balthazard, & Parker, 1990), and in personal accounts of celebrities (it is well known, for example, that Estée Lauder, founder of the giant cosmetic firm, was known for her intuitive ability to outpredict any market research on which fragrance would sell). Notwithstanding, many researchers have pointed out that reliance on intuition can misguide us and be a systematic source of error in human judgment (Ross, 1977, cited by Bowers et al., 1990).

There is no agreement on what intuition is or how it develops (Goldberg, 1983). The literature is characterized by many notable points of contention clustered within three main themes of study: intuition versus reason and logic (Nutt, 1989; Simonton, 1980); intuition and creativity (Bastick, 1982; Finke, Ward, & Smith, 1992); and intuition and tacit knowledge (Reber, 1989; Shirley & Langan-Fox, 1996).

Goldberg (1983) distinguishes multiple facets (or functions) of intuition. He has suggested that inquiries into intuition could be classified into six categories in which intuition is viewed as a means of discovery, creativity, evaluation, operation, prediction, and illumination. The first two facets of intuition stress its links to creative processes – intuition is a part and the center of the creative process. The sixth facet of intuition, illumination, has to do with self-realization (Goldberg uses such synonyms as *samadhi*, *satori*, nirvana, cosmic consciousness, union with God). The third, fourth, and fifth facets of intuition, however, in Goldberg's interpretation, appear to relate intuition and tacit knowledge, even though the author himself does not use this terminology.

Describing the evaluation facet of intuition, Goldberg refers to the experiences of financial planners, who make contingency plans on the basis of a formal analysis of technical data but use their feelings (intuition) in making the actual decision (commit vs hold off vs abandon). In operation, intuition leads people to actions the reasoning behind which is difficult to explain verbally. Operative intuition might be responsible for what often seems like luck. Goldberg suggests that people who seem to be in the right place at the right time and whose lives are marked by seemingly fortuitous accidents are equipped with this facet of intuition. Predictive intuition, the last category of intuition, is related to both creativity and practicality. An illustration of this can be found in professors' evaluations of their students' potentials. Such evaluations, of course, take into account the available logical evidence (e.g., grades, ideas, dedication), but they are always more than that.

The link between intuition and tacit knowledge appears to be very important in theorizing about the development of practical problem solving. Tacit knowledge is action-oriented, typically acquired without direct help from others, and allows individuals to achieve goals they personally value (Sternberg et al., 1995). Tacit knowledge has three main features: it is procedural; it is relevant to the attainment of goals people value; and it typically is acquired with little help from others. Tacit knowledge forms an important part of practical intelligence (Sternberg, 1995c, 1997a, 1997b). Intuitive thought is said to be the end product of learning (both formal and informal) and experience (Reber, 1989); the learner has gained the knowledge necessary for an intuitive judgment on a particular matter. In the modern world, those professionals who are capable of highly reliable intuitive judgments are increasingly prized within organizations (Rockenstein, 1988). Many managers admit now that they rely on their intuition and "gut feelings" (Ray & Myers, 1989). Moreover, it has been shown that intuitive managers, who rely on intuition as well as analysis when making high-risk decisions, make more profit than those who do not (Ray & Myers, 1989).

A number of researchers, including Shirley and Langan-Fox (1996), have written on the overlap between tacit knowledge and intuition. Reber (1989), for example, defines intuition as a cognitive state that emerges under specifiable conditions and operates to assist an individual to make choices and to carry out a particular course of behavior. To have an intuitive sense of what is right and proper, to have a feeling for what is going to work and what is not going to work, to comprehend the situation holistically, to "get the point" without really being able to verbalize the steps leading to this realization – all of these experiences suggest implicit learning and the development of a requisite tacit knowledge base.

Wisdom

Yet another concept that has been referred to as a higher-level outgrowth of practical intelligence is wisdom. The most extensive program of empirical research on wisdom has been conducted by Baltes and his colleagues. This program of research is related to Baltes's long-standing program of research on intellectual abilities and aging. For example, Baltes and Smith (1987, 1990) presented adult participants with life management problems, such as "A fourteen-year-old girl is pregnant. What should she, what should one, consider and do?" and "A fifteen-year-old girl wants to marry soon. What should she, what should one, consider and do?" This same problem might be used to measure the pragmatics of intelligence, about which Baltes has written at length. Baltes and Smith tested a five-component model of wisdom on participants' protocols in answering these and other questions, based on a notion of wisdom as expert knowledge about fundamental life matters (Smith & Baltes, 1990) or of wisdom as good judgment and advice in important but uncertain matters of life (Baltes & Staudinger, 1993).

Three kinds of factors – general personal factors, expertise-specific factors, and facilitative experiential contexts – were proposed to facilitate wise judgments. These factors are used in life planning, life management, and life review. Wisdom, in turn, is then reflected in five components: (1) rich factual knowledge (general and specific knowledge about the conditions of life and its variations); (2) rich procedural knowledge (general and specific knowledge about strategies of judgment and advice concerning matters of life); (3) life-span contextualism (knowledge about the contexts of life and their temporal [developmental] relationships); (4) relativism (knowledge about differences in values, goals, and priorities); and (5) uncertainty (knowledge about the relative indeterminacy and unpredictability of life and ways to manage them). An expert answer should reflect more of these components, whereas a novice answer should reflect fewer of them. The data collected to date generally have been supportive of the model. These factors seem to reflect the pragmatic aspect of intelligence but go beyond it, for example, in the inclusion of the factors of relativism and uncertainty.

Baltes, Smith, and Staudinger (1992), Baltes and Staudinger (1993), and other colleagues of Baltes have, over time, collected a wide range of data showing the empirical usefulness of the proposed theoretical and measurement approaches to wisdom. For example, Staudinger, Lopez, and Baltes (1997) found that measures of intelligence (as well as personality) overlap with, but are not identical to, measures of wisdom in terms of constructs measured, and Staudinger, Smith, and Baltes (1992) have shown that human services professionals outperformed a control group on wisdom-related tasks. They also showed that older adults performed as well on such tasks as did younger adults, and that older adults did better on such tasks if there was a match between their age and the age of the fictitious characters about whom they made judgments. Baltes, Staudinger, Maercker, and Smith (1995) found that older individuals nominated for their wisdom performed as well as did clinical psychologists on wisdom-related tasks. They also showed that up to the age of 80, older adults performed as well on such tasks as did younger adults. In a further set of studies, Staudinger and Baltes (1996) found that performance settings that were ecologically relevant to the lives of their participants and that provided for actual or virtual interaction of minds increased wisdom-related performance substantially.

Thus, wisdom seems to behave more like crystallized than like fluid intelligence in its development over the life course (Horn, 1994; Horn & Cattell, 1966). In particular, crystallized intelligence, like wisdom, appears to increase during most of the life-span and then perhaps to level off near its end (cf. Meacham, 1990). Fluid intelligence, in contrast, appears to decline after some point in adulthood.

Sternberg (1990b) also proposed an explicit theory of wisdom, suggesting that the development of wisdom can be traced to six antecedent components: (1) knowledge, including an understanding of its presuppositions and meaning as well as its limitations; (2) processes, including an understanding of which problems should be solved automatically and which problems should not be so solved; (3) a judicial thinking style, characterized by the desire to judge and evaluate things in an in-depth way; (4) personality, including tolerance of ambiguity and of the role of obstacles in life; (5) motivation, especially the motivation to understand what is known and what it means; and (6) environmental context, involving an appreciation of the contextual factors in the environment that lead to various kinds of thoughts and actions. The first two of these components correspond very roughly to crystallized and fluid aspects of intelligence, whereas the other components go beyond intelligence as it is usually understood.

Whereas an earlier theory of Sternberg (1990b) specified a set of antecedents of wisdom, his balance theory (Sternberg, 1998b, 1999b) specifies the processes (balancing of interests and of responses to environmental contexts) in relation to the goal of wisdom (achievement of a common good). Correspondingly, the earlier Sternberg (1990b) theory is incorporated into the balance theory as specifying antecedent sources of developmental and individual differences.

Sternberg's current view of wisdom has at its core the notion of tacit knowledge (Polanyi, 1976) about oneself, others, and situational contexts. The balance theory views wisdom as inherent in the interaction between an individual and a situational context, much as intelligence (Sternberg, 1997a; Valsiner & Leung, 1994) involves a person–context interaction, as does creativity (Csikszentmihalyi, 1996; Sternberg & Lubart, 1995). For this reason, the balances proposed by the theory are in the interaction between a person and his or her context, rather than, say, in internal systems of functioning (such as cognitive, conative, and affective). In the current view, people could be balanced in terms of the internal systems by which they process information but not in the products that result from these processes. Because wisdom lies in the interaction of person and situation, information processing in and of itself is not wise or unwise; its degree of wisdom depends on the fit of a wise solution to its context.

In this view, the same balance of cognitive, conative, and affective processes that in one situational context might result in a wise solution, in another context might not. This result might derive, for example, from a lack of tacit knowledge or incorrect tacit knowledge about one situation but not another. Judgments in any domain require a substantial tacit knowledge base in order consistently to be wise. In particular, wisdom is defined as the application of tacit knowledge as mediated by values toward the goal of achieving a common good through a balance among multiple interests (intrapersonal, interpersonal, and extrapersonal) in order to achieve a balance among responses to environmental contexts (adaptation to existing environmental contexts, shaping of existing environmental contexts, and selection of new environmental contexts).

Thus, wisdom is like all practical intelligence (Sternberg, 1985a) in requiring a balancing of responses to environmental contexts, but it only comprises that subset of practical intelligence that involves balancing of interests, something that is not a necessary aspect of all practical intelligence.

The balance theory suggests a number of sources for developmental and individual differences in wisdom. In particular, there are two kinds of sources, those that directly affect the balance processes and those that are antecedent to them.

Five sources of individual and developmental differences directly affect the balance processes. The first is goals. People may differ in terms of the extent to which they seek a common good and thus in the extent to which they aim for the essential goal of wisdom. The seeking of a common good does not apply to intelligence in general, however. One can be analytically, creatively, or even practically intelligent without looking out for the interests of others. Second, people may differ in their balance of responses to environmental contexts. Responses always reflect an interaction of the individual making the judgment with the environmental context, and people can interact with contexts in myriad ways. Such balancing is a hallmark of all uses of practical intelligence. Third, people may balance interests in different ways. This balancing is unique to wisdom and does not necessarily apply to analytical, creative, or other kinds of practical intelligence. Fourth, people bring different kinds and levels of tacit knowledge to judgmental situations that are likely to affect their responses. This aspect of wisdom applies to all practical intelligence but typically does not apply to analytical or creative intelligence. Finally, people have different values that mediate their utilization of tacit knowledge in the balancing of interests and responses. Values covertly enter into all aspects of intelligence just as soon as intelligence is measured, because any test of intelligence reflects someone's (usually the author's) values as to what is worth measuring on a test of intelligence.

These sources of differences produce variation in how wise people are and in how well they can apply their wisdom in different kinds of situations. To the extent that wisdom typically is associated with greater intellectual and even physical maturity, this presumably is because the development of tacit knowledge and of values is something that unfolds over the course of the life-span, not just in childhood or even in the early years of adulthood.

The above sources of individual differences pertain to the balancing processes. Other sources (knowledge, triarchic abilities, judicial thinking styles, personality variables, motivation to think wisely, and environmental variables), specified in Sternberg's (1990b) earlier theory, are antecedent to these processes.

Some theorists have viewed wisdom in terms of post-formal operational thinking, thereby viewing wisdom as a form of intellectual functioning that extends the development of thinking beyond the Piagetian stages of intelligence (Piaget, 1972). These theorists seem to view wisdom in a way that is similar or even identical to the way they perceive the development of intelligence past the Piagetian (1972) stage of formal operations. For example, some authors have argued that wise individuals are those who can think reflectively or dialectically, in the latter case with the individuals' realizing that truth is not always absolute but rather evolves in a historical context of theses, antitheses, and syntheses (Basseches, 1984; Kitchener, 1983, 1986; Kitchener & Brenner, 1990; Kitchener & Kitchener, 1981; Labouvie-Vief, 1980, 1982, 1990; Pascual-Leone, 1990; Riegel, 1973). Consider a very brief review of some specific dialectical approaches.

Kitchener and Brenner (1990) suggested that wisdom requires a synthesis of knowledge from opposing points of view. Similarly, Labouvie-Vief (1990) has emphasized the importance of a smooth and balanced dialogue between logical forms of processing and more subjective forms of processing. Pascual-Leone (1990) has argued for the importance of the dialectical integration of all aspects of a person's affect, cognition, conation (motivation), and life experience. Similarly, Orwoll and Perlmutter (1990) have emphasized the importance to wisdom of an integration of cognition with affect. Kramer (1990) has suggested the importance of the integration of relativistic and dialectical modes of thinking, affect, and reflection. And Birren and Fisher (1990), combining a number of views of wisdom, have suggested as well the importance of the integration of the cognitive, conative, and affective aspects of human abilities. A common feature of these models is the balancing of different aspects of the mind – what Baltes (in press) refers to as the orchestration of the mind. In contrast, the balance theory described in this chapter (Sternberg, 1998b) views balance as referring to competing interests and reactions to the environment in response to these competing interests.

Other theorists have suggested the importance of knowing the limits of one's own extant knowledge and of then trying to go beyond it. For example, Meacham (1990) has suggested that an important aspect of wisdom is a kind of metacognition, that is, an awareness of one's own fallibility and a knowledge of what one does and does not know. Similarly, Kitchener and Brenner (1990) have also emphasized the importance of knowing the limitations of one's own knowledge. Arlin (1990) has linked wisdom to problem finding, the first step of which is recognition that how one currently defines a problem may be inadequate. This view perhaps links wisdom not just with intelligence but with creativity, in that problem finding is often viewed as important to creative thinking (Getzels & Csikszentmihlayi, 1976; Sternberg, 1999a; Sternberg & Lubart, 1995). Arlin sees problem finding as a possible stage of post-formal operational thinking. Such a view is not necessarily inconsistent with the view of dialectical thinking as such a post-formal operational stage. Dialectical thinking and problem finding could represent either two distinct post-formal operational stages or two manifestations of the same post-formal operational stage. These operations provide a transition for the kinds of skills that will be needed, beyond formal operational skills, in the workplace.

CHAPTER 4

Practical Intelligence in the Workplace

For the last 50 years, the field of management has been split in two. The split is between those who perceive managers to be rational technicians, whose job is to apply the principles of management science in the workplace (Taylor, 1947), and those who view managers as craftsmen, who practice an art that cannot be captured by a set of scientific principles (Schön, 1983). This split has had profound implications for managerial theory, practice, and training (Wagner, 1991). In this chapter, we review some of the approaches to understanding management that highlight the importance of practical abilities.

This chapter is divided into two parts. In the first part, we review rational approaches to managerial problem solving and consider some possible limitations of these approaches. The goal of this part is to provide a historical perspective from which to view the development of alternative approaches. In the second part, we review approaches that emphasize the art of managerial problem solving. Our focus here is on approaches that attempt to examine practical intelligence or competence as it is applied in the workplace to solve managerial problems.

RATIONAL APPROACHES TO MANAGEMENT

The management science movement has produced a number of approaches that collectively are referred to as rational approaches to problem solving (Isenberg, 1984). The hallmark of rational approaches to managerial problem solving is a set of problem solving principles alleged to have near universal applicability. Two examples of rational approaches will be described for purposes of illustration.

The Rational Manager

Kepner and Tregoe (1965) proposed a system for solving managerial problems in their classic text on rational management, which consists of five key principles.

1. *Problems are identified by comparing actual performance with an expected standard of performance.* The most important thing effective managers do continuously is to compare what should be happening with what is happening. A problem is identified when a significant discrepancy is found.

2. *Problems are defined as deviations from expected standards of performance.* Problem definition is based on an analysis of the discrepancy between actual and expected performance that alerted a manager to the existence of a problem in the first place. For example, assume that the normal percentage of defective jeans produced in a Texas plant is 5%. If the percentage of defective jeans increases to 15%, the problem is defined as "a tripling in the percentage of defective jeans produced at the Texas plant."

3. *Prerequisite to identifying the cause of a problem is generating a precise and complete description of the problem.* Describing a problem precisely and completely consists of describing four things. What is happening? Where is it happening? When is it happening? To what extent is it happening? To provide a boundary for the problem, an effort is made also to describe what is not happening, that is, what is not problematical.

4. *The cause of the problem will be found by comparing situations in which the problem is found with similar situations in which the problem is not found.* Problems rarely affect everything. Most problems can be isolated to a particular plant, shift, product, time, and so forth. Searching out potential causes of the problem involves identifying what differentiates the situation in which the problem is found from similar situations in which the problem is not found. This is the key to determining the cause of the problem. For example, searching for a problem isolated to night shift workers would begin with an analysis of differences between them and day shift workers, including differences in their supervision and the nature of their work.

5. *Problems are the result of some change that has caused an unwanted deviation from expectations.* Assuming the problem is of recent origin, something must have changed to produce it. Thus, a quality control problem may have begun when a new employee was hired on the suspect shift. Perhaps the new employee has been poorly trained or is careless.

Kepner and Tregoe illustrate the application of their principles using a problem involving rancid butterfat. The example begins with the vice-president of a butterfat manufacturer receiving a call from a customer of her midwestern plant informing her that butterfat is turning rancid during the manufacture of various food products. The vice president defined the problem in terms of a deviation from the expected standard. The problem therefore was that some bags of butterfat produced in the midwestern plant turned rancid before they should have.

Having identified that a problem existed and having defined it, the next step was to describe the problem as precisely and completely as possible. By talking with individuals on the scene, the vice-president learned four important facts: (1) The problem was limited to bags of butterfat that were produced at the company's midwestern plant; (2) the problem affected only the single customer; (3) the problem butterfat was limited to 20% of the bags that the customer used; and (4) the problem had begun about 1 week previously.

Having generated a precise problem description, the next step was to search for factors that differed when the problem occurred and when it did not. This investigation revealed, first, that the customer was the midwestern plant's largest customer, a consequence of which was that the customer's bags were handled differently from those of other customers. The bags for the large customer were stacked in cubes on pallets before being frozen for shipment. However, this fact did not really explain the problem because the customer's bags had been handled this way for several years, and yet the problem had appeared only 1 week previously. Second, the midwestern plant's quality control inspector was a new employee who had begun work 1 week previously. However, even if the quality control inspector was not doing his job, that fact would only explain why it was a customer rather than plant personnel who discovered the problem and not why a plant that typically turns out good butterfat began turning out bad butterfat. Third, a new, more cost-effective freezer that had been brought on line 1 week previously in the midwestern plant had been used to freeze the bags of butterfat before shipping. If the new machine was not working as effectively as the old one, some of the bags of butterfat might not have been completely frozen and thus could have turned rancid. However, why would only the one customer be affected?

A potential cause was identified by combining the facts that the customer's bags were stacked and that a new freezer was in operation. The vice-president asked the plant manager to insert temperature probes into one of the cubes, with some probes near the center of the cube and others near the outside, and then to use the new freezer to freeze the cube. The results of this test indicated that the bags near the outside froze very quickly, but that the bags near the center were not cooled at all. The frozen bags on the outside of the cube insulated the inner bags from the cold of the freezer. The problem was solved by having bag handlers leave at least 1 inch of space between the columns of bags as opposed to their previous method of stacking them into a solid cube. A subsequent test using temperature probes showed that the space between columns resulted in all bags being frozen completely.

The Proactive Manager

A second example of a rational approach to managerial problem solving is provided by Plunkett and Hale (1982). Their system of managerial problem solving is based on the following seven steps:

1. *State the problem.* The first step in problem solving is to state the problem and the desired resolution. Problem identification and formulation are assumed to be perfunctory parts of the problem solving process, as was true for the previous approach.

2. *Describe the problem.* The second step is to describe the problem carefully. Key facts to be determined include (1) what object, unit, or person appears to be affected by the problem; (2) what exactly is wrong; (3) where the problem is found; (4) when the problem began; and (5) how many of the total number of objects, units, or persons that could be affected by the problem actually are affected.

3. *Identify differences between affected and unaffected objects, units, or persons.* The cause of the problem is identified by examining differences between affected and unaffected objects, units, or persons.

4. *Identify changes that are associated with the problem.* When something is operating at the expected level of performance, it will continue to do so unless something changes. Whatever changes will be the origin of the problem.

5. *Generate likely causes.* Once changes that are associated with the problem have been identified, the problem solver attempts to determine how a particular change, either alone or in combination with other changes or factors, might have caused the problem.

6. *Consider the most likely cause.* Here the problem solver determines whether the most likely cause provides an adequate explanation for the problem, focusing on whether the cause can explain why the problem appears in some situations and not in others.

7. *Verify the most likely cause.* The goal here is to find some independent means to verify that one has uncovered the actual cause of the problem rather than a potential cause.

Rational approaches to managerial problem solving such as those proposed by Kepner and Tregoe (1965) and Plunkett and Hale (1982) have a number of obvious strengths. First, the approaches are explicit and thus readily communicated to others. Second, the approaches are general, applying universally to all problems and potential problem solvers. The same principles apply regardless of the nature of the specific problem or of the characteristics of the manager who is responsible for solving the problem. The generality of rational approaches to managerial problem solving has served as a rationale for creating a class of general managers who can move from position to position and yet be effective problem solvers. This generality provides an organization with considerable flexibility in staffing managerial positions. Third, the approaches are based on principles of logic and scientific reasoning. Managers attempt to minimize bias and avoid jumping to conclusions prematurely. They generate alternative potential explanations of a problem and they search for independent confirmation of the explanation on which they settle.

Given these obvious strengths, it is perhaps surprising that support for the rational management approach appears to be on the decline. For example, rational approaches have received little consideration in handbooks of managerial problem solving (Albert, 1980; Virga, 1987). What has limited the influence of rational approaches to managerial problem solving?

One problem for rational approaches is evidence that effective problem solvers often deviate from rational approaches in significant ways. For example, Mintzberg's (1973) influential studies of what managers actually do, as opposed to what they are supposed to do or what they say they do, showed that managers rarely, if ever, employed rational approaches. Rather than following a step-by-step sequence from problem definition to problem solution, managers typically grope along with only vague impressions about the nature of the problems they are dealing with and with little idea of what the ultimate solution will be until they have found it (Mintzberg, Raisinghani, & Theoret, 1976). Isenberg (1984) reached a similar conclusion in his analysis of how senior managers solve problems. The senior managers he studied did not follow the rational model of first defining problems, next assessing possible causes, and only then taking action to solve the problem. Instead they proceeded from general overriding concerns and worked simultaneously on a number of problems. The senior managers often took action throughout the problem solving process. In fact, evaluating the outcomes of their preliminary actions appeared to be one of their more useful tools for problem formulation.

A second problem for rational approaches to managerial problem solving is growing skepticism about the power of general principles of problem solving in the absence of content knowledge of the problem solving domain (McCall & Kaplan, 1985). Proponents of rational approaches have argued that one of the major strengths of such approaches is that managers can apply these approaches without having prior knowledge of or experience with the problems they confront. For example, Kepner and Tregoe (1965) found it notable that a particular manager was able to solve a problem with "...no special know-how or detailed technical information about this problem. He relied instead on a thorough knowledge of the process of problem analysis."

The growing awareness of the limitation of rational approaches to managerial problem solving has led to an interest in closer study of the art of managerial problem solving, with a focus on how practical intelligence or competence actually is applied in the workplace.

APPLYING PRACTICAL INTELLIGENCE IN THE WORKPLACE

We now turn to a description of alternative approaches for studying the application of practical competence in the workplace. The first approach to be considered, that of Isenberg (1986), suggests that managers deviate most strongly from the rational model in terms of their propensity to act before the facts are in.

Thinking While Doing

Isenberg (1986) used a variety of methods for studying how experienced managers solve problems. For example, he compared the thinking-aloud protocols of 12 general managers and of 3 college students who planned to pursue business careers as they solved a short business case. The case involved the Dashman Company (Harvard Business School Case Services, 1947):

Mr. Post was recently appointed vice-president of purchasing. The Dashman Company has 20 plants, and in an effort to avoid shortfalls in essential raw materials required by the plants, Mr. Post decided to centralize part of the purchasing process the plants must follow. Mr. Post's experienced assistant objected to the change, but Mr. Post proceeded with the new procedures anyway. He sent a letter describing the new purchasing process to plant managers responsible for purchasing and received supportive letters from the managers of all 20 plants. However, none of the managers complied with the new purchasing process.

The case was presented in parts on cards. The participants' task was to identify Mr. Post's problems and to determine what he should do about them. The participants' verbal protocols were transcribed and coded into categories that covered encoding information (e.g., ponders specific information, clarifies meaning, evaluates information), reasoning (e.g., causal reasoning, conditional reasoning, analogical reasoning), and planning action (e.g., makes reference to goals when planning, puts self in place of another when deciding what to do, establishes contingencies). In addition to coding the verbal protocols, the effectiveness of the participants' solutions to Mr. Post's problems was rated by several professors at the Harvard Business School who had used the Dashman case in their teaching over the years. As compared with a control group of students, the experienced managers began planning action sooner; asked for less additional information; drew more inferences from the data; and were less reflective about what they were doing and why. In many cases, managers began suggesting problem solutions after reading only half of the cards containing the case, even though they were not under time pressure and additional information was available merely by turning over the remaining cards.

Thus, experienced managers behaved differently from the way that a rational model of managerial problem solving would suggest. They were very soon action-oriented into the problem solving process. Their analyses were cursory rather than exhaustive and were based on their personal experience with analogous problems rather than on more formal principles of problem solving. As is consistent with Mintzberg

(1973), these results suggest that managers are people of action rather than of analysis. Peters and Waterman (1982) noted that effective organizations capitalize on mangers' penchant for action by promoting a "bias for action."

Isenberg (1984) documented other ways that managers depart from traditional conceptions of managerial problem solving. The traditional view is that managers carefully choose a strategy, formulate well-specified goals, establish clear and quantifiable objectives, and determine the most effective way to reach them. Whereas the traditional view might present an accurate picture of how junior managers approach problems, senior managers do their jobs differently. Using detailed interviews and observation, Isenberg demonstrated that senior managers work from one or a small number of very general concerns or preoccupations.

Nonlinear Problem Solving

Solving managerial problems by proceeding linearly through the stages of problem recognition, analysis, and solution is the exception rather than the rule. Typically, problem solving is recursive, with repeated delays, interruptions, revisions, and restarts (Mintzberg et al., 1976). For example, few of the problems presented to managers are correctly formulated. Most problems are formulated in ways that make reaching a solution nearly impossible. Whether a formulation is the optimal one is rarely apparent until attempts have been made at finding and implementing solutions.

Identifying potential problem solutions also becomes a recursive operation. Managers produce solutions bit by bit, as they are guided only by a vague notion of some ideal solution. Managers often do not know what the ultimate solution will look like until it has been completely crafted together. The recursive nature of problem solving continues through to the implementation of solutions. Solutions cannot be implemented without authorization, and for important problems, managers usually must seek authorization from others. The authorization process can be recursive, cycling back and forth among several levels of the organization and the manager. To make matters worse, interruptions and delays are common to all phases of managerial problem solving.

McCall and Kaplan's (1985) extensive interviews with working managers confirmed Mintzberg's observations about the nonlinear character of managerial problem solving, especially when the problems are important ones. McCall and Kaplan characterized the process as convoluted action. Convoluted action occurs over significant time periods, typically months or even years as opposed to days or weeks. Many people are involved, with different interest groups competing for their stake in the outcome. Exhaustive searches are carried out to find solutions to problems, each of which is scrutinized before implementation is considered.

An advantage of convoluted action is that it appears to meet organizational needs. Problems often are caused by and affect a web of interrelated groups and individuals in an organization. Solutions to such problems must involve the cooperative efforts of many parties if they are to succeed. Convoluted action provides the opportunity for all interested parties to attempt to influence the process. A disadvantage of convoluted action is the frequency with which the process breaks down before a solution is identified and implemented. Because so many individuals are involved and because each has the opportunity to derail or at least delay the process, it is not unusual for a solution to be put on the shelf rather than to be implemented – that is, if the process even reaches to the point of solution implementation. Problems are much more likely to be solved through convoluted action if they have a champion who refuses to let the problem solving process be derailed until it has been completed (Peters & Waterman, 1982).

Not all problem solving in organizations involves convoluted action. Some problems simply cannot wait for convoluted action to run its course. These problems require quick action, the characteristics of which are just the opposite of those of convoluted action (McCall & Kaplan, 1985). The goal of the manager is to implement a solution to the problem as quickly as possible. The manager takes sole responsibility for deciding on a solution and makes the decision unilaterally, although others may be consulted for advice if they are available. The search for information and alternative solutions is necessarily cursory. There simply is no time to obtain all of the information that might be helpful, so the manager must focus on a few key facts and must rely heavily on past experience.

An advantage of quick action is that it is not thwarted by problems that are not clearly understood, and more may be learned about the nature of some problems by studying the response to a quick action than by analysis without action. A political advantage of quick action is that it informs others in the organization that the problem is being dealt with. The obvious disadvantages of quick action include the facts that the chances of choosing an ineffective or even a deleterious solution are nontrivial and that the manager who takes quick action is likely to bear complete responsibility for a failure.

McCall and Kaplan (1985) identified several characteristics of managers who seem to be able to make quick action work. These managers rely on one or two individuals who can provide trustworthy information about the problem. They drop everything and attend to the problem directly rather than delegating parts of the problem solving process. And although it may seem counterintuitive, they avoid taking unnecessarily quick action. When presented with an emergency, their first response is to question why the situation must be handled the same day, as opposed to the next day or the next week. Often, only one aspect of the problem is really urgent, and that aspect can be dealt with by some limited response that will buy some time for addressing the complete problem.

Reflection in Action

Schön (1983) described the environment that managers confront as comprising dynamic situations involving many complex, interwoven problems, each of which must be restructured to make it soluble. Because problems are complex and interconnected and environments are turbulent, rational analytic methods will not suffice. What is required is a manager who can imagine a more desirable future and invent ways of reaching it.

Much of managerial competence appears as action that is nearly spontaneous and is based more on intuition than on rationality (Schön, 1983). When asked to explain their behavior, managers either are at a loss for words or will make up an explanation that may be fictitious. They do not invent such explanations intentionally but only in the spirit of trying to satisfy the questioner. To use Schön's own words, "Our knowing is ordinarily tacit, implicit in our patterns of action and in our feel for the stuff with which we are dealing. It seems right to say that our knowing is *in* our action."

Schön is not the first to make this observation. For example, Barnard (1938, 1968) believed such knowledge to come from nonlogical processes that cannot be expressed in words but are demonstrated in judgment and action. Thus, people are able to make quite accurate judgments of things such as the distance to the pin in golf and the trajectory to throw a ball so that it reaches its intended target. Yet they are not able to describe how they make their judgments.

Although managers cannot accurately describe how they are able to do what they do, many managers do occasionally attempt to reflect on their actions as they perform them. These reflections in action are on-the-spot examinations and testing of a manager's intuitive understanding of a situation, often in the form of a reflective conversation about the situation (Schön, 1983). They are the cornerstone of Schön's analyses. For example, a manager might ask herself why she feels uneasy about a decision she is about to make or whether she might come up with a new way of framing an intractable problem. Although the practice of reflection in action is widespread among managers, managers rarely, if ever, reflect on their reflection in action.

One of the best examples of the importance of reflection in action is provided by marketing. Businesses depend on their ability to identify, create, and adapt to markets. The study of market phenomena is a highly specialized one; the field of marketing research has generated quantitative models of market phenomena and methods for predicting the response of a particular market to a particular product. However, the vast majority of the work managers do during the course of product development and marketing requires them to transcend the techniques and knowledge of market research. One reason for the limited effectiveness of market research on product development is a mismatch in timing. To be of much use in development, knowledge about a product's potential markets needs to be available early in product development, before considerable resources have been invested in a particular design. Yet market researchers cannot make accurate predictions until the product has been fully developed and can be test marketed. Market researchers can ask individuals how interested they would be in a yet to be developed product that will do x, y, and z, but the individuals' responses are poor predictors of their subsequent behavior, should the product subsequently appear in a store.

As an example, Schön (1983) described the marketing of a new type of tape by 3M (Minnesota Mining and Manufacturing Co.) shortly after World War II as an example of reflection in action. The company had developed a clear cellulose acetate tape that was coated on one side with an adhesive. The intended use of the product, named Scotch Tape, was for mending books that might otherwise be thrown away. The initial marketing plan, which reflected the intended use of mending books, did not succeed because not many people were interested in mending their books. However, some Scotch Tape was being bought by consumers who used it for a variety of other purposes, such as wrapping packages or holding curlers in their hair. The marketing managers reacted by dropping the original marketing plan and bringing out different types of Scotch Tape, each designed optimally for a particular use, such as wrapping packages or curling hair.

In summary, managerial problem solving often is not characterized by a linear progression through the stages of problem formulation, solution search, and solution implementation but instead may be characterized by either a recursive and interrupted cycling through the various stages (i.e., convoluted action) or by a compressed response that truncates part of the problem solving process (i.e., quick action). The results of the approaches that have been discussed suggest that managers do not follow a rational model of first reflecting and then acting. Schön (1983) suggests that managers do reflect, but this reflection occurs primarily during as opposed to before taking action.

A common theme of these more practical approaches to understanding managerial problem solving is that the rational theories espoused in some business schools do not necessarily apply in real-world managerial situations. Managers seem to learn how to adapt to the various demands of each situation – to take quick action and to adjust their plans of action as necessary. But what is it that successful managers learn that enables them to respond effectively? In chapter 4, we discuss various approaches to understanding real-world problem solving ability, including those pertaining to social intelligence, emotional intelligence, and successful intelligence.

CHAPTER 5

Approaches to Studying Practical Intelligence

During the past two decades, there has been a growing interest (and in part a renewed interest) in nonacademic forms of intelligence. Several distinct but arguably overlapping constructs have been proposed to capture this nonacademic intelligence. One of these constructs is Sternberg's (1985a, 1997a) concept of practical intelligence. Alternative related conceptualizations of nonacademic or practical intelligence include social intelligence (Cantor & Kihlstrom, 1987; Ford & Maher, 1998; Kihlstrom & Cantor, in press), emotional intelligence (Goleman, 1995; Salovey & Mayer, 1990; Mayer, Salovey, & Caruso, in press), and intrapersonal and interpersonal intelligences (Gardner, 1983, 1993). Jones and Day (1997) noted the similarities among the various conceptualizations of nonacademic intelligence. They suggested that practical, social, and emotional intelligence share a focus on declarative and procedural knowledge, flexible knowledge retrieval capabilities, and problem solving involving more than one correct interpretation or solution. In this chapter we discuss the different conceptualizations of practical intelligence and the methods researchers have used to study them.

SOCIAL INTELLIGENCE

Interest in the construct of social intelligence has fluctuated since the concept was first introduced by Thorndike (1920), who defined social intelligence as comprising the abilities to understand others and to act or behave wisely in relation to others. He also distinguished social from abstract and mechanical forms of intelligence. Several other definitions and expansions of Thorndike's definition followed. These expanded definitions included the ability to get along with others (Moss & Hunt, 1927), the ability to deal with people (Hunt, 1928), knowledge about people (Strang, 1930), ease with other people, insights into the states and traits of others (Vernon, 1933), and the ability to judge correctly the feelings, moods, and motivations of others (Wedeck, 1947). Wechsler's (1958) definition seemed to capture these various conceptualizations in the single definition of social intelligence as one's facility in dealing with human beings.

Some researchers sought to understand the meaning of social intelligence by studying people's implicit concepts or theories (Bruner, Shapiro, & Tagiuri, 1958; Cantor, 1978). In a study by Sternberg et al. (1981), discussed previously, experts and laypersons were asked to rate to what extent various behaviors were characteristic of intelligent, academically intelligent, and everyday intelligent people. A factor of *social competence* emerged from the factor analyses of the ratings in each aspect of intelligence.

More recently, Kosmitzki and John (1993) attempted to clarify some of the inconsistency in the literature regarding definitions of social intelligence. They identified seven components that seemed to be most central to people's implicit conceptions of social intelligence. These components included both cognitive elements (perspective taking, understanding people, knowing social rules, and openness to others) and behavioral elements (ability to deal with people, social adaptability, and interpersonal warmth). These implicit conceptions overlap, to some extent, with scientists' explicit theories, but suggest some additional aspects previously not included, such as interpersonal warmth and openness to others. Although these last two aspects have yet to be tested empirically, most studies have focused on some variation of the five remaining components (perspective taking, understanding people, knowing social rules, ability to deal with people, and social adaptability).

Throughout its history, the study of social intelligence has periodically fallen out of favor with researchers. This lack of interest can be attributed to failed attempts to distinguish measures of social from measures of academic or abstract intelligence. The difficulty in making this distinction can be explained by efforts that focus primarily on cognitive aspects of social intelligence and methods that rely heavily on verbal assessment. Researchers as early as Thorndike (1920) acknowledged the multidimensional nature of social intelligence. Until recently, however, the approaches to studying social intelligence have emphasized cognitive aspects, such as social perception (Chapin, 1942) and moral reasoning (Keating, 1978). In order to assess these cognitive dimensions, researchers relied to a large extent on verbal measures.

Measures of behavioral aspects of social intelligence also have relied somewhat on verbal forms of assessment (e.g., self-report). As becomes clear from a brief review of the literature, research efforts that consider behavioral and nonverbal measures of social intelligence have had greater success in establishing discriminant validity from measures of abstract intelligence than have the more cognitive, verbal measures of social intelligence.

Cognitive–Verbal Measures of Social Intelligence

Many approaches to understanding social intelligence follow the tradition of intelligence testing by developing instruments to assess individual differences in social intelligence. One of the first and better known tests of social intelligence was the George Washington Social Intelligence Test (GWSIT) (Moss, Hunt, Omwake, & Woodward, 1949). This test consists of a number of subtests that assess judgment in social situations, recognition of the mental states behind messages, memory for names and faces, observation of human behavior, and sense of humor. Early research with the GWSIT suggested that it could not be distinguished easily from measures of abstract intelligence (Thorndike & Stein, 1937).

A set of social intelligence tests emerged within the context of Guilford's (1967) Structure of Intellect model of intelligence. Within Guilford's framework, social intelligence is viewed as comprising those abilities that fall within the domain of behavioral operations. O'Sullivan, Guilford, and deMille (1965) developed tests to measure behavioral cognition, which they defined as the ability to judge people. More specifically, the tests measured ability to decode social cues, including facial expressions, vocal inflections, posture, and gestures. In a study with 306 high school students, O'Sullivan et al. (1965) found evidence that their factors of social intelligence were distinct from measures of abstract cognitive ability. Later research, however, found contradictory results (Riggio, Messamer, & Throckmorton, 1991).

Riggio et al. (1991) administered several measures of social intelligence and several measures of academic intelligence to undergraduate students. Academic intelligence was measured by the Shipley–Hartford Institute of Living Scale (Shipley, 1940), which measures verbal and abstract reasoning, and the vocabulary subscale of the WAIS-R (Wechsler, 1981). Measures of social intelligence included four tests of the Factor Tests of Social Intelligence (O'Sullivan & Guilford, 1976); Riggio's (1986, 1989) Social Skills Inventory (SSI), which assess six social communication skills (emotional expressivity, emotional sensitivity, emotional control, social expressivity, social sensitivity, and social control); and a social etiquette–tacit knowledge test, which measured knowledge of appropriate behaviors in social situations. Riggio et al. (1991) found comparable intercorrelations *within* measures of both academic and social intelligence as they did *between* measures of these types of intelligence. An exploratory factor analysis suggested two factors: One included the Shipley-Hartford Abstract Reasoning Scale and the Guilford measures and was labeled *abstract reasoning intelligence,* and the second included the Shipley-Hartford Verbal Scale and the SSI, which was labeled *verbal intelligence.* These findings suggested that academic and social intelligence are overlapping domains. At the same time, these researchers found little evidence of convergent validity among the measures of social intelligence, which likely reflects the complexity of the construct and the various ways it has been operationalized in the literature.

Similar results were obtained by Keating (1978), using a different set of social intelligence measures. Keating administered the Social Insight Test (Chapin, 1967), which asks individuals to read about problem situations and to select the best from among four alternative interpretations of the situation; the Defining Issues Test (Rest, 1975), based on Kohlberg's (1963) theory of moral development; and the Social Maturity Index (Gough, 1966), which is a self-report measure of effective social functioning. Keating failed to find substantial intercorrelations among the social intelligence measures, and found no evidence, from either a multitrait-multimethod analysis or a factor analysis, that social intelligence was distinct from academic intelligence. All of Keating's measures, like those of Riggio et al. (1991), were verbal, which may have contributed to their inability to discriminate between abstract and social intelligence.

Behavioral Approaches to Measuring Social Intelligence

As a result of frustrations in trying to distinguish social from academic intelligence, many researchers returned to Thorndike's (1920) definition and considered the behavioral as well as cognitive dimension of the construct. These researchers (Ford & Tisak, 1983; Frederickson, Carlson, & Ward, 1984) proposed that cognitive aspects of social intelligence might expectedly be more closely associated with abstract intelligence, whereas behavioral aspects would represent a more distinct construct.

A supplementary set of tests to those of O'Sullivan et al. (1965) emerged from Guilford's (1967) Structure of Intellect model. These tests focused on behavioral rather than cognitive abilities and defined social intelligence as the ability to cope with people (Hendricks, Guilford, & Hoepfner, 1969). Hendricks et al. administered their tests to 252 high school students. Through principal-components analysis they identified factors that readily were interpretable as divergent production abilities and found that these factors were independent of behavioral cognition. These findings were later confirmed by Chen and Michael (1993).

A study by Ford and Tisak (1983) took the next step by distinguishing a behavioral measure of social intelligence from academic intelligence. The investigators conducted their study with more than 600 high school students. Their measure of social intelligence included self, peer, and teacher ratings of social competence, Hogan's (1969) empathy test, and a judgment of social competence from an individual interview. In addition, they obtained measures of verbal and mathematical ability from school grades and standardized test scores. The measures of academic and social intelligence were found to load on separate factors. They further found that the ratings of social competence and scores on the empathy scale were more predictive of interview ratings than were the measures of verbal and mathematical ability. Ford and Tisak suggested that the difference between their findings and those of Keating (1978) were attributable to their use of a behavioral rather than a cognitive measure of social intelligence.

A number of subsequent studies obtained findings consistent with Ford and Tisak (1983). Marlowe (1986), for example, found that scores on several self-report measures of social intelligence were unrelated to scores on measures of verbal and abstract intelligence. Similarly, Frederickson et al. (1984) did not find significant correlations between ratings of interview behavior and measures of scholastic aptitude, achievement, or problem solving. However, Stricker and Rock (1990) did find a correlation between verbal ability and participants' ability to judge accurately a person and a situation from a videotaped interview.

Stricker and Rock (1990) administered a behavioral situational judgment test, the Interpersonal Competence Instrument (ICI), to 131 undergraduates, along with other measures of social intelligence (e.g., peer and self-ratings, accuracy in decoding nonverbal communication) and measures of general ability (e.g., verbal comprehension, general reasoning). Using multidimensional scaling analysis, they found little evidence of convergent or discriminant validity among the measures of social intelligence and general ability. Some of the social intelligence measures appeared to tap verbal ability, whereas others seemed to measure general reasoning ability. In contrast to the findings of Ford and Tisak (1983), these results failed to support the hypothesis that behavioral measures of social intelligence would be more distinguishable from measures of general academic intelligence than would be verbal measures of social intelligence.

Brown and Anthony's (1990) findings suggested that the constructs of social and academic intelligence are distinct but potentially interrelated. They evaluated the relationship of grade point average (GPA) and American College Test (ACT) English and mathematics scores of college freshman to self and peer ratings of personality and behavioral dimensions of social intelligence. Using a principal-components analysis, they identified three distinct components in their data, represented by an academic component, a peer-ratings component, and a self-ratings component. They concluded that social intelligence could be separated from academic intelligence. Social intelligence as perceived by others was also distinct from one's own assessment of social skills. However, they also found that GPA was the best predictor of self and peer ratings on behavioral aspects of social intelligence, which suggests a relationship between social skills and school performance.

Nonverbal Approaches to Measuring Social Intelligence

In addition to behavioral approaches to measuring social intelligence, researchers have also sought to distinguish social from academic intelligence by pursing nonverbal measures. Nonverbal approaches to measuring social intelligence assess primarily nonverbal decoding skills (Archer, 1980; Archer & Akert, 1980; Barnes & Sternberg, 1989; Rosenthal, 1979; Rosenthal, Hall, DiMatteo, Rogers, & Archer, 1979; Sternberg & Smith, 1985). Rosenthal et al. developed the Profile of Nonverbal Sensitivity (PONS) test, which presents a single woman in a variety of poses. Participants are asked to decode the implicit signals being emitted and to figure out which of two alternative descriptions better characterizes what the test taker has seen and/or heard. The PONS has been found to have weak to moderate correlations with other measures of social and cognitive competence (Halberstadt & Hall, 1980; Rosenthal et al., 1979).

Archer (1980) and Archer and Akert (1980) developed an alternative to the PONS test called the Social Interpretation Test (SIT). The SIT presents participants with visual and auditory information regarding a social situation. For example, the participants might see a picture of a woman talking on the phone and hear a fragment of the woman's conversation. The participants are asked to judge whether the woman is talking to another woman or to a man. In another situation, participants are asked to judge whether a man and woman shown in a picture are strangers, acquaintances, or friends. Research using the SIT has focused primarily on the accuracy of participants' judgments based on verbal versus nonverbal information.

Using a task similar to the SIT, Sternberg and Smith (1985) developed a measure of decoding skills and assessed the relationship of such skills to other measures of social and cognitive intelligence. They presented participants with two types of photographs. In one type, a man and woman were shown posing as if they were in a close relationship. Participants were asked to judge if the two persons shown were a real couple or only playing the roles. In the second type, the picture showed a supervisor and his or her supervisee. Participants were asked to judge which of the two individuals was the supervisor. Accuracy was assessed as the percentage of pictures the participant judged correctly. Participants were also given several measures of social and cognitive intelligence, including the PONS (Rosenthal et al., 1979); the Social Insight Test (Chapin, 1967); the GWSIT (Moss et al., 1949); the Group Embedded Figures Test (Oltman, Raskin, & Witkin, 1971); and the Cattell Culture Fair Test of g (Cattell & Cattell, 1963). Nonverbal decoding accuracy correlated significantly with performance only on the Embedded Figures Test. Sternberg and Smith (1985) concluded that there was insufficient evidence to suggest that nonverbal decoding skills provided a valid measure of the construct of social intelligence.

A subsequent study by Barnes and Sternberg (1989) was more successful. Participants were given the same set of pictures used by Sternberg and Smith (1985), one set portraying heterosexual couples and the other supervisors and supervisees. In addition to judging the pictures, participants were asked to rate their degree of confidence in their judgments; to indicate what features in each picture they used to make their judgment; to rate the importance of those features in their decision; and to assign a weight based on how much the feature was exhibited in the picture. Participants also completed several measures of social and academic intelligence. They were assigned scores on social competence based on the 13 behaviors from Sternberg et al.'s (1981) Social Competence Factor; situational competence based on the

Social Competence Nomination Form (Ford, 1982); overall social competence based on the Empathy Scale (Hogan, 1969) and the Self-Monitoring scale (Snyder, 1974); and overall cognitive intelligence based on educational background, school performance, and the Henmon-Nelson Test of Mental Ability (Nelson & Lamke, 1973). Barnes and Sternberg obtained significant correlations between accuracy at nonverbal decoding in the couples' task and all measures of social competence, except for situational competence. Decoding accuracy did not correlate with any of the cognitive intelligence measures. There was, however, a correlation between the quantity of features identified by participants and cognitive intelligence scores. These investigators concluded that the ability to accurately decode nonverbal communication is an indicator of social intelligence.

Wong, Day, Maxwell, and Meara (1995) attributed previous failures to discriminate the two forms of intelligence to the use of paper-and-pencil measures of social as well as academic intelligence. They conducted two studies to examine the relationships between cognitive and behavioral measures of social intelligence and academic intelligence. In the first study, they administered verbal, nonverbal, self-report, and other-report measures of academic intelligence, social perception (cognitive social intelligence), and effectiveness in heterosexual interactions (behavioral social intelligence) to undergraduate students. Using confirmatory factor analysis, they found that the model that best fitted the data consisted of three separate factors: social perception, effectiveness in heterosexual interaction, and academic intelligence. In the second study, they focused on three cognitive aspects of social intelligence: social knowledge (knowledge of etiquette rules), social perception (the ability to understand the emotional states of others), and social insight (the ability to comprehend observed behaviors in a social context). The best-fitting model consisted of three factors: academic intelligence, a combined social perception-social insight factor, and social knowledge. In their studies, Wong et al. were able to discriminate not only behavioral but also cognitive aspects of social intelligence from academic intelligence.

Jones and Day (1997) attempted further to understand the cognitive and behavioral aspects of social intelligence. They examined the relationship between two dimensions of social intelligence, Crystallized Social Knowledge (declarative and procedural knowledge about familiar social events) and Social-Cognitive Flexibility (the ability to apply social knowledge to relatively novel problems). They proposed that these two dimensions of social intelligence could be distinguished from academic problem solving, which depends on fluid abilities to solve novel, abstract problems that generally have a single correct solution. They administered pictorial, verbal, self-report, and teacher-report measures of Crystallized Social Knowledge, Social-Cognitive Flexibility, and Academic Problem Solving to 169 high school students. In addition, they obtained a measure of social competence from the teachers. Confirmatory factor analyses of the correlation matrix among these measures indicated that the Social-Cognitive Flexibility factor could be discriminated from both Crystallized Social Knowledge and Academic Problem Solving, but that the latter were not discriminable from each other. They further found that all three factors were significantly related to social competency ratings.

Although Jones and Day's (1997) findings suggest that there are processes associated with solving novel social problems that are different from those used to solve familiar social problems or novel academic problems, there are some limitations to their study. First, the sample (high school students) may represent individuals who are relative novices when it comes to social problem solving, so that their level of knowledge may reflect abstract concepts that are similar to academic-type problems. Individuals who have more expertise in social problems may have knowledge that is more distinct from academic problem solving ability. Second, the method of measuring each of these factors may have contributed to the findings. Both Crystallized Social Knowledge and Academic Problem Solving involved items with one correct answer, whereas the measures of Social-Cognitive Flexibility asked respondents to provide their own interpretation, rate the importance of different social goals, and identify the most effective solution to achieve the social goal. The similarity in the measurement format for the former two measures may have created an artificially higher validity estimate among them.

The limitations identified by Jones and Day (1997) are some of the concerns that Kihlstrom and Cantor (in press) raise about relying on psychometric approaches to study social intelligence. Cantor and Harlow (1994), Cantor and Kihlstrom (1987) and Kihlstrom and Cantor (in press) take a social intelligence view of personality. These researchers do agree that social behavior is intelligent because it is mediated by cognitive processes such as perception, memory, reasoning, and problem solving. They argue that psychometric approaches to understanding social intelligence inappropriately focus on how much social intelligence a person has rather than what social intelligence the person possesses. Individual differences in social behavior can be attributed to differences in knowledge and strategies needed to accomplish social tasks.

Cantor and Harlow (1994) proposed that intelligent behavior involves attunement to the consequences of one's actions, the implications of those consequences for other goals, and the goal-fulfilling potentials of different situations. Attunement allows for flexibility in terms of what tasks to pursue, where and when opportunities are present to work on various tasks, and how to pursue the tasks. Therefore, attunement and flexibility are critical aspects of personality and intelligence, allowing individuals successfully to pursue goal and solve problems. Cantor and Harlow argued that owing to the varied tasks and settings in which individuals behave, it is difficult to obtain a general, stable measure of social intelligence.

Rather than developing instruments to assess individual differences in social intelligence, Cantor and her colleagues have chosen to study the cognitive processes that support intelligent social behavior (Kihlstrom & Cantor, in press). They focus on life tasks as their unit of analysis for studying social intelligence. Life tasks are identified by the individual as meaningful and serve to organize one's daily activities. They allow researchers to observe the ability of people to solve problems of a social nature and the knowledge they have of how to solve them. Life tasks include things such as making friends, finding a spouse, establishing a career, and getting good grades. Cantor and her colleagues have chosen to focus on periods of transition (e.g., from high school to college) to observe individual differences in life tasks (Kihlstrom & Cantor, in press). They have found that people formulate action plans, monitor their progress, and assess the outcomes of their actions. They draw on their autobiographical memory to evaluate various causes of those outcomes and alternative courses of action. When their pursuit of a life task is obstructed, they are able to alter plans or choose a new plan of action. As we discuss later in this chapter, the processes identified by Cantor and her colleagues are consistent with the metacomponents identified by Sternberg (1985a) as underlying successful intelligence.

Unfortunately, recent efforts to define and measure social intelligence have not led to any substantial improvement in our understanding of the construct. There appear to be as many definitions and operationalizations of social intelligence as there are researchers. The definitions of social intelligence refer to dimensions such as social perception, social knowledge, social insight, empathy, social memory, and social adaptation. Furthermore, there is little consistency regarding the relationships among measures of social intelligence or their relations to measures of academic intelligence. Although we acknowledge Cantor and Harlow's (1994) concern regarding the difficulty in measuring social intelligence, the construct of tacit knowledge, elaborated on in other chapters, represents an attempt to quantify context-specific knowledge that is an aspect of practical intelligence. Tests of tacit knowledge have been successful in predicting performance (behavioral outcomes) and discriminating practical from abstract or academic intelligence (Sternberg et al., 1993; Sternberg et al., 1995). Before considering the measurement of practical intelligence, we discuss another related construct, that of emotional intelligence.

EMOTIONAL INTELLIGENCE

Research and theorizing on the construct of emotional intelligence has a much shorter history as compared with social intelligence. According to Mayer, Salovey, and Caruso (in press), the history of emotional intelligence research spans less than a decade. As such, the numbers of definitions of and approaches to studying emotional intelligence are delineated more readily.

Mayer et al. (in press) distinguished between two general models of emotional intelligence. *Ability models* view emotional intelligence as the intersection of cognition and emotion. *Mixed models* define emotional intelligence as a combination of mental ability and personality traits. We talk first about the mixed models (Bar-On, 1997; Goleman, 1995) and their associated measures of emotional intelligence. Then we discuss the work of Mayer and Salovey as they attempt to characterize emotional intelligence as distinct from personality.

Goleman (1995) brought popular attention to the concept of emotional intelligence. He argued, as have other researchers (Gardner, 1983; Sternberg, 1997a), that IQ tests and similar tests, such as the Scholastic Assessment Tests (SATs), fail to predict accurately who will succeed in life. Goleman suggested that part of the 80% variance in success unaccounted for by IQ could be explained by other characteristics, one of which is emotional intelligence. He defined emotional intelligence as including "abilities such as being able to motivate oneself and persist in the face of frustrations; to control impulses and delay gratification; to regulate one's moods and keep distress from swamping the ability to think; to empathize and to hope." Although Goleman did not point to any specific test of emotional intelligence, he cited support for the construct in research on related factors, such as empathy and ego resilience, which suggests that emotional intelligence is distinct from IQ.

Interestingly a study by Davies, Stankov, and Roberts (1998) used a scale Goleman created to measure emotional intelligence. The items consisted of hypothetical situations to which individuals responded. Davies et al. found that Goleman's measure correlated with self-reported empathy and emotional control. Mayer et al. (in press) noted that it is not clear whether Goleman's scale was intended for empirical use, so the findings of Davies et al. are tentative.

A more measurement-based approach was used by Bar-On (1997), who defined emotional intelligence as all noncognitive abilities, skills, and competencies that enable one to cope successfully with life. Bar-On identified five broad areas of skills or competencies, and within each, more specific skills that appear to contribute to success. These include intrapersonal skills (emotional self-awareness, assertiveness, self-regard, self-actualization, independence); interpersonal skills (interpersonal relationships, social responsibility, empathy); adaptability (problem solving, reality testing, flexibility); stress management (stress tolerance, impulse, control); and general mood (happiness, optimism). According to Mayer et al. (in press), Bar-On's model combines skills that can be characterized as mental abilities (e.g., problem solving) and others that can be considered personality traits (e.g., optimism), which makes it a mixed model.

Bar-On (1997) developed the Emotional Quotient Inventory (EQ_i) based on his broad-based model of noncognitive skills. Thirteen subscales of the EQ_i were identified, roughly corresponding to the specific skills in his model. These subscales were found to be highly intercorrelated, and thus a single test score is computed. Bar-On has found that scores on his test correlate negatively with measures of negative affect, such as the Beck Depression Inventory (Beck, Ward, Mendelson, Mock, & Erbaugh, 1961) and the Zung Self-Rating Depression Scale; positively with measures of positive affect (such as emotional stability, extraversion); and nonsignificantly with measures of general intelligence such as the WAIS-R (Wechsler, 1981). Again, it is clear from these results that Bar-On's EQ_i measures aspects of personality and possibly mental ability. Because the measure is one of self-report, it is difficult to assess how generalizable the results would be to behavior.

Initial theorizing by Salovey and Mayer (1990) also related emotional intelligence to personality factors such as warmth and outgoingness. But since then, these authors have argued that these personality factors are distinct from emotional intelligence. They consider the latter to be more strictly an ability (Mayer & Salovey, 1997; Mayer et al., in press). They define emotional intelligence as the ability to recognize the meanings of emotions and to use that knowledge to reason and solve problems. They have proposed a framework of emotional intelligence to organize the various abilities involved in the adaptive processing of emotionally relevant information.

Emotional intelligence consists of four main classes of abilities. These abilities pertain to (1) the accurate appraisal and expression of emotions in oneself and in others; (2) assimilation of emotional experience into cognition; (3) recognition, understanding, and reasoning about emotions; and (4) the adaptive regulation of emotions in oneself and in others (Mayer et al., in press; Salovey & Mayer, 1994).

Mayer and Salovey (1993) offered several mechanisms underlying emotional intelligence that suggest its association with mental abilities. First, emotions are associated with thought processes – certain emotions may increase thoughts and direct attention to certain tasks. Second, the effective regulation of emotions may be related to other abilities, such as empathy and openness. Third, research on alexithymia (the inability to appraise and verbally express emotions) suggests possible disconnections between areas of the brain that prohibit the integration of thoughts and emotions.

Mayer and Salovey (1997) and Mayer, Caruso, and Salovey, (in press) have developed their own test of emotional intelligence, called the Mutifactor Emotional Intelligence Scale (MEIS). It consists of 12 ability measures, which fall into the four classes of abilities identified above (perception, assimilation, understanding, and managing emotions). Perception is measured by presenting various stimuli, including faces, abstract designs, music, and stories, and asking people to judge the emotional content reflected in those stimuli. Assimilation is measured by *synesthesia judgments* (describing emotional sensations and their relations to other sense modalities) and *feeling biases* (judgment of how the individual feels toward a fictional person). Understanding is measured by *blends*, the ability to blend emotions (sample question: Optimism most closely combines which two emotions?); *progressions* (understanding how emotional reactions progress over time); *transitions* (understanding how emotions flow from one to another); and *relativity* (estimating the feelings of people depicted in a conflictual social encounter). Finally, managing emotions is measured in reference to others and to oneself. Managing feelings of others is measured by using brief vignettes about fictional people in need of assistance and asking respondents to rate the effectiveness of alternative courses of action. Managing feelings of self is measured similarly, but the vignettes describe emotional problems that the individual might encounter.

Mayer et al. (1998) validated the MEIS with 503 adults and 229 adolescents. From a factor analysis of the MEIS, they identified three primary factors, corresponding to *perception of understanding, managing* emotion, and a higher-order, general factor of *Emotional Intelligence* (g_{ei}) (Mayer et al., in press). General emotional intelligence correlated significantly with a measure of verbal intelligence, the Army Alpha vocabulary scale (Yerkes, 1921) and a measure of self-reported empathy (Caruso & Mayer, 1997). The investigators also found that the emotional intelligence of adults was higher than that of adolescents, which suggests age-related changes. Of the three specific factors, understanding correlated most highly with verbal intelligence, followed by managing emotions and then perception. These investigators concluded that emotional intelligence can be characterized appropriately as a mental ability because their results follow the patterns of other well established measures of intelligence. The specific abilities in the MEIS are intercorrelated; scores on the MEIS develop with age, as do scores on other standard intelligence tests; and emotional intelligence overlaps to some extent with traditional intelligence.

Schutte et al. (1998) developed their own measure of emotional intelligence based on Salovey and Mayer's (1990) model. Their 33-item self-report measure correlated significantly with eight theoretically related constructs, including awareness of emotion, outlook on life, depressed mood, ability to regulate emotions, and impulsivity. They also showed differences on their measure with groups expected to differ in emotional intelligence (e.g., psychotherapists and prisoners, men and women). They further showed that scores on indexes of emotional intelligence were predictive of end-of-year GPAs of college freshman but were unrelated to SAT or ACT scores. Finally, they found that of the five main personality traits, emotional intelligence related significantly only to openness to experience.

There appears to be some support for the constructs of both social intelligence and emotional intelligence. As yet, there have been no direct efforts aimed at distinguishing social from emotional intelligence, and often the two are treated interchangeably. However, there is evidence to suggest that both social and emotional intelligence overlap to some extent with abstract, academic intelligence. This interdependence is not surprising if we take the position that similar mental processes are employed in solving problems of a social, emotional, or academic nature. Sternberg's (1997a) theory of successful intelligence and the triarchic theory subsumed within it specify these processes and their relation to successful performance of everyday tasks. Before considering his theory, we briefly review some alternative frameworks of competence or intelligence, which provide a different perspective on social, emotional, and even abstract intelligence.

COMPREHENSIVE FRAMEWORKS OF ABILITIES

Some researchers have attempted to define nonacademic forms of intelligence within broader models of personal competence (Greenspan, 1981; Greenspan & Driscoll, 1997; Greenspan & Granfield, 1992) or human functioning (Ford, 1987, 1994; Ford & Ford, 1987; Ford & Maher, 1998). We briefly review two of these frameworks here.

Greenspan and Driscoll's Model of Personal Competence

Greenspan (1981), Greenspan and Driscoll (1997), and Greenspan and Granfield (1992) view personal competence as comprising the skills involved in attaining goals and solving problems, whereas intelligence refers to the subcomponent of these skills involved in thinking and understanding. A recent version of their model (Greenspan & Driscoll, 1997) consists of four broad domains of competence: physical competence, affective competence, everyday competence, and academic competence. These broad domains are further divided into eight subdomains. Physical competence consists of organ (e.g., vision, heart functioning) and motor competence (e.g., strength, coordination). Affective competence consists of temperament (e.g., emotionality, distractibility) and character (e.g., gregariousness, social orientation). Everyday competence includes practical intelligence (the ability to think about and understand problems in everyday settings) and social intelligence (the ability to think about and understand social problems). Academic competence involves conceptual intelligence (the ability to think about and understand problems of an academic or abstract nature) and language (the ability to understand and participate in communications).

Greenspan and Driscoll's (1997) model takes into account Cantor and Kihlstrom's (1989) suggestion that social intelligence forms a link between intelligence and personality. The tendency to view personality as a disposition and intelligence as an ability has led most researchers to treat the constructs as separate. The Greenspan-Driscoll model recognizes that social competence consists of both intellective and nonintellective components.

The Living Systems Framework

In the Living Systems Framework (LSF) of human functioning and development (Ford, 1987, 1994; Ford & Ford, 1987), intelligence is viewed as the effective pursuit of goals within some setting or domain of activity (Ford & Maher, 1998). The key aspect of the LSF is the *behavior episode,* a context-specific, goal-directed pattern of behavior. Everyday life consists of a continuous series of behavior episodes. Behavior episodes can involve motor or communicative activity, information seeking, or thought processes. Multiple behavior episodes form a *behavior episode schema* (BES), which directs attention and guides thoughts, feelings, and actions and consists of both declarative and procedural knowledge. The combination of a number of BESs allows for flexibility in dealing with various types of everyday problems, which is considered a major component of social and practical intelligence (Ford, 1986).

Neither the Greenspan model nor that of Ford and Maher (1998) seems to capture emotional intelligence as defined by Mayer et al. (in press). It is likely that Greenspan and Driscoll would consider emotional intelligence as they view social intelligence, that is, as located at the intersection of personality and intelligence. Both these models and the approaches to social and emotional intelligence discussed earlier in this chapter recognize the importance of nonacademic or nontraditional intelligence in determining success in life. This view also forms the basis of Sternberg's (1997a) aptly named theory of successful intelligence.

STERNBERG'S THEORY OF SUCCESSFUL INTELLIGENCE

Consistent with Greenspan and Driscoll's distinction between academic and everyday competence is Sternberg's (1985a) distinction between academic and practical intelligence. Practical intelligence, however, is part of a more comprehensive theory of successful intelligence (Sternberg, 1997a). According to this theory, also termed the *triarchic theory*, successful intelligence is the ability to achieve success in life, given one's personal standards, within one's sociocultural context. Ability to achieve success depends on capitalizing on one's strengths and correcting or compensating for one's weaknesses through a balance of analytical, creative, and practical abilities in order to adapt to, shape, and select environments.

The theory of successful intelligence, first introduced in chapter 2, serves as the basis for the work described throughout this book on practical intelligence and tacit knowledge. We describe in greater detail in this chapter the main components of the theory. Then we describe a measure designed to assess these components, including the ability to apply knowledge to real-world, practical problems.

Subtheories

Sternberg's theory of successful intelligence (Sternberg, 1988, 1997a, in press-c) seeks to explain in an integrative way the relationship between intelligence and (1) the internal world of the individual, or the mental mechanisms that underlie intelligent behavior; (2) experience, or the mediating role of one's passage through life between the internal and external worlds; and (3) the external world of the individual, or the use of cognitive mechanisms in everyday life in order to attain a functional fit to the environment. These three parts of the theory are referred to, respectively, as the componential subtheory, the experiential subtheory, and the contextual subtheory.

THE COMPONENTIAL SUBTHEORY. The componential subtheory seeks to elucidate the mental processes that underlie intelligent behavior by identifying three basic kinds of information processing components, which are referred to as metacomponents, performance components, and knowledge acquisition components.

Metacomponents are higher-order, executive processes used to plan what one is going to do, to monitor it while doing it, and to evaluate it after it is done. These metacomponents include (1) recognizing the existence of a problem; (2) deciding on the nature of the problem; (3) selecting a set of lower-order processes to solve the problem; (4) selecting a strategy into which to combine these components; (5) selecting a mental representation on which the components and strategy can act;

(6) allocating one's mental resources; (7) monitoring one's problem solving as it is happening; and (8) evaluating one's problem solving after it is done.

Performance components are lower-order processes, which execute the instructions of the metacomponents. These components solve the problems according to the plans laid out by the metacomponents. Whereas the number of metacomponents used in the performance of various tasks is relatively limited, the number of performance components is probably quite large, and many are relatively specific to a narrow range of tasks (Sternberg, 1985a). Inductive reasoning tasks such as matrices, analogies, series completion, and classifications involve a set of performance components that provide potential insight into the nature of the general factor of intelligence. That is, induction problems of these kinds show the highest loading on the general intelligence factor, or *g* (Jensen, 1980; Snow & Lohman, 1984; Sternberg & Gardner, 1982). The main performance components of inductive reasoning are encoding, inference, mapping, application, comparison, justification, and response.

Knowledge acquisition components are used to learn how to do what the metacomponents and performance components eventually do. Three knowledge acquisition components seem to be central in intellectual functioning: selective encoding, selective combination, and selective comparison.

Selective encoding involves sifting out relevant from irrelevant information. When new information is presented in natural contexts, relevant information for one's given purpose is embedded in the midst of large amounts of purpose-irrelevant information. A critical task for the learner is to sift the "wheat from the chaff," recognizing just what among the pieces of information is relevant for one's purposes (Schank, 1990).

Selective combination involves combining selectively encoded information in such a way as to form an integrated, plausible whole. Simply sifting out relevant from irrelevant information is not enough to generate a new knowledge structure. One must know how to combine the pieces of information into an internally connected whole (Mayer & Greeno, 1972).

Selective comparison involves relating new information to old information already stored in memory. It is not enough to encode and combine new information; the information has to be tied to some preexisting knowledge base. A good selective comparer recognizes how existing knowledge can be brought to bear on the present situation, whereas a poor selective comparer does not readily see the relations between existing and new information. For example, a competent lawyer looks for past precedents, a competent physician for old cases that shed light on new ones.

The various components of intelligence work together. Metacomponents activate performance and knowledge acquisition components. These latter kinds of components in turn provide feedback to the metacomponents. Although one can isolate various kinds of information processing components from task performance by using experimental means, in practice the components function together in highly interactive ways and are not readily isolated. Thus, diagnosis, as well as instructional interventions, needs to consider all three types of components in interaction rather than any one kind of component in isolation. However, understanding the nature of the components of intelligence is not, in itself, sufficient to understand the nature of intelligence because there is more to intelligence than a set of information processing components. One could scarcely understand all of what makes one person more intelligent than another by understanding the components of processing on, say, an intelligence test. The other aspects of the triarchic theory address some of the other aspects of intelligence that contribute to individual differences in observed performance, outside testing situations as well as within them.

THE EXPERIENTIAL SUBTHEORY. Components of information processing are always applied to tasks and situations with which one has some level of prior experience (including the null level). Hence, these internal mechanisms are closely tied to one's experience. According to the experiential subtheory, the components are not equally good measures of intelligence at all levels of experience. Assessing intelligence requires one to consider not only components but also the level of experience at which they are applied.

According to the experiential subtheory, intelligence is best measured at those regions of the experiential continuum that involve tasks or situations that are either relatively novel, on the one hand, or in the process of becoming automatized, on the other.

Several sources of evidence converge on the notion that ability to deal with relative novelty is a good way of measuring intelligence. Davidson and Sternberg (1984) found that gifted children had greater insight to deal with novel problems than did nongifted children.

Research on fluid intelligence, which is a kind of intelligence involved in dealing with novelty (Cattell, 1971), suggests that tests that measure the ability to deal with novelty fall relatively close to the so-called general factor of intelligence (Snow & Lohman, 1984).

There are also converging lines of evidence that automatization ability is a key aspect of intelligence. Sternberg (1977) found that the correlation between performance on an analogy problem and a measure of general intelligence increased with practice. The first stage of Ackerman (1987) and Kanfer and Ackerman's (1989) model of automatization also is related to intelligence. Theorists such as Jensen (1982) and Hunt (1978) attribute the correlation between such tasks as choice reaction time and letter matching to the relation between speed of information processing and intelligence. An alternative explanation is that some of the correlation is due to the effects of automatization of processing.

The ability to deal with novelty and the ability to automatize information processing are interrelated. If one is able to automatize well, one has more resources left over for dealing with novelty. Similarly, if one is well able to deal with novelty, one has more resources left over for automatization.

THE CONTEXTUAL SUBTHEORY. According to the contextual subtheory, intelligent thought is directed toward one or more of three behavioral goals: adaptation to an environment, shaping of an environment, or selection of an environment. These three goals may be viewed as the functions toward which intelligence is directed. Intelligence is not aimless or random mental activity that happens to involve certain components of information processing at certain levels of experience. Rather, it is purposefully directed toward the pursuit of these three global goals, all of which have more specific and concrete instantiations in people's lives.

Most intelligent thought is directed toward the attempt to adapt to one's environment. The requirements for adaptation can differ radically from one environment to another, regardless of whether environments are defined in terms of families, jobs, subcultures, or cultures. According to the triarchic theory and in particular the contextual subtheory, the processes, experiential facets, and functions of intelligence remain essentially the same across contexts, but the particular instantiations of these processes, facets, and functions can differ radically. Thus, the content of intelligent thought and its manifestations in behavior will bear no necessary resemblance across contexts. To understand intelligence, one must understand it not only in relation to its internal manifestations in terms of mental processes and its experiential manifestations in terms of facets of the experiential continuum, but also in terms of how thought is intelligently translated into action in a variety of different contextual settings. The difference in what is considered adaptive and intelligent can extend even to different occupations within a given cultural milieu.

Shaping of the environment is often used as a backup strategy when adaptation fails. If one is unable to change oneself to fit the environment, one may attempt to change the environment to fit oneself. Shaping, however, is not always used in lieu of adaptation; it may be used before adaptation is tried. In science, the distinction can be made between those who set the paradigms (shape) and those who follow them (adapt) (Sternberg, 1999a).

Selection involves renunciation of one environment in favor of another. Selection is sometimes used when both adaptation and shaping fail. Failure to adjust to the demands of a work environment or to change the demands to fit one's interest, values, expectations, or abilities may result in a decision to seek a new job. However, selection is not always used as a last resort. It may reflect an intelligent person's recognition that a situation is not suitable and that no attempt to change oneself would improve the fit.

Adaptation, shaping, and selection are functions of intelligent thought as it operates in context. It is through adaptation, shaping, and selection that the components of intelligence as employed at various levels of experience become actualized in the real world. This is the definition of practical intelligence used by Sternberg and his colleagues (Sternberg, 1997a; Sternberg & Wagner, 1986).

Sternberg Triarchic Abilities Test

A measure has been developed to assess the components of Sternberg's theory (Sternberg, 1985a, 1988). The Sternberg Triarchic Abilities Test (STAT) (Sternberg, 1991a, 1991b, 1993) measures three domains of mental processing, namely, analytical, creative, and practical, which reflect the subtheories outlined above. Analytical questions address the ability to learn from context and reason inductively (i.e., the relation of intelligence to the internal world); creative questions address the ability to cope with novelty (i.e., the relation of intelligence to experience); and practical questions address the ability to solve real-world, everyday problems (i.e., the relation of intelligence to the external world)

The current version of the STAT (1993) has nine four-option multiple-choice subtests, each consisting of four items, plus three essays. The nine multiple-choice subtests represent a crossing of three kinds of process domains (analytical, creative, and practical) with three major content domains (verbal, quantitative, and figural). The three essays assess performance in analytical, creative, and practical domains. We describe each of the subtests, which are organized around the process domains.

There are four analytical subtests of the STAT, one for each content area (multiple-choice verbal, multiple-choice quantitative, multiple-choice figural, and essay). Traditional verbal ability tests (e.g., synonym–antonym tests) correlate highly with overall IQ (Sternberg & Powell, 1983), but they are more measures of achievement than of ability. In other words, they emphasize the products over the process of learning. Analytical-verbal abilities are measured in the STAT by assessing the ability to learn from context. Vocabulary is viewed as a proxy for the ability to pick up information from relevant context (Sternberg, 1987). The analytical-quantitative section consists of items that measure inductive reasoning ability in the numerical domain. The analytical-figural items similarly measure inductive reasoning ability with either figure classification or figure analogy problems. In the figure classification test, the examinee must indicate which figure does not belong with the others. The four analytical subtests are:

1. *Analytical-verbal (neologisms)*. Students see a novel word embedded in a paragraph and have to infer its meaning from the context.
2. *Analytical-quantitative (number series)*. Students have to say what number should come next in a series of numbers.
3. *Analytical-figural (matrices)*. Students see a figural matrix with the lower right entry missing, and have to say which of the options fits into the missing space.
4. *Analytical essay*. Students are required to analyze the advantages and disadvantages of having police or security guards in a school building.

The creative portion of the STAT also consists of four subtests (multiple-choice verbal, multiple-choice quantitative, multiple-choice figural, and essay). The creative-verbal questions require counterfactual reasoning and attempt to assess the ability to think in relatively novel ways. In the creative-quantitative questions, symbols are used in place of certain numbers requiring the examinee to make a substitution. The creative-figural items require the examinee to complete a series in a domain separate from the one in which they inferred the completion rule. The four creative subtests are:

5. *Creative-verbal (novel analogies).* Students are presented with verbal analogies preceded by counterfactual premises (e.g., money falls off trees) and must solve the analogies as though the counterfactual premises were true.
6. *Creative-quantitative (novel number operations).* Students are presented with rules for novel number operation (e.g., flix, for which numerical manipulations differ depending on whether the first of two operands is greater than, equal to, or less than the second). Students have to use the novel number operations to solve presented mathematical problems.
7. *Creative-figural (novel series completion).* Students are first presented with a figural series that involves one or more transformations; they then must apply the rule of the original series to a new figure with a different appearance to complete a new series.
8. *Creative essay.* Students are required to describe how they would reform their school system to produce an ideal one.

Finally, the practical portion of the STAT is designed to assess ability to apply knowledge to problems with practical relevance. Practical-verbal items require the examinee to answer everyday inferential reasoning problems. Practical-quantitative items require the examinee to reason quantitatively with practical everyday problems of the kind that might be faced in everyday life. Items in the practical-figural portion require the ability to plan a route efficiently, given the information in a map or diagram. The four practical subtests are:

9. *Practical-verbal (everyday reasoning).* Students have to solve a set of everyday problems in the life of an adolescent (e.g., what to do about a friend who seems to have a substance abuse problem).
10. *Practical-quantitative (everyday mathematics).* Students have to solve mathematical problems based on scenarios requiring the

use of mathematics in everyday life (e.g., buying tickets for a ball game or making chocolate chip cookies).
11. *Practical-figural (route planning).* Students are presented with a map of an area (e.g., an entertainment park) and have to answer questions about navigating effectively through the area depicted by the map.
12. *Practical essay.* Students are required to specify a problem in their life and to state three possible practical solutions for it.

The multiple choice questions are scored by using an answer key. The essays are scored by trained raters according to the extent to which the answer reflects analytical, creative, and practical thinking. In a pilot use of the STAT (Sternberg & Clinkenbeard, 1995), a variety of ability tests were administered to 64 participants. The other tests used were the Terman Concept Mastery Test (primarily a test of crystallized abilities), the Watson-Glaser Critical Thinking Appraisal (a verbal test of critical thinking), the Cattell Culture Fair Test of g (primarily a test of fluid abilities), and a homemade test of insight problems (adapted from Sternberg, 1986). Respective correlations of the STAT with these tests were for the analytical, .49, .50, .50, and .47 (all significant); for the creative, .43, .53, .55, and .59 (all significant); and for the practical .21, .32, .36, and .21 (the second and third significant). Of the three processing domains measured by the STAT, the one that correlated the least with more traditional measures of general intelligence was practical ability.

In a subsequent study (Sternberg, Ferrari, Clinkenbeard, & Grigorenko, 1996; Sternberg, Grigorenko, Ferrari, & Clinkenbeard, 1999), the STAT was administered to 324 children around the United States and in some other countries who were identified by their schools as gifted by any standard whatsoever. Children were selected for a summer psychology program at Yale (college level) if they fell into one of five ability groupings: high analytical, high creative, high practical, high balanced (high in all three abilities), or low balanced (low in all three abilities). Students who came to Yale were then divided into four instructional groups. Students in all four instructional groups used the same introductory psychology textbook (a preliminary version of Sternberg [1995b]) and listened to the same psychology lectures. What differed among them was the type of afternoon discussion section to which they were assigned. They were assigned to an instructional condition that emphasized either memory, analytical, creative, or practical instruction. For example, in the memory condition, they might be asked to describe the main tenets of a major theory of depression. In the analytical condition, they might be asked to compare and contrast two theories of depression. In the creative condition, they might be asked to formulate their own theory of depression. In the practical condition, they might be asked how they could use what they had learned about depression to help a friend who was depressed.

Students in all four instructional conditions were evaluated in terms of their performance on homework, a midterm examination, a final examination, and an independent project. Each type of work was evaluated for memory, analytical, creative, and practical quality. Thus, all students were evaluated in exactly the same way.

Sternberg et al. (1996) performed a principal components factor analysis and found a weak general factor, which suggested that the general factor of intelligence is probably relevant only when a fairly narrow range of abilities is measured, as is typically the case with conventional tests. They found that the testing format had a large effect on results: Multiple choice tests tended to correlate with other multiple choice tests, almost without regard to what they measure. Essay tests showed only weak correlations with multiple choice, however. These investigators further found that after they controlled for modality of testing (multiple choice versus essay), the correlations between the analytical, creative, and practical sections were very weak and generally nonsignificant, supporting the relative independence of the various abilities. All three ability tests – analytical, creative, and practical – significantly predicted course performance. When multiple-regression analysis was used, at least two of these ability measures contributed significantly to the prediction of each of the measures of achievement. Perhaps as a reflection of the difficulty of deemphasizing the analytical way of teaching, one of the significant predictors was always the analytical score. Most importantly, there was an aptitude–treatment interaction whereby students who were placed in instructional conditions that better matched their pattern of abilities outperformed students who were mismatched. In other words, when students are taught in a way that fits how they think, they do better in school. Children with creative and practical abilities, who are almost never taught or assessed in a way that matches their pattern of abilities, may be at a disadvantage in course after course, year after year.

Thus the results of the studies involving the STAT suggest that the theory of successful intelligence is valid not just in its parts but as a whole. Moreover, the results suggest that the theory can make a difference not only in laboratory tests but also in school classrooms.

More recently, the triarchic theory of intelligence was tested with an adult population, with use of measures of analytical, creative, and practical intelligence that differed from the STAT questions described above. Grigorenko and Sternberg (in press) administered measures of analytical, creative, and practical intelligence to 452 women and 293 men between the ages of 26 and 60 in a large industrial city in Russia. The environment in Russia is characterized by financial, institutional, political, and societal uncertainty and instability. The investigators hypothesized that in such environments, practical and creative intelligence would play as important a role as analytical intelligence, if not a greater role, in successful adaptation to the changing social context.

Grigorenko and Sternberg measured analytical ability using the *Series* and *Matrices* subtests of the Test of *g:* Culture Fair, Level II (Cattell, 1940; Cattell & Cattell, 1973) to measure fluid abilities. A test of crystallized intelligence was adapted from existing traditional tests of analogies and synonyms–antonyms used in Russia. Creative intelligence was measured by asking participants to describe the world through the eyes of insects and to describe who might live and what might happen on a fictitious planet called "Priumliava." Responses were rated for novelty, quality, and sophistication. For practical intelligence, participants were asked to report their practical skills in the social domain (e.g., effective and successful communication with other people), in the family domain (e.g., how to fix household items, how to run the family budget), and in the domain of effective resolution of sudden problems (e.g., organizing something that has become chaotic). The participants were also asked to respond to four vignettes, based on themes of (1) how to maintain the value of one's savings; (2) what to do when one makes a purchase and discovers that the item one has purchased is broken; (3) how to locate medical assistance in a time of need; and (4) how to manage a salary bonus one has received for outstanding work. Participants were asked to select the best option among five presented for each vignette. The most frequently chosen option was used as the keyed answer. Finally, self-report measures of physical and mental health were used to assess successful adaptation. Participants received a summary score on their physical health based on reports of chronic illness and other debilitating injuries or diseases. They also completed the Beck Anxiety Scale (BAS) (Beck, Epstein, Brown, & Steer, 1988) and the Beck Depression Inventory (BDI) (Beck, Ward,

Mendelson, Mock, & Erbaugh, 1961), as well as five items that measured their self-efficacy for adaptation.

Grigorenko and Sternberg found that practical intelligence consistently predicted self-reported adaptive functioning on all indicators, with higher practical intelligence associated with better physical and mental health. Analytical intelligence was associated with lower anxiety and higher self-efficacy on two items. Creative intelligence was marginally associated with poorer physical health but lower anxiety. When the data were analyzed separately by sex, creative ability was found to be associated with lower anxiety for women but poorer physical health and lower self-efficacy for men. The results suggest that both analytical and practical intelligence have a positive effect on adaptive functioning. Evidence regarding the role of creative intelligence is inconclusive.

Measures of Practical Intelligence

In addition to the STAT and self-report questions, Sternberg and his colleagues have developed measures targeted specifically at practical intelligence (Sternberg et al., 1993; Sternberg et al., 1995; Wagner, 1987). Practical intelligence is viewed as relevant to successful performance of everyday problems, whether the problems are of a social, emotional, or task-related nature. Therefore, measures of practical intelligence hold promise for elucidating some of the unexplained portions of success that have not been accounted for by traditional intelligence tests. Sternberg and colleagues have taken a knowledge-based approach to measuring practical intelligence. *Tacit knowledge,* as an aspect of practical intelligence, is experience-based knowledge relevant to solving practical problems. As such, tacit knowledge can pertain to social or emotional information. Therefore, tacit knowledge may provide a common approach to understanding various forms of nonacademic intelligence. In the chapters that follow, we delineate further the construct of tacit knowledge, describe methods of measuring tacit knowledge, and review a program of research that provides growing support for the validity of tacit knowledge and, consequently, practical intelligence.

CHAPTER 6

Understanding Practical Intelligence
The Role of Tacit Knowledge

What distinguishes people who are more successful from those who are less successful in their everyday lives? Sternberg and his colleagues (Sternberg et al., 1993; Sternberg et al., 1995; Wagner & Sternberg, 1985; Wagner, 1987) have taken a knowledge-based approach to addressing this question. They have found in their research that much of the knowledge needed to succeed in real-world tasks is tacit. It is acquired during performance of everyday activities but typically without conscious awareness of what is being learned. And although people's actions may reflect their knowledge, they may find it difficult to articulate what they know. The notion that people acquire knowledge without awareness of what is being learned is reflected in the common language of the workplace as people speak of "learning by doing" and "learning by osmosis." Terms such as *professional intuition* and *professional instinct* further imply that the knowledge associated with successful performance has a tacit quality.

The term *tacit knowledge,* introduced by Polanyi (1966), has been used to characterize the knowledge gained from everyday experience that has an implicit, unarticulated quality (Neisser, 1976; Schön, 1983; Sternberg, 1985a, 1988, 1997a). Sternberg and his colleagues (Sternberg, 1997a, 1997b; Sternberg & Horvath, 1999; Wagner & Sternberg, 1985) view tacit knowledge as an aspect of practical intelligence. It is knowledge that reflects the practical ability to learn from experience and to apply that knowledge in pursuit of personally valued goals. Tacit knowledge is needed to successfully adapt to, select, or shape real-world environments. Because tacit knowledge is an aspect of practical intelligence, it provides insight into an important factor underlying the successful performance of real-world tasks. Research by Sternberg and his colleagues (Sternberg et al., 1993; Sternberg et al., 1995), which we review in later chapters, has shown that tacit knowledge can be applied to understanding performance in a variety of job domains.

Support for the importance of the tacit knowledge concept is found also in research on expertise and implicit learning. Research with experts in a variety of knowledge-intensive domains has shown that reasoning and problem solving in such domains depend on proceduralized skills and schematically organized knowledge, both of which may operate outside of focal awareness (Chi, Glaser, & Farr, 1988). Furthermore, expert knowledge appears to reflect the structure of the operating environment or situation more closely than it does the structure of formal, disciplinary knowledge (Groen & Patel, 1988).

Research on implicit learning focuses on the phenomenon of learning without intention or awareness. Tacit knowledge may be, but need not be, acquired implicitly. Reber and his colleagues' work on the acquisition of stochastic grammars and of event sequences suggested that human beings are capable of acquiring knowledge of a very complex nature without conscious intention or awareness of learning (Reber, 1967, 1969; Reber & Millward, 1968). Researchers subsequently applied the paradigm to study learning of meaningful information (e.g., information about other people and information about the behavior of an economic system) and replicated the basic pattern of results (Broadbent & Aston, 1978; Broadbent, Fitzgerald, & Broadbent, 1986). The research on implicit learning suggests that knowledge can be acquired in the absence of awareness or intention to learn and thus can have a hidden or tacit quality.

In this chapter, we begin by discussing the type of theoretical concept we consider tacit knowledge to be. Next, we describe the characteristic features of tacit knowledge and how it is distinguished from related concepts. Then, we consider how tacit knowledge is represented at different levels of abstraction. We present a cognitive model that relates the key features of tacit knowledge to the acquisition, storage, and retrieval of knowledge in and from memory.

TACIT KNOWLEDGE AS A THEORETICAL CONCEPT

In research by Sternberg and his colleagues (Sternberg et al., 1993; Sternberg et al., 1995; Wagner & Sternberg, 1985), the term tacit knowledge has been used to characterize a type of knowledge the possession of which distinguishes more from less practically successful individuals.

In order to understand better the theoretical concept of tacit knowledge, we begin with a distinction between nominal and natural concepts.

Nominal concepts are used attributively. For example, we use the term *bachelor* to attribute certain features (i.e., male, adult, unmarried) to some persons. The instances of a nominal concept often share features that are both necessary (i.e., all valid instances must have these features) and sufficient (i.e., having these features is enough to qualify something as a valid instance). Membership in a nominal concept is all-or-none – either an instance possesses the critical features or it does not.

Natural concepts, in contrast, are used ostensively. For example, we use the term *furniture* to refer to objects that we view as equivalent (e.g., dresser, chair, table). The instances of a natural concept share characteristic features, but these features are not necessary or sufficient for membership. Membership in a natural concept is not all-or-none, but rather, instances are judged in terms of the strength of their resemblance to the concept. This means that some instances, namely, those with high resemblance, will be judged as better examples of the concept than will other instances with low resemblance. For example, most people would agree that *armchair* is a more typical example of the concept *furniture* than is *bean bag chair*.

Tacit knowledge is a natural concept. It is used to denote a type of knowledge that is held together by the resemblance of items to one another and not by a set of individually necessary and jointly sufficient features. This lack of necessary and sufficient features does not mean that as a concept tacit knowledge is incoherent or meaningless. Two people may not be able to identify the critical features that all items of furniture share, but they can still agree that furniture exists and that a coffee table is furniture and a toaster oven is not.

Because tacit knowledge is a natural concept, we do not expect that judgments about what is and is not tacit knowledge will be all-or-none. Rather, judgments should depend on the item's strength of resemblance to the concept. Some knowledge will seem to represent a particularly clear example of tacit knowledge and other knowledge will seem marginal. For marginal items, individuals may disagree about whether the item is a valid instance of tacit knowledge. Given a high level of agreement among judges, the tacit quality of knowledge items can be determined with some degree of confidence.

We describe below three key features that are commonly shared by items of tacit knowledge. These features are used to judge the resemblance of items to the concept. In other words, items that possess these features are more likely to be characteristic of tacit knowledge.

THE CHARACTERISTIC FEATURES OF TACIT KNOWLEDGE

We identify three key features of tacit knowledge. These features of tacit knowledge relate to the conditions under which it is acquired, its cognitive structure, and the conditions of its use. First, tacit knowledge generally is acquired on one's own with little support from the environment (e.g., through personal experience rather than through instruction). Second, tacit knowledge is viewed as procedural in nature. It is associated with particular uses in particular situations or classes of situations. Third, because it generally is acquired through one's own experiences, tacit knowledge has practical value to the individual. We will now expand upon each of these features.

Tacit Knowledge Typically Is Acquired with Little or No Environmental Support

Tacit knowledge generally is acquired on one's own. That is, it is acquired under conditions of minimal environmental support. By environmental support, we mean either people or media that help the individual to acquire the knowledge. As such, tacit knowledge tends to be unspoken, underemphasized, and poorly conveyed relative to its importance for practical success.

When people or media support the acquisition of knowledge, they facilitate three knowledge acquisition components: selective encoding, selective combination, and selective comparison (Sternberg, 1988). When an individual is helped to distinguish more from less important information (selective encoding), to combine elements of information in useful ways (selective combination), and to identify knowledge in memory that is relevant to the present situation (selective comparison), that individual has been supported in acquiring knowledge. In performing real-world tasks, individuals often must engage in these processes on their own in order to make sense of and respond to situations. The resulting knowledge may reflect the use of these processes, but the individual may not be able to express how the knowledge was acquired.

Tacit Knowledge Is Procedural

The second feature of tacit knowledge is its close association with action. Tacit knowledge takes the form of knowing how rather than knowing that. Anderson (1983) has characterized these two types of knowledge as procedural and declarative, respectively. More precisely, procedural knowledge is knowledge that is represented in a way that commits it to a particular use or set of uses. It is knowledge that guides behavior, usually without being readily available to conscious introspection. People may not know they possess and/or may find it difficult to articulate such knowledge. We view procedural knowledge as a superset of tacit knowledge. All tacit knowledge is procedural, although not all procedural knowledge is tacit.

The characterization of tacit knowledge as procedural derives from our research. We have found that when individuals are queried about the knowledge they have acquired through their experiences, they often begin by articulating general rules in roughly declarative form (e.g., "A good leader needs to know people"). When these general statements are probed, the statements often reveal themselves to be more abstract or summary representations of a family of complexly specified procedural rules (e.g., rules about how to judge people accurately for a variety of purposes and under a variety of circumstances). These procedural rules, we believe, represent the characteristic structure of tacit knowledge and serves as the basis for identifying and measuring tacit knowledge.

We can represent tacit knowledge in the form of condition–action pairings:

IF *<antecedent condition>* THEN *<consequent action>*

For example, the knowledge of how to respond to a red traffic light could be represented as:

IF *<light is red>* THEN *<stop>*

Of course, the specification of the conditions and actions that make up proceduralized knowledge may be quite complex. In fact, much of the tacit knowledge that we have observed seems to take the form of complex, multicondition rules (production systems) for how to pursue particular goals in particular situations. In other words, tacit knowledge is more than a set of abstract procedural rules. It is context-specific knowledge about what to do in a given situation or class of situations. For example, knowledge about confronting one's superior might be represented in a form with a compound condition:

IF *<you are in a public forum>*
AND

IF <*the boss says or does something that you perceive is wrong or inappropriate*>
AND
IF <*the boss does not ask for questions or comments*>
THEN <*speak directly to the point of contention and do not make evaluative statements about your boss's, staff's, or peers' character or motives*>
BECAUSE <*this saves the boss from embarassment and preserves your relationship with him or her.*>

Tacit Knowledge Is Practically Useful

The third characteristic feature of tacit knowledge is its instrumental value in attaining personal goals. The more highly valued the goal is and the more directly the knowledge supports the attainment of the goal, the more useful is the knowledge. For example, knowing that seeking input from subordinates makes them feel valued is practically useful for those supervisors who want their subordinates to feel valued but is not practically useful for supervisors who do not value this goal.

We do not believe that practically useful knowledge must be acquired in any particular context or forum. Useful knowledge is, of course, acquired in classrooms, from experience on the job, through mentoring relationships, and through self-study. We distinguish practically useful knowledge not from formally acquired knowledge but rather from knowledge (however acquired) that is not relevant to the practical goals that an individual values.

Tacit Knowledge Involves Coherent Relations among Its Features

The three features of tacit knowledge, namely, acquisition on one's own, procedural structure, and practical value, are related to one another in a nonarbitrary way. That is, we can explain why these features go together in the specification of a meaningful natural concept of tacit knowledge.

First, there is a natural correspondence between the features of procedural structure and practical value. Procedural knowledge tends to be practically useful – it contains within it the specification of how it is to be used. Declarative knowledge, in contrast, is not specific with respect to use and, as a consequence, may remain inert or unused.

Therefore, procedural knowledge is more likely to be relevant in the pursuit of personally valued goals.

Second, knowledge acquired under low environmental support is more likely to have practical value. When knowledge must be acquired on one's own, the probability increases that some individuals will fail to acquire it. When some individuals fail to acquire knowledge, those who succeed may gain a comparative advantage. This advantage is expected to be lower when the knowledge is highly supported by the environment (i.e., explicity and effectively taught) because more people would be expected to acquire and use it. At the same time, knowledge acquired through one's own experiences should have more personal relevance to the types of situations one encounters in everyday life.

Finally, we associate knowledge acquired through experience with knowledge that is procedural in structure. Because procedural knowledge is more difficult to articulate and more poorly conveyed relative to declarative knowledge, its acquisition is more likely to be a function of experiential learning. By the same token, knowledge acquired through experience is more likely to be related to action because originally it was obtained in the context of performing a practical, everyday task.

Each of these features is viewed as a continuous rather than a discrete dimension of tacit knowledge. That is, knowledge is not categorized as either possessing or not possessing these features, but rather it is a matter of degree. Some knowledge may be better supported by the environment than other knowledge. Similarly, some knowledge may have more practical value to the individual than other knowledge. Knowledge that is closer to one end of the continuum is considered more representative of tacit knowledge.

WHAT TACIT KNOWLEDGE IS NOT

We have identified the features that help describe what type of knowledge we consider tacit knowledge to be. It is helpful also to distinguish tacit knowledge conceptually from other related concepts, such as job knowledge, general intelligence, and performance.

Tacit Knowledge Is Not Synonymous with Job Knowledge

Schmidt and Hunter (1993) suggested that tacit knowledge is merely a type of job knowledge. However, tacit knowledge and job knowledge are viewed more appropriately as overlapping concepts. First, some, but not all, tacit knowledge pertains to job-related activities. Tacit knowledge can pertain to any personally valued activity, including academic and social activities; it is more than job knowledge. Second, some, but not all, job knowledge is tacit. Job knowledge includes declarative and procedural knowledge, with some of the latter characterized as tacit. Job knowledge may be explicit and readily verbalized, as in the rules for operating a lathe or the steps used to compute simple interest, or the knowledge may be tacit, as in knowing what package design will likely sell a product.

Measures of tacit knowledge have the potential to explain individual differences in performance that are not explained by traditional measures of job knowledge, which tend to assess more declarative, explicit forms of knowledge (Schmidt & Hunter, 1998). Individual differences in the ability or inclination to acquire and use tacit knowledge make it a potentially useful construct for understanding intelligent behavior in real-world settings, as well as for predicting success in such settings.

Tacit Knowledge Is Not a Proxy for General Intelligence

The ability or propensity to acquire tacit knowledge is viewed as a dimension of practical intelligence that conventional ability tests do not adequately measure. Instruments such as IQ tests and similar tests, which are intended to measure so-called general intelligence (g), are composed of problems that can be characterized as largely academic or abstract. As discussed earlier, academic problems are well defined, abstract problems, which do not necessarily reflect real-world tasks (Neisser, 1976; Sternberg, 1988, 1997a). Therefore, IQ and similar tests measure problem-solving skills that are relatively different from the skills needed to solve everyday, practical problems. For this reason, we do not view measures of tacit knowledge as proxies for measures of academic intelligence. Although general cognitive ability may support the acquisition and use of tacit knowledge in important ways, tacit knowledge is not reducible to academic intelligence. Of course, it is an empirical question whether measures of tacit knowledge do in fact correlate with measures of crystallized intelligence. This question is addressed in subsequent chapters.

Tacit Knowledge Is Not Sufficient for Effective Performance

Although we do not consider tacit knowledge to be a proxy for general intelligence, we do recognize that g and other factors contribute to successful performance in many jobs, as defined by traditional criteria of success such as performance ratings. The performance of many everyday tasks requires general academic intelligence in at least the normative range, motivation to succeed, nontacit domain knowledge, and many other resources. We recognize and basically are in agreement with the results of numerous meta-analyses that show the significant contribution of these variables to understanding performance (Schmidt & Hunter, 1998). However, we attempt to supplement these variables and improve on conventional approaches to understanding, predicting, and improving performance in real-world settings.

Measures of practical intelligence, like all measures of intelligence, are at best indicators of the underlying cognitive functions we seek to understand. As such, we can talk about practical intelligence, and more specifically tacit knowledge, at different levels of abstraction. That is, we can conceptualize tacit knowledge at the level of its cognitive representation and at the level at which it is measured in the behavior and articulated knowledge of the individual. We now discuss these different levels of abstraction.

DESCRIBING TACIT KNOWLEDGE AT DIFFERENT LEVELS OF ABSTRACTION

Tacit knowledge can be conceptualized at qualitatively different levels of abstraction. At the lowest, least abstract level, tacit knowledge can be described as mentally represented knowledge structures. We believe that these knowledge structures take the form of complex, condition–action mappings. At this level of description, tacit knowledge takes on its psychological reality and has its consequences for intelligent behavior.

Ideally, we would measure the possession of tacit knowledge directly at the level of its cognitive representation. However, we must infer possession of tacit knowledge from the knowledge that people articulate. When knowledge is articulated, often it is greatly simplified. That is, the complex knowledge structures that map sets of antecedent conditions onto consequent actions are summarized and abbreviated into general rules and procedures. It is at this level that we measure people's tacit knowledge.

At a higher, more abstract level of description, tacit knowledge items can be grouped into categories of functionally related items. Describing tacit knowledge at this level adds value to the identification of tacit knowledge by highlighting the broad, functional areas or competencies that it represents. In other words, in addition to specific items of tacit knowledge, we can identify more generally the types of knowledge that are likely to be tacit.

Before considering how we identify and measure tacit knowledge, we discuss briefly what we view as the underlying cognitive representation of tacit knowledge.

A Cognitive Representation of Tacit Knowledge

We present a model of tacit knowledge in terms of the mental processes of encoding and storing information in and retrieving it from memory. The proposed model of tacit knowledge draws on the basic distinction between episodic, semantic, and procedural memory, attributable to Tulving (1972, 1995).

Episodic memory is memory for specific, personally experienced events, that is, memory for the episodes that make up one's experience. For example, an army officer's memory of the unpleasant working conditions (e.g., sweltering heat, long hours) surrounding his last assignment can be classified as episodic. The hypothesized contents of episodic memory are often described as cases, situations, or event representations.

Semantic memory is memory for general, impersonal knowledge—memory for information that transcends particular episodes. For example, an officer's memory of which acts of insubordination are subject to what disciplinary action is classified as semantic because it is generalized knowledge and does not depend on memory of a particular situation (such as having previously reprimanded a disobedient soldier). Semantic memory also does not address how the action is performed, such as how an officer goes about disciplining soldiers. The latter is the realm of procedural memory, that is, memory for specific behaviors and actions.

Procedural memory is memory for specific condition–action pairings that guide a person's actions in a given situation. It includes learned skills, such as driving a car, and acquired knowledge, such as how to induce one's superior to change directives. An officer's memory of the actions used successfully to bring disobedient soldiers into compliance is classified as procedural. The individual does not need to recall specific episodes in which the action was performed in order to respond to new situations based on those experiences.

Figure 1 shows the three memory stores (episodic, semantic, and procedural), along with arrows indicating relations among them in terms of encoding, storage, and retrieval processes. The top of Figure 1

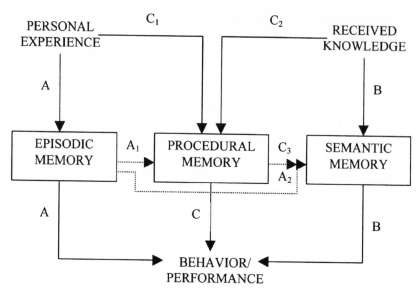

Figure 1. Memory structures and knowledge acquisition pathways in a cognitive model of tacit knowledge.

represents the stimulus environment (the source of inputs to the memory system), and the bottom of the figure represents behavioral consequences of learning (the output of the memory system). We do not intend with this model to introduce a new theory of knowledge acquisition, storage, and retrieval. Instead, we use the model, which is based on existing theory, to illustrate how tacit knowledge is represented cognitively and how it can be identified and measured.

We identify three major pathways through the memory system. The first pathway, labeled A in Figure 1, corresponds to the process by which personally experienced events are stored in episodic memory. Over time, these memories of specific events may be used to construct more generalized knowledge structures in procedural or semantic memory (indicated by paths A_1 and A_2). According to models of inductive learning (Holland, Holyoak, Nisbett, & Thagard, 1986), the transition from event knowledge to generalized knowledge involves mental processes that are sensitive to the covariance structure of the environment, to what goes with what in the world. These processes, variously referred to as induction, abstraction, or extraction of invariants, isolate shared features and/or structure across episodes and construct abstract or general representations of that shared structure. Thus, path A can be seen as one pathway by which personal experience comes to influence behavior, either directly, or indirectly through further encoding in procedural and semantic memory.

Path B corresponds to the process by which generalized knowledge of the world is acquired directly, most typically through a process of formal instruction. For example, a civilian researcher might have no personal experience in dealing with soldiers but may still acquire knowledge about which behaviors are subject to disciplinary action by reading army doctrine. Such knowledge, according to our model, takes the form of received knowledge, which is input, more or less directly, to semantic memory.

Path C corresponds to the process by which knowledge, acquired either directly or through personal experience, becomes stored in procedural memory. It is knowledge about how to perform certain behaviors or tasks. For example, army doctrine may specify step-by-step procedures for disciplining soldiers who fail to comply with directives. In other words, the steps are made explicit. Over instantiations, these steps are committed to memory, and the officer is able to take appropriate disciplinary action without thinking through each step. Alternatively, memory of how to discipline a soldier may be derived from personal experience. For example, an officer may find that disciplinary tactics that are unfamiliar to soldiers have a greater impact on their behaviors than tactics that are familiar to them and expected.

Knowledge in procedural memory may also be derived from episodic memory (path A_1). That is, memory of various experiences may become encoded as a set of complex procedural rules for how to respond to different situations. For example, after several confrontations with insubordinate soldiers, an officer may derive a set of rules for what disciplinary actions to take depending on the situation. Information in procedural memory also may be further encoded into general knowledge (path C_3). An officer's knowledge about disciplinary action may be expressed as a generalized rule that withholding privileges is more effective than requiring additional physical activity.

The model recognizes both direct and indirect influences of knowledge acquisition on behavior. Knowledge from personal experience can exert a direct influence on behavior through its representation in episodic or procedural memory. Experience-based knowledge that is encoded initially in episodic memory can also influence behavior indirectly through its transfer to procedural or semantic memory. Received knowledge can influence behavior through its encoding in either procedural or semantic memory. For example, officers may discipline soldiers for insubordination because they have been taught that ignoring acts of insubordination threatens their authority.

In general, individuals are able to articulate the general knowledge represented in semantic memory more readily than knowledge represented in episodic or procedural memory. But the behaviors exhibited by those individuals reflect more than simply generalized knowledge. Researchers have shown that even when memory for individual episodes appears to be lost, information about those episodes continues to influence behavior (Jacoby, 1983; Schacter, 1987). The most direct support is found in studies of implicit memory, in which participants have reported knowing that a word appeared on a list without being able to recall the event of having studied the list (Gardiner, 1988; Tulving, 1985).

Procedural knowledge, as indicated earlier, guides behavior without necessarily being accessible to conscious awareness. Officers may know at what point to respond to soldiers' insubordination but not be able to express how they know when it is the right time to take action. Knowledge received through path C_2 can be linked to its original source in which the information was preprocessed into a set of explicit procedures and taught directly to the individual. Knowledge acquired through personal experience (C_1) is less easily traced because the processing was done by the learner. The individual is the only source for finding out about that knowledge but may not be able to articulate what he or she knows.

The proposed model helps to illustrate the characteristic features of tacit knowledge. Tacit knowledge is a subset of procedural knowledge that is acquired through personal experience (via either path A_1 or C_1), is not readily articulated, and directly influences behavior. According to the model, knowledge acquired via path A_1 or C_1 is knowledge acquired through personal experience. Furthermore, knowledge that is acquired via path A_1 or C_1 takes the form of knowing how and guides behavior without being available to conscious introspection. Finally, knowledge that is acquired via path A_1 or C_1 is likely to be knowledge that supports action directed toward personally valued goals because such knowledge is acquired during the course of goal-directed activity. Knowledge acquired by paths B and C_2, on the other hand, is not acquired through personal experience but through the communication of generalized knowledge based on someone else's experience. Because it has been formulated for communication, knowledge acquired through paths B and C_2 is in a form that is readily and openly articulated. Such knowledge also may vary in its relevance to personally valued goals, depending on the similarity of those goals to the goals of instruction.

Knowledge acquired via paths A_1 or C_1 (i.e., tacit knowledge) is likely to confer a performance advantage to those who possess it. First, because tacit knowledge is not well supported in its acquisition (i.e., taught directly), it is likely that some individuals will fail to acquire it. Second, knowledge acquired through personal experience is more likely to include conditional information about the types of problems or situations to which the knowledge is relevant. When "behavior/performance" in Figure 1 is a response to a realistic, contextualized problem, knowledge that includes contextual information likely will be more useful than knowledge that is not contextualized. Finally, to the extent that one's past experiences, as opposed to someone else's experiences, are more predictive of one's future experiences, knowledge acquired via path A_1 or C_1 should be more applicable to the pursuit of one's personal goals than knowledge acquired via path B or C_2.

Identifying and Measuring Tacit Knowledge

Measuring tacit knowledge takes into account the realistic, contextualized quality of the knowledge. Responses to realistic problem situations are used as indicators of an individual's possession of tacit knowledge. Wagner and Sternberg (1985) devised a method of presenting scenarios to individuals that depict the types of problems they face in their given pursuits. These scenarios reflect the types of situations in which recognized domain experts have acquired knowledge characterized as tacit. Because tacit knowledge is not readily articulated, we rely on observable indicators, such as responses to the scenarios, to assess whether an individual possesses knowledge characterized as tacit and can apply that knowledge to the situation at hand. The responses reflect an individual's ability to recognize and take appropriate action in a given situation and presumably also reflect that person's procedural knowledge.

Deriving the information for these scenarios poses a challenge in that the tacit knowledge of domain experts must somehow be identified. Domain experts are appropriate sources for identifying tacit knowledge because in order to achieve their expert status, they likely have acquired knowledge that others have not (i.e., knowledge without direct support). As a subset of procedural knowledge that is not readily articulated, tacit knowledge is not likely to be elicited directly from individuals. However, since tacit knowledge is experience-based, we attempt to identify the knowledge in the recalled experiences of individuals. In other words, when individuals have difficulty expressing their action-oriented knowledge, we attempt to elicit memories for the particular episodes that produced that knowledge.

In chapter 7, we describe methods used to elicit examples of tacit knowledge from domain experts and to develop instruments to measure the acquisition and use of tacit knowledge within a given domain. The methods, which have been applied in domains ranging from education to military leadership, have evolved over the course of our tacit knowledge research, resulting in a refined and detailed methodology for eliciting and measuring tacit knowledge. We devote chapter 7 to describing this methodology because it plays an important role in understanding the findings from tacit knowledge research and offers a tool for studying tacit knowledge in any domain.

Measuring Tacit Knowledge

One of the goals of our research is to show that tacit knowledge contributes to successful performance in a variety of domains. That is, we aim to establish a relationship between the possession of tacit knowledge and performance. But how does one proceed to develop a test to measure tacit knowledge? This chapter addresses the development of tools to measure the amount of tacit knowledge of various kinds that an individual has acquired. We begin by reviewing some approaches that have been used to measure the competencies considered to be relevant to the performance of real-world tasks and contrasting them with our knowledge-based approach. We then discuss what tacit knowledge tests are intended to measure, and we offer a general framework for developing and validating such a test.

METHODS OF MEASURING REAL-WORLD COMPETENCIES

The tacit knowledge approach to understanding practical intelligence is based on several methods of measuring real-world competencies. These include the use of the critical incident technique, simulations, and situational judgment tests. We review briefly each of these methods and then discuss how the tacit knowledge approach draws certain aspects from these methods.

Critical Incident Technique

The critical incident technique is an approach that seeks to identify the behaviors associated with effective performance. According to Flanagan (1954), a critical incident describes the behavior, the setting in which the behavior occurred, and the consequences of the behavior. Critical incidents are generated by asking individuals, typically subject matter experts, to provide examples of effective and ineffective behaviors. More specifically, individuals are asked, through interviews or open-ended survey questions, to describe several incidents that they or someone else handled particularly well, as well as several incidents that they or someone else handled poorly (Flanagan, 1954; McClelland, 1976). Boyatzis (1982) used a variation on the critical incident technique, called the *behavioral event interview,* in which he obtained behavioral incidents from individuals identified a priori as either high, medium, or low in effectiveness. He then examined the incidents generated from each group to identify traits and skills that distinguished between effective and ineffective managers.

The critical incidents generated from observations, interviews, or surveys are analyzed qualitatively to determine the nature of the competencies that appear important for success in a given task domain. The incidents typically are grouped on the basis of similar behavioral content. For example, an incident that pertains to assigning a task to a subordinate and an incident about monitoring task completion by a subordinate might be grouped into a category of supervising subordinates. These categories are used to draw general conclusions about the behaviors that are characteristic of effective and ineffective performers.

Limitations of the critical incident technique are its assumptions that people can and will provide incidents that are critical to success in their particular jobs and that qualitative analysis is sufficient for identifying the underlying competencies. However, the value of the critical incident technique lies in its use to identify the strategies individuals use to perform various tasks and to examine specific, situationally relevant aspects of behavior. The critical incident technique has been used successfully in the development of several performance assessment tools, including behaviorally anchored rating scales (BARS) (Smith & Kendall, 1963) and situational judgment tests (SJTs) (Motowidlo, Dunnette, & Carter, 1990), the latter of which is described in more detail in connection with simulations.

Simulations

Simulations have been used both as assessment tools and as training methods. Simulations are aimed at assessing job behaviors directly. They involve observing people in situations that have been created to simulate aspects of the actual job situation. Responses to these simulations are considered to represent the actual responses that individuals would exhibit in real situations. Simulations can take the form of in-basket tests, situational interviews, group discussion, assessment centers, and SJTs. Motowidlo et al. (1990) distinguished between high-fidelity and low-fidelity simulations. In high-fidelity simulations, the stimuli presented to the respondents closely replicate the actual situation, and the individuals have an opportunity to respond as if they were in the actual situation. In low-fidelity simulations, the stimuli are presented in written or oral form, and the individuals are asked to describe how they would respond to the situation rather than actually to carry out the behavior.

At the high-fidelity end of the continuum is the assessment center. Assessment centers present small groups of individuals with a variety of tasks, including in-basket tests, simulated interviews, and simulated group discussions (Bray, 1982; Thornton & Byham, 1982). The simulation approach has the advantage of more closely representing actual job performance. However, it is not always clear what aspects of the job should be chosen to simulate or how performance should be evaluated.

In-basket tests have a moderate level of fidelity. In these tests, the participant is presented with various materials (memos, financial reports, letters) and is asked to respond to them (Frederiksen, 1966; Frederiksen, Saunders, & Wand, 1957). The individual, however, has a limited amount of time to deal with the problems presented in the in-basket, giving him or her some of the constraints of actual job situations. Performance is evaluated on the basis of how the items are handled. For example, does the participant respond to a letter from the director of finance requesting fourth-quarter financial records with complete and accurate information?

Situational judgment tests have been considered low-fidelity simulations (Motowidlo et al., 1990). These tests present descriptions of situations, typically work-related, in which a problem exists (Chan & Schmitt, 1998; Legree, 1995; Motowidlo et al., 1990). The descriptions may be of actual situations or may be written to approximate actual situations in the domain of interest (e.g., a salesperson making a phone solicitation). Situations typically are selected on the bases of a critical incident analysis. Following each situational description is a set of options (i.e., strategies) for solving the problem. Respondents are asked to indicate their endorsement of the options, either by selecting the best and possibly the worst from among a few strategies or by rating the effectiveness of each alternative. Traditionally, SJTs have been scored by awarding points based on the correct choice of the best and worst options (Motowidlo et al., 1990) or by awarding points based on the percentage of experts who endorse the option (Chan & Schmitt, 1998).

Tacit Knowledge Approach

The tacit knowledge approach draws on aspects of the already discussed approaches in order to measure the level of domain-specific procedural knowledge that individuals have acquired from solving everyday problems. It is based on theoretical and empirical claims that the amount and organization of knowledge differs between experts and novices (Chi et al., 1988; Ericsson, 1996; Ericsson & Smith, 1991) and that these knowledge differences reflect differences in the developed abilities of experts and novices (Sternberg, 1998a; in press-b).

The tacit knowledge approach relies on a critical incident technique to identify examples of tacit knowledge acquired in solving real-world problems. That is, we interview domain experts to identify incidents that reflect important lessons and ask them to express in their own words the knowledge gained from those situations. We do not rely solely on the individuals who provided the incidents to determine which items of knowledge are more and which are less effective. We use subsequent analyses to identify the items that are critical to performance.

The tacit knowledge approach shares with the simulation approach the view that measuring practically relevant behavior in a test situation depends in part on the extent to which the task resembles those tasks found in everyday life. As such, we attempt to include sufficient detail in our measure to provide respondents with a realistic picture of the situation. However, we have relied primarily on a paper-and-pencil format to present this information rather than simulations for reasons of practicality, with the exception of our tacit knowledge acquisition task for sales (Sternberg et al., 1993). We have chosen to provide better coverage of the performance domain at the potential cost of lower fidelity. Future testing, however, is moving in the direction of more performance-based, high-fidelity assessment.

The tacit knowledge approach is linked most closely to that of SJTs. We present situation descriptions, often based on actual situations of position incumbents, followed by several possible responses to those situations. The number of response options ranges between 5 and 20. Individuals are asked to rate on a Likert scale the quality or appropriateness of each option for addressing the problem presented in the situation.

In a hypothetical example, an administrative assistant realizes that there is a factual error in a memorandum that her boss has written and that needs to be sent out immediately. The boss is in a closed door meeting. The respondent is asked to rate several options (usually on a 1 = low to 9 = high scale) for solving the problem. Examples of responses include interrupting the meeting to show the boss the error; fixing the error oneself and sending out the revision; and fixing the error but waiting to send out the memo until the assistant can consult the boss.

The set of ratings the individual generates for all the situations is used to assess the individual's tacit knowledge for that domain. As with SJTs, the scoring of tacit knowledge tests often relies on the judgments of experts. In general, tacit knowledge tests have been scored in one of three ways: by correlating participants' responses with an index of group membership (i.e., expert, intermediate, novice), by judging the degree to which participants' responses conform to professional rules of thumb, or by computing the difference between participants' responses and an expert prototype. To understand better what tacit knowledge tests are designed to measure, we consider tacit knowledge as a measurement construct.

TACIT KNOWLEDGE AS A MEASUREMENT CONSTRUCT

Drawing on our description of the key features of tacit knowledge and the cognitive model presented in chapter 6, we discuss tacit knowledge as a measurement construct. In other words, what are tacit knowledge tests and the items contained within them intended to measure?

This question can be answered by considering a traditional distinction between achievement testing and intelligence testing. In achievement testing, items are presumed to exemplify the measurement construct (e.g., knowledge of world history) but are not commonly viewed as predictors. For example, when individuals correctly answer a factual multiple-choice question about world history, we assume that they possessed prior knowledge of either the fact in question or related facts that enabled them to rule out incorrect alternatives. We do not commonly view the history question as predictive of performance on other tests or tasks. In intelligence testing, by contrast, items are presumed to predict performance but are not commonly viewed as exemplars of the measurement construct. For example, when individuals correctly solve a figural analogy problem, we do not assume that they possessed prior knowledge of the analogical relationship in question. However, we do view such analogy problems as predictive of performance on other tests and tasks of general mental ability.

Is a measure of tacit knowledge an intelligence test or an achievement test? Having drawn a distinction between intelligence and achievement testing, we must point out that neither type of test exists in a pure form (Sternberg, 1998a). All achievement tests measure underlying abilities, if only the abilities necessary to acquire and display mastery of the tested content, and so tend to have predictive value. Likewise, all intelligence tests measure acculturated knowledge, if only the knowledge necessary to make sense of items and testing conventions, and so tell us something about the knowledge content of individuals rated high and low in general intelligence. All these tests measure a form of developing expertise (Sternberg, 1998a). Tacit knowledge tests break down the artificial boundaries between achievement and ability testing.

Tacit knowledge tests are knowledge-based tests built on a theory of human intelligence (Sternberg, 1995c). They are intended to measure both practical, experience-based knowledge and the underlying dispositions or abilities that support the acquisition and use of that knowledge. Thus, scores on tacit knowledge tests are expected to predict performance on tests or tasks that draw on either tacit knowledge or the mental abilities that supported its development and use. These abilities are hypothesized to differ from those implicated in the so-called general factor in human intelligence commonly referred to as g and often approximately measured, in norm-referenced fashion, as IQ. Research by Sternberg and his colleagues has produced support for the hypothesis that the abilities associated with tacit knowledge test performance are different from those associated with tests of g (Hedlund et al., 1999; Sternberg et al., 1993; Sternberg et al., 1995).

Because tacit knowledge items are considered to measure both acquired knowledge and practical ability, we propose that tacit knowledge tests have the potential to shed light on both the content of tacit knowledge and the events or experiences through which it was acquired. Few would contest that tacit knowledge items reflect the knowledge of the respondents from whom the items were obtained (in the course of a story-telling exercise focusing on personal experiences). The items came from these respondents' memories and so must reflect the content of those memories. What remains to be determined is the degree to which tacit knowledge items measure the acquisition and use of tacit knowledge by those who did not produce but rather endorsed or rated the items. This question is being addressed by our numerous research studies in both civilian and military sectors, which we discuss in subsequent chapters.

DEVELOPING TACIT KNOWLEDGE INVENTORIES

We have developed tests to assess tacit knowledge for academic psychology, elementary school teaching, business management, sales, entry level jobs in organizations, college education, and military leadership. In this section we present a framework for developing tacit knowledge tests of the format described above, a framework that is based on the techniques we have used to measure tacit knowledge in the various domains we have studied.

The development of tacit knowledge inventories readily may be understood as a production process, beginning with the raw materials of experience-based tacit knowledge elicited from successful practitioners in a given domain and culminating in a revised and validated inventory. At each step in the development process, value is added through the conduct of research and analysis. Figure 2 shows, in schematic form, the major phases of the development process, the constituent research activities within each phase, and the informational products that are produced at various points in the process.

All the phases indicated in Figure 2 are designed to support the development of assessment instruments based both on the theory and methods of tacit knowledge research and on the substantive knowledge in the domain of interest. Specifically, the steps are intended to aid in selecting the content that is most promising with respect to the goals of the assessment phase, that is, in measuring an individual's possession of tacit knowledge. The term *promising* is used here to refer to that subset of tacit knowledge with the highest probability of yielding or contributing to tacit knowledge test questions that, taken together, constitute a valid measure of the underlying, domain-relevant tacit knowledge of respondents. This process was developed over the course of several research projects and is applicable to the identification and assessment of tacit knowledge in any performance domain. We now describe each stage in the process, from the identification of exemplars of tacit knowledge to the construction of the final inventory.

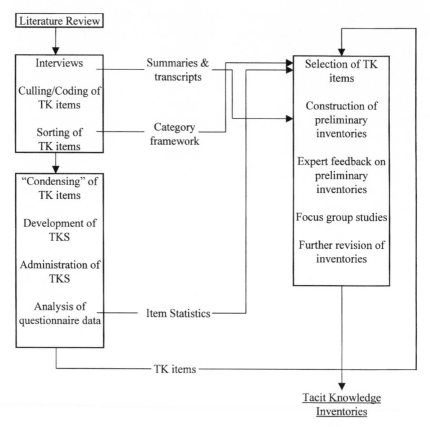

Figure 2. *Flow chart showing phases, activities, and sources of information in the inventory development process.*

Knowledge Identification

As shown in Figure 2, we generally begin with a review of job-relevant literature (e.g., sales manuals, army trade publications) to identify on a preliminary basis the experience-based, tacit knowledge for the relevant profession (e.g., salespersons, army leaders). This review may suggest some of the content for use in a tacit knowledge inventory and may provide a preliminary taxonomy, or category framework, for organizing the knowledge. For example, in research with managers, Wagner and Sternberg (1986) proposed a framework of practically intelligent behavior consisting of tacit knowledge about managing oneself, managing others, and managing one's career.

Typically, a review of the literature does not provide a sufficient number of examples of knowledge that meet our criteria or include enough detail from which to create tacit knowledge questions of the format that we have described. We have found that the practical advice presented in the professional literature tends to be decontextualized and already converted to semantic knowledge. We also surmise that the politics of professional print may keep some truly tacit knowledge – knowledge that contradicts doctrine, for example – out of print altogether. Therefore, the next step is to conduct interviews with successful practitioners in the domain to generate a larger body of knowledge from which to draw in developing the tacit knowledge inventories. We describe here a method for conducting these interviews.

A METHOD FOR ELICITING TACIT KNOWLEDGE. In selecting individuals to interview, it is important to identify a sample that is likely to possess a certain amount of tacit knowledge. We seek to identify individuals who are both experienced and successful in their domain. Individuals who are more successful likely have acquired some important knowledge relevant to success that individuals who are less successful have not. Furthermore, individuals who are currently practicing in the domain of interest are more appropriate sources for understanding the tacit knowledge of that domain than are individuals who hold other positions (e.g., supervisor) or previously held the position of interest. The latter may consider different knowledge to be relevant on the basis of their different perspectives. Once a relevant pool of practitioners is identified, experts can be chosen either by nomination (by peers or superiors) or on the basis of existing performance criteria (e.g., performance evaluation, salary). In research by Sternberg and colleagues (Hedlund et al., 1999; Sternberg et al., 1993; Sternberg et al., 1995; Wagner, 1987), interviews were conducted with academic psychologists deemed successful on the basis of their tenure and affiliation (e.g., full professors at Yale); with business managers who were considered successful on the basis of their position in the company; with salespersons who were successful in their sales performance; with successful college students selected on the basis of grades and school affiliation; and with successful military leaders identified through a nomination process.

All these experts were asked to consider what it takes to succeed in their respective domains and to provide typical performance-related situations and possible responses to those situations that exemplify tacit knowledge. In recent research, we have developed a structured interview in which participants are provided with more explicit instructions about the knowledge we seek to identify and with prompts to elicit more in-depth responses.

We rely generally on a two-person interview team, with one person designated as the lead interviewer and the other as the notetaker. The lead interviewer directs the interview and the notetaker takes written notes, asks for clarification, and, along with the lead interviewer, asks follow-up questions. The interviews are taped when possible, with the interviewees' consent, so that questions and clarifications can be addressed once the interview is completed. It is also helpful for one of the interviewers to be familiar with the domain in order to understand any technical language or the jargon of the interviewee.

We present below a protocol for conducting the interviews. We use specific examples from our work with military leaders to illustrate the steps involved.

1. *Introduction.* When the participant arrives, members of the interview team introduce themselves and give a standardized introduction to the study and the interview. This introduction should state the purpose of the research, preempt likely misunderstandings, and orient the participant to the purpose of the interview. For example:

We are trying to understand the key lessons that leaders acquire from their experience on the job. If we can identify these lessons, we will try to find ways to use them to strengthen leader development efforts.

This is not an evaluation of you as a leader. This is not a study comparing leaders from your organization with those from another organization.

We want to identify specific examples of informal knowledge about leadership at your level. We want to find examples of things about leadership that are not written in books or taught in classes. Our belief is that this knowledge is often not discussed openly, but nevertheless is used by leaders as they meet the demands of their jobs. This knowledge may have been learned because of some challenge or problem you faced. It may have been acquired by watching someone else's successes or failures.

We are not interested in the party line or doctrine. We also are not interested in the purely technical things you learned from experience, for example, how to tune up an engine. We are really interested in the problems and challenges you face and what you have learned about leadership at your level from these experiences.

2. *Request for Stories.* The purpose of the interview is to elicit stories or cases from the participants' experiences and to explore the unspoken, practical knowledge gained from or reflected in those cases. We ask participants, for example, "Tell us a story about a leadership experience you have had as a leader in your current position from which you learned a lesson." The aim is to keep the focus on the stories rather than on theories or generalizations about effective performance. In this way, the responses are more closely tied to the tacit knowledge construct (i.e., in the knowledge based on personal, practical experience). Because the values in the recalled experiences are sometimes unclear, we seek the participant's help in making sense of each story and identifying the lesson associated with the story.

3. *Follow-up Questions.* Follow-up questions are used to focus on key contextual variables in the stories (e.g., "Tell us more about the climate in your unit"); the goals and alternative courses of action reflected in the stories (e.g., "What exactly did you hope to accomplish?" and "What else did you consider doing at the time?"); and on identifying practical knowledge with broader applicability (i.e., lessons learned) derived from the experiences described in the stories (e.g., "What do you think you learned from this experience?" and "How has this experience affected your approach to leadership?"). Once it appears that no more information can be gained from a story, the interviewer, given time allowances, may ask the participant to share another story from personal experience.

At the completion of each interview, the notetaker summarizes the interview. An interview summary might contain the following information: participant information (e.g., position, time in job, race, sex); a summary of each story; annotations to each story based on follow-up questions; and any comments from the interviewer. It is useful for the notetaker and lead interviewer to review the summaries and resolve any disagreements over details or interpretations from the interview.

The identification of tacit knowledge does not end with the summarized interviews. Even with explicit instructions about what the interviewer is looking for, not all of the stories generated from the interviews provide examples of tacit knowledge. Therefore, the interview summaries are submitted to a panel of experts who are familiar with both the performance domain and the tacit knowledge construct. These experts are asked to judge whether the interview summary represents knowledge that is intimately related to action, is relevant to the goals that the individual values, is acquired with minimal environmental support, and is relevant to performance in the domain under study (e.g., academic psychology, military leadership).

PRODUCTS OF THE INTERVIEWS. The products of the interviews are transcripts and summaries containing numerous potential examples of tacit knowledge. These summaries serve two purposes in instrument development. First, tacit knowledge items (essentially pieces of advice) may be extracted from the summaries and used in a number of later analyses. Second, the summaries themselves (consisting of stories that the professionals shared about their experiences) can be used directly in the construction of the inventory.

A useful interim step is to ask a panel of experts (members of the research team or practitioners familiar with the tacit knowledge construct) to review the knowledge compiled from the interview summaries to ensure that it meets the criteria for tacitness. These criteria are (1) that the knowledge should have been acquired with little environmental support, (2) that it should be related to action, and (3) that it should have relevance to the goals that the person values. Often, on further review, a knowledge example may be judged by experts to fail to meet one of these criteria. For example, consider the following story told by a military officer.

> I had a lieutenant who was screwing up big-time. He would take sensitive items, for example, weapons, night vision devices, etc., home. He even lost sensitive items. He lost a pistol, and rather than stop the mission and look for it, he continued on with the mission. As we all know, when you lose a sensitive item, you stop everything and look for it until you find it.

The above story was deemed to lack the necessary criteria for tacitness. The interviewee indicated that the knowledge he referred to is generally known by leaders. It even may represent an official procedure. Therefore, we have no evidence that this knowledge is attributable to the officer's experience in dealing with sensitive items that are missing. On the other hand, consider a story from another officer about a similar issue.

> It is important for a commander to know when to report bad news to the boss and when to withhold it. My unit had just completed a night move and had been in position for about two hours. A weapon was

identified as missing around midnight. The section chief told me that the weapon was in the current position because he had seen it during the sensitive item checks. I talked to each member of the section and determined that the weapon was in the position. We looked for the weapon from about midnight until 0300 hours. During this time I chose not to notify the battalion commander because I was confident that the weapon would be found. However, a sensitive item report was due at 0400 hours, so, for ethical reasons, I notified the battalion commander at 0300 hours that the weapon was missing. I told the battalion commander what I had done so far and that I was confident that the weapon would be found at first light. He was not upset. We found the weapon within ten minutes after the sun came up and the battalion commander was pleased we followed the standard operating procedures for dealing with a missing weapon.

In this story, the officer clearly expresses some knowledge he has acquired through previous experience in dealing with missing sensitive items (e.g., weapons). He has learned that, under some circumstances, it is best to hold off reporting a problem until it becomes necessary, as long as appropriate steps are taken to resolve the problem in the interim.

CODING THE INTERVIEW SUMMARIES. After determining which examples of knowledge meet the established criteria, it is useful to transform the summaries into a more usable form for the purpose of later analyses. We have used a format that is based on the procedural feature of our definition of tacit knowledge. That is, the knowledge is expressed as a mapping between a set of antecedent conditions and a set of consequent actions. An example of a tacit knowledge story and the item derived from it is shown in Table 1.

As the example shows, the item of knowledge is represented by one or more antecedent condition or IF statements, by one or more consequent action or THEN statements, and by a brief explanation or BECAUSE statement. The logical operators AND and OR are used in the coding to signal relationships of conjunction and disjunction, respectively. The operator ELSE is employed in the coding to connect sets of condition–action mappings into more complex procedures. Each individual piece of tacit knowledge is rewritten into this procedural form. This coding allows the researcher to analyze more readily the content of the tacit knowledge for the purpose of identifying categories of knowledge and selecting examples of knowledge that may be useful as items in a tacit knowledge inventory. The result of this phase is a set of coded tacit knowledge items.

The coded tacit knowledge items then may be subjected to a sorting process to identify major categories of tacit knowledge. This sorting may entail asking a group of experts to organize the items according to categories of their own devising. The results of the independent sortings may be analyzed by using hierarchical or other cluster analyses, a

---

TABLE 1. Example Leadership Story with Coded Knowledge Item

Story Summary

The battalion commander noticed that his company commanders were trying so hard to be successful that they would accept missions that their units did not have the capabilities to execute. Thus, the companies and the commanders would expend a great deal of effort and time to accomplish the mission without asking for help from the battalion in order to demonstrate their talents as leaders. The battalion commander gave one of his commanders a mission, and the commander worked his unit overtime for 2 weeks to accomplish it. The battalion commander realized that the same mission could have been accomplished in 2 days if the commander had requested resources from the battalion. After that incident, the battalion commander made it a point to ask the company commanders to realistically assess their units' resources before taking on a mission. The battalion commander felt that all commanders wanted to succeed and earn the top block rating due to the competitive environment in today's army.

Coded Item

IF your company commanders have a strong desire to be successful and earn top block ratings

AND

IF they also have a tendency to take on resource-intensive missions that exceed their capabilities

AND

IF they are reluctant to ask higher headquarters for help when they have missions that tax their units' resources

THEN require commanders to conduct resource assessments before they take on missions

BECAUSE an accurate resource assessment should indicate whether or not the unit has the resources to handle the mission. This assessment may prevent commanders from taking on a mission that would overburden their unit.

---

family of techniques for uncovering the natural groupings in a set of data (Hartigan, 1975). This type of analysis may produce hierarchically organized clusters of items that can be expressed in the form of a tree. The clusters can be interpreted by experts and assigned labels that represent different categories of tacit knowledge. The categories may provide an indication of the major areas of learning that occur in one's respective field. The category framework is also useful in selecting items for test development that provide a broad representation of the performance domain.

Item Selection

Although one may proceed to develop test questions directly from the tacit knowledge items generated from the interviews, a further selection process may be necessary for a number of reasons. First, the interview study may yield too many items of tacit knowledge to include in a tacit knowledge inventory of reasonable length, depending on the context in which the test might be used. Second, we cannot determine on the basis of the interviews alone what tacit knowledge is diagnostic of experience or predictive of effective performance in a given domain, or alternatively, what tacit knowledge is not related to these criteria. Managers, for example, may have learned that subordinates are more likely to come to them with problems if they leave their doors open. However, the extent to which this practice contributes to the manager's success is unclear. By leaving the door open, a manager may become the repository for problems that are the responsibility of other managers, which may create a job distraction. Third, the results of the preliminary sorting of interview data may not be sufficient for determining the internal structure of the tacit knowledge construct domain. That is, for the purposes of test construction, we would want further evidence of the structure of the performance domain to ensure that our items are representative. For these reasons, we take an additional step to narrow down the pool of items from which test questions will be constructed.

The next step in the process of selecting items for instrument development is more quantitative than qualitative. It entails surveying job incumbents to assess the quality of each tacit knowledge item. In order to develop a questionnaire that can be administered to job incumbents, the tacit knowledge items may need to be condensed. For example, if we want professionals to evaluate 100 examples of tacit knowledge, it would be unreasonable to ask them to read 100

items of the form shown in Table 1. Therefore, it may become necessary to condense the items into briefer descriptions. Condensing the
items involves extracting only the most important information and
deleting unnecessary information. Attempts should be made to
increase the comprehensibility of the items for the intended audience
and to preserve the intent of the interviewee who provided the
knowledge. As shown in the example of a condensed tacit knowledge
item for military leaders (Table 2), the procedural structure that we
consider to be characteristic of tacit knowledge is maintained in the
rewriting of items.

TABLE 2. Example Question from the Tacit Knowledge Survey

TACIT KNOWLEDGE SURVEY

Military Leaders

If a training event scheduled by your battalion commander conflicts
with a training event scheduled by your supported-unit commander and
if the event scheduled by the supported-unit commander has potentially
greater training value, then take a risk and give priority to the supported-unit commander's training event. By taking a risk to provide
your soldiers with the best training, you earn their trust.

1. How *good* is this advice for company commanders?

1	2	3	4	5	6	7
Extremely bad			Neither bad nor good			Extremely good

2. How *commonly known* is this advice among company commanders?

1	2	3	4	5	6	7
Known by almost none			Known by some			Known by almost all

3. How *often* do company commanders face situations like this?

1	2	3	4	5	6	7
Almost never			Sometimes			Almost all the time

4. To what extent does this advice match *your concept* of leadership?

1	2	3	4	5	6	7
Does not match my concept of leadership at all			Matches my concept of leadership somewhat			Matches my concept of leader-ship very closely

The condensed items are compiled into a survey, which we refer to as a Tacit Knowledge Survey (TKS) (Table 2). The TKS differs from a tacit knowledge inventory in that respondents are asked to rate the perceived quality of the tacit knowledge in the former, whereas they are asked to rate the quality of responses to the problem in the latter. Job incumbents can be asked to rate each item on a number of dimensions (as shown in Table 2). We have used four 7-point scales, which ask for the following judgments: (1) How good does the respondent think the advice is? (2) How commonly known does the respondent think the advice is? (3) How often, in the judgment of the respondent, do incumbents at the specified level face situations such as the one described? and (4) To what extent does the advice match the respondent's personal concept of job performance? Each of the scales is intended to provide a different sort of information about the tacit knowledge item being rated. The *good* scale is intended to assess the overall quality of the knowledge being rated. The *known* scale is intended to assess one possible index of tacitness (on the theory that knowledge whose acquisition is not well supported by the environment may be less commonly known than other knowledge). The *often* scale is intended to assess the generalizability or applicability of knowledge items across job settings within the domain. Finally, the *concept* scale is intended to assess respondents' implicit theories of performance. Together, the four rating scales are intended to provide a comprehensive but nonredundant picture of each tacit knowledge item for the purpose of evaluating each item's potential for development into tacit knowledge test questions.

We are interested in items that are (1) rated as better advice by those considered to be successful in their domain; (2) not viewed as common knowledge by individuals in the domain; (3) representative of the situations faced by most individuals in the domain; and (4) a good fit to the concept of performance held by successful individuals in the domain. In order to identify items that are endorsed by individuals who are successful in a domain, we obtain data on a relevant performance criterion. In our research with military leaders, we obtained two criterion measures, experience and performance ratings. Experience was expressed in terms of expert–novice differences, and performance was assessed from ratings of leadership effectiveness by other leaders. Responses to the TKS are analyzed along with the criterion measure to identify items that have promise for inclusion in the tacit-knowledge inventory. This analysis generates a number of item statistics that can be used in the selection process.

In our research, we used discriminant analysis to identify items that distinguish individuals with more from those with less experience (Hedlund et al., 1999). In the discriminant analysis, a linear combination of the discriminating variables (e.g., TKS items) is derived that maximizes the divergence between groups (e.g., experienced vs. novice). The linear combination of the discriminating variables (the canonical discriminant function) can be tested for significance to determine if the set of variables distinguishes between groups. In addition, the correlations between discriminating variables and the canonical discriminant function can be computed to assess the discriminating power of individual variables (e.g., TKS items).

We used point-biserial correlations between ratings on the items and ratings of effective performance to identify items that reflected the responses of effective performers. Item statistics such as these can be used, along with the category framework developed in the interview phase, to select items that have the most potential to explain successful performance and provide the best coverage of the tacit knowledge domain.

Instrument Construction

The knowledge identification and item selection phases in the development of tacit knowledge inventories generate several outputs that serve as materials for the final phase of instrument construction. These outputs include interview transcripts and interview summaries; the category framework derived from expert sortings and cluster analyses; a set of item statistics for use in the selection of content for the inventories; and the knowledge items retained on the basis of the category framework and item statistics from the questionnaire study. In the next phase of test development, preliminary inventory questions are constructed by using both selected knowledge items and the interview summaries from which they were drawn. A tacit knowledge question consists of a situation description followed by several potential responses to that situation. Although the condensed tacit knowledge item may serve to describe the situation, it is preferable to include the details from the original story to provide a richer, more in-depth problem description. Including more contextual and situation-specific information in the question provides the respondent with a clearer basis on which to evaluate the appropriateness of potential responses to the situation. The original story also provides a source for developing the response options to a question.

Once the researchers are satisfied with the form of the preliminary inventory, it is useful to circulate the inventory among experts in the domain. One method of obtaining feedback is to convene a focus group of experts to review and discuss the inventory. In our research, focus group participants were given a brief introduction to the goals of the project and an explanation of the tacit knowledge construct in non-technical language. They were asked to judge the construct-relatedness of the inventory questions by considering whether each question addresses knowledge gained through experience and fits the definition of tacit knowledge provided. In addition, focus group participants were asked to help fill gaps and fix problems in the inventory. In particular, they were asked to provide additional, plausible response options for any question; identify areas of confusion or lack of clarity; (c) identify problems of sexual, racial, or ethnic bias; and identify anything that did not ring true in the inventory questions.

The researcher can use the feedback from the focus group to revise the inventories. For example, inventory questions for which judgments of construct-relatedness are not unanimous and positive may be omitted from the inventory. Similarly, a response option or scenario feature that is objected to by two or more participants may be omitted. The focus group may suggest additional response options or scenario features, which can be added to the inventory. The final result of this test development process is a revised tacit knowledge inventory, which can be administered to position incumbents and used to address further research questions, such as those regarding criterion-related construct validity.

Summary of Tacit Knowledge Inventory Construction

The phases that we have described are all designed to support the construction of tacit knowledge tests. The tacit knowledge items acquired in the interview study form the raw materials for this construction process, during which the tacit knowledge items are subjected to qualitative analysis (sorting into categories) and quantitative analysis (obtaining quality ratings). The various phases serve to address two basic questions about the pool of tacit knowledge from which an instrument will be developed. First, which items are most promising for use in the construction of tacit knowledge test questions? Second, what does the underlying structure represented by the tacit knowledge items tell us about the structure of the construct domain so that we can design our tacit knowledge tests to capture this domain?

The result of this process is an inventory that has greater likelihood of possessing both internal and external validity, an issue discussed in the last part of this chapter.

ESTABLISHING THE VALIDITY OF TACIT KNOWLEDGE INVENTORIES

An important part of developing any test is to establish its construct validity. Unlike the development of many intelligence-type tests, we do not rely solely on the qualifications that items should load heavily on a single factor and predict some external performance criteria as justification for concluding that a test measures the construct of interest. As Nunally (1970) and others have argued, such a criterion-based approach to test development is problematic and often produces measurement instruments of inferior quality. Specifically, such an approach may yield tests that suffer from low internal consistency, poor factor structure, and fragility with respect to criteria other than those on which the selection of items was based.

We rely on both theoretical and empirical justifications to establish the validity of tacit knowledge tests. We use Messick's (1995) unified validity framework to show how tacit knowledge theory and the phases of test development that we have outlined contribute to the validity of our tacit knowledge tests. Messick's framework treats the traditionally separate forms of validity (content, construct, and criterion) as aspects of a more comprehensive kind of construct validity. According to this framework, the essential goal of test validation is to support, through a combination of theoretical rationale and empirical evidence, the interpretation of test scores and the uses of scores under that interpretation.

The Content Aspect

The content aspect of validity refers to evidence that test content is relevant to and representative of the focal construct. It addresses the concerns that fall under the traditional heading of content validity. In the context of tacit knowledge test development, the goal of *construct relevance* calls for tacit knowledge test questions that are sensitive to knowledge of the type specified by the focal construct and insensitive to knowledge that falls outside the focal construct. A first step toward this goal is taken during the identification phase of test development, in interviews with job incumbents, when we orient participants toward personal experiences and away from formal principles or theory within their performance domains. A second step is taken in the item selection phase, when job incumbents are asked to rate the quality of tacit knowledge items. These ratings (i.e., item means and variances) may provide evidence regarding the relevance of tacit knowledge items to the underlying construct. For example, tacit knowledge items with low mean ratings (items containing knowledge that respondents, on average, consider to present bad advice) may not be relevant to successful performance. Also, items with low variances (items for which respondents agree highly about the quality, good or bad, of the knowledge reflected in the item) may not reflect knowledge gained through personal experience if the knowledge is generally agreed on as good. In addition to these steps, the goal of establishing construct relevance also is supported by asking domain experts, at various stages in the test development process, to judge the relevance of the items to the tacit knowledge construct.

The goal of *construct representativeness* calls for tacit knowledge items that are typical rather than atypical of knowledge-based items specified by the focal construct. An initial step toward this goal is taken in the identification phase by interviewing job incumbents who are representative of the range of specialty areas within the domain. For example, military leaders in the same position (e.g., platoon leader) may serve in one of many branches (e.g., infantry, engineering). Therefore, in our research, we sought to interview officers from these various branches to increase the representativeness of the knowledge that was elicited. A second step is taken during the item selection phase, when participants are asked to rate how often a situation presented in a tacit knowledge item occurs. Items that receive both a low mean and a small variance, for example, are ones that most incumbents agree almost never occur and therefore may not be representative of the knowledge domain. The categories derived from cluster analyses of the tacit knowledge items also provide a source for ensuring construct representativeness. Items can be chosen to represent each of the major categories of tacit knowledge, thus providing better coverage of the construct domain. Finally, at several points during test development, expert judgments are sought regarding the construct representativeness of the items. After an initial pool of potential tacit knowledge items is obtained from the interviews, an expert panel is asked to judge the representativeness of each item. The experts are asked to eliminate items that are too narrow or technical in focus (e.g., how to safely store chemical weapons) and knowledge that is relevant to a small proportion of job incumbents (e.g., how to manage stress at work if you are a single parent). Experts again are asked to evaluate the representativeness of the items after preliminary test questions have been developed.

The Substantive Aspect

The substantive aspect of validity refers to the theoretical rationale behind tacit knowledge and its relationship to task (test) performance. A step toward the goal of substantive validity is provided by our cognitive model and the characterization of tacit knowledge presented in chapter 6. The model illustrates how tacit, procedural knowledge is acquired and how it comes to be applied in solving everyday problems. The model also helps to illustrate how tacit knowledge confers a performance advantage (relative to that conferred by nontacit, procedural knowledge) in people's ability to respond to contextualized problems of realistic complexity. The characteristic features of tacit knowledge (acquisition on one's own, procedural nature, and instrumental value) further highlight its potential contribution to successful performance. The cognitive model of tacit knowledge, on which the identification and measurement of tacit knowledge is based, provides a theoretical rationale for tacit knowledge test performance and, as such, directly serves the goal of substantive validity. Substantive validity also may be supported by showing, through empirical research, the extent to which participants draw on personally experienced rather than received knowledge in performing everyday, real-world tasks.

The Structural Aspect

The structural aspect of validity refers to the level of fit between the internal structure of the test and the internal structure of the construct domain. It is related to the issue of construct representativeness discussed earlier. A first step toward the goal of structural validity is taken by interviewing and eliciting knowledge from job incumbents in all areas that represent the performance domain. For example, in our study with military leaders, we interviewed officers in all three of the major branch categories within the army (combat arms, combat support, combat service support). The goal of structural validity also is served by administering measurement instruments (e.g., the Tacit Knowledge Survey) to a wide variety of job incumbents. By using broad samples of job incumbents, we are able to avoid basing our analyses and test development on a restricted subset of the tacit knowledge domain. Of course, the structural aspect of validity is addressed most directly through statistical techniques, such as cluster analysis and multidimensional scaling, that identify the internal structure of the sample of items. By examining the internal structure, we cast a wider net in our selection of tacit knowledge items, and in so doing, we have improved our prospects for developing tacit knowledge tests that mirror the structure of the construct domain (the domain of practical, action-oriented knowledge that individuals acquire from personal experience).

The Generalizability Aspect

The generalizability aspect of validity refers to the extent to which score properties and interpretations generalize across groups, settings, and tasks. The generalizability aspect includes concerns that traditionally fall under the heading of *reliability*. In the context of tacit knowledge test development, the goal of generalizability calls for tacit knowledge test scores that generalize across roles within the organization, repeated administrations, and alternate forms of the test. Test development efforts relevant to the content, substantive, and structural aspects of validity also are relevant to the generalizability aspect. In general, by seeking to specify and measure the construct rather than merely pursuing correlation with an external criterion, we presumably increase the generalizability of score interpretations for our tacit knowledge tests.

The External Aspect

The external aspect of validity refers to the issue of criterion-related validity. That is, we seek to establish that the test relates to an external criterion. More specifically, the goal is to obtain evidence of convergent and discriminant validity. Establishing criterion-related validity entails showing that tacit knowledge test scores correlate more highly (converge) with theoretically related constructs such as performance and correlate less highly with (diverge) from theoretically distinct constructs such as general intelligence or formal job knowledge.

Test development efforts to specify and measure the tacit knowledge construct also support the goal of criterion validity. For example, job incumbents are asked to provide examples of important lessons they learned in the course of performing their job rather than examples of knowledge they gained in school. These instructions increase the likelihood that the tacit knowledge items obtained will be related to performance criteria and be distinct from formally acquired knowledge. Research during the item selection phase involves assessing more directly the relation of these items to external criteria. This step helps to identify tacit knowledge items that are indicative of successful performance.

Beyond these efforts during test development, additional steps should be taken to provide evidence of convergent and discriminant validity. For tacit knowledge tests, possible discriminant evidence would be that which discounts the effects of general intelligence, reading comprehension, and formally acquired knowledge on tacit knowledge test scores. Evidence of convergent validity would include a correlation between tacit knowledge test scores and variables such as perceived job effectiveness, degree and rate of career advancement, and performance on job-relevant tasks. To obtain such evidence requires conducting a validation study in which measures of these variables are administered to or obtained from individuals. For example, in our research with managers and military leaders, we administered the tacit knowledge inventory, along with a measure of general intelligence and related constructs, and obtained various performance criteria such as supervisor ratings, salary, and productivity. Correlational and hierarchical regression analyses can be used to assess convergent and discriminant validity. Convergent validity is supported by a significant relationship between tacit knowledge test scores and the performance criterion (e.g., supervisor ratings). Discriminant validity is supported by zero to moderate correlations with measures such as general intelligence and general job knowledge, as well as the incremental validity of tacit knowledge test scores beyond these measures.

The Consequential Aspect

The consequential aspect of validity refers to the value implications of the intended use of score interpretation as a basis for action. Because tacit knowledge tests may be used for employee assessment and development or even selection, it is important to consider how the knowledge included in those tests fits into the culture and rules of the organization. For example, if an item of tacit knowledge meets all the criteria that we have discussed (e.g., satisfies the definition of tacit, exhibits a strong positive correlation with effective performance) but conflicts with the organizational culture (e.g., suggesting that females should be given less responsibility than males) or involves disobeying a regulation (e.g., suggesting that financial figures should be tampered with when information is unavailable), then it may be inappropriate to include the item in a tacit knowledge test. Relying on experts to review the tacit knowledge items throughout the test development process helps to ensure that issues related to the consequential aspect of validity are addressed.

SUMMARY

The goal of the test development process outlined in this chapter is to support the construction of valid tacit knowledge tests. Our theoretical model of tacit knowledge, described in chapter 6, constitutes, we believe, a step in the direction of this goal. By elaborating on what we consider to be tacit knowledge at a theoretical level, we set the stage for a more detailed consideration of item content during the selection process and in so doing, increase the substantive validity of our tests. The analysis of item ratings and performance data constitutes a second step toward measuring the construct. By identifying those items with the strongest association with performance criteria, we increase the probability that we will select items and construct test questions that embody the construct, given that tacit knowledge has clear benefits for performance. The analysis of the underlying structure by sorting items into categories constitutes a third step toward our goal. By examining the structure of the tacit knowledge space (based on the data from our sample), we are able to make more informed decisions about the distribution of item content in our tacit knowledge tests and in so doing, increase the structural validity and generalizability of score interpretations. Finally, by conducting validation studies we provide support that tacit knowledge is relevant to understanding performance in the domain of interest and that it contributes to that understanding beyond traditional indicators of performance. In chapters 8 and 9 we discuss the development and validation of tests to measure tacit knowledge in civilian and military domains.

CHAPTER 8

The Role of Practical Intelligence in Civilian Settings

Our program of research is based on the notion that there is more to successfully predicting performance than just measuring the so-called general factor from conventional psychometric tests of intelligence (Sternberg & Wagner, 1993). We propose that tacit knowledge, as an aspect of practical intelligence, is a key ingredient of success in any domain. Of course, there are those who disagree with this position (Jensen, 1993; Ree & Earles, 1993; Schmidt & Hunter, 1993, 1998), suggesting that individual differences in performance are explained primarily by general cognitive ability. Some proponents of using general cognitive ability tests argue further that the value of these tests is that they are applicable for all jobs, have lowest cost to develop and administer, and have the highest validity (Schmidt & Hunter, 1998). However, even Schmidt and Hunter acknowledge that alternative measures such as work sample tests and job knowledge tests have comparable and perhaps even higher validities than general ability tests and provide incremental prediction above the latter.

A program of research by Sternberg and his colleagues has conducted tacit knowledge research with business managers, college professors, elementary school students, salespeople, college students, and general populations. In study after study, this important aspect of practical intelligence has been found generally to be uncorrelated with academic intelligence as measured by conventional tests in a variety of populations and occupations and at a variety of age levels (Sternberg et al., 1993; Sternberg et al., 1995; Wagner, 1987; Wagner & Sternberg, 1985). A major task of this tacit knowledge research has been to identify the content of tacit knowledge and develop ways to measure the possession of tacit knowledge. Tacit knowledge tests present a set of problem situations and ask respondents to rate the quality or appropriateness of a number of possible responses to those situations. (The format and development of tacit knowledge tests was discussed in the previous chapter.) In this chapter we review the tacit knowledge studies that have been conducted in civilian settings, and in the next chapter we present a specific example of a tacit knowledge project with military leaders.

ACADEMIC PSYCHOLOGISTS

One of the first studies in the program of tacit knowledge research was conducted by Wagner and Sternberg (1985) with academic psychologists. These investigators developed a test of tacit knowledge for academic psychologists, which was based on interviews with five full professors, and administered the test to three groups. The first group consisted of 54 faculty members from 20 psychology departments, identified as either among the top 15 nationally ranked colleges or outside the top 15. The second group consisted of 104 psychology graduate students from the same departments as the faculty members. The third group consisted of 29 Yale undergraduates. Each participant was given 12 work-related situations, each with 6 to 20 response options. For example, one question described a second-year assistant professor who in the past year had published two unrelated empirical articles, who had one graduate student working with him, and who had not yet received external funding. His goal was to become a top person in his field and to obtain tenure in his department. Participants were asked to rate on a scale from 1 to 9 the value of several pieces of advice regarding what the professor could do in the next 2 months. Examples of advice included (1) improve the quality of his teaching; (2) write a grant proposal; (3) begin a long-term research project that might lead to a major theoretical article; (4) concentrate on recruiting more students; (5) serve on a committee studying university–community relations; and (6) begin several related short-term projects, each of which might lead to an empirical article.

Responses to the test were scored by correlating ratings on each item with an index variable for group membership (1 = undergraduate, 2 = graduate student, 3 = aculty member). A positive correlation between item and group membership indicated that higher ratings on the item were associated with more expertise, and a negative correlation indicated the opposite. Wagner and Sternberg (1985) validated the test using several criteria. They obtained from faculty members citation rates, the number of publications, number of conferences attended in the last year, number of conference papers presented, distribution of time across teaching and research, academic rank, year Ph.D. was obtained, and level of institutional affiliation (high or low). For undergraduates, they obtained scores on the verbal reasoning section of the Differential Aptitude Test (DAT) (Bennett, Seashore, & Wesman, 1974).

Wagner and Sternberg (1985) found that tacit knowledge test scores correlated significantly and positively with number of publications (.33), number of conferences attended (.34), rated level of institution (.40), and proportion of time spent in research (.39). For the undergraduates, tacit knowledge tests scores did not correlate significantly with verbal reasoning scores ($r = -.04$, ns).

In a follow-up study by Wagner (1987), a revised version of the test was administered to 91 faculty members, 61 graduate students, and 60 Yale undergraduates. The revised test contained 12 situations with 9 to 10 response options. Wagner obtained ratings for both conceptions of what the subjects would do in their actual jobs and what they would do in their ideal jobs. Scores were obtained for the overall test and for six subscales, which crossed three kinds of tacit knowledge – tacit knowledge about managing oneself, managing others, and managing tasks – with two orientations of tacit knowledge, local tacit knowledge, pertaining to the situation at hand, versus global tacit knowledge, pertaining to a wider set of circumstances.

A different scoring method was used than in the study by Wagner and Sternberg (1985). An expert profile was created by administering the test to a sample of professors who were nominated as high on practical intelligence. A distance score (d^2) was computed between the ratings of the participants and the mean of the experts' ratings. The mean d^2 values for the three groups were 339 for faculty, 412 for graduate students, and 429 for undergraduates, indicating that tacit knowledge increased, on average, with level of experience (a smaller value representing greater tacit knowledge). There were exceptions in each group, however, suggesting that what mattered was not merely experience but what one had learned from experience.

Wagner then examined the relationship of tacit knowledge with the same criterion measures that were used in Wagner and Sternberg (1985). Because the tacit knowledge test was scored by using a distance measure, a lower distance, or smaller value, represents a better tacit knowledge score. Therefore, negative correlations reflect a positive association between tacit knowledge scores and the criterion.

For the actual-job ratings, significant correlations were obtained between tacit knowledge scores and ratings of department (–.48), number of citations (–.44), number of publications (–.28), proportion of time spent on research (–.41), and number of papers presented. The correlations for ideal-job ratings were slightly lower but comparable. Again, the tacit knowledge scores did not correlate with verbal reasoning ability. Wagner did find significant intercorrelations among the six subscales, ranging from .2 to .4. He interpreted these correlations to indicate a weak general factor for tacit knowledge, a factor that appears to be distinct from the general factor measured by traditional intelligence tests.

BUSINESS MANAGERS

Wagner and Sternberg (1985) and Wagner (1987) conducted studies with business managers in parallel to the studies with academic psychologists. The studies involved similar methods but with a different performance domain.

Wagner and Sternberg (1985) developed a tacit knowledge test for business managers based on interviews with five experienced and successful mid-level managers. The test consisted of 12 work-related situations with 9 to 20 response options and was administered to 54 managers (19 of whom were from among top 20 Fortune 500 companies), 51 graduate students from five business schools varying in prestige, and 22 Yale undergraduates. The criteria obtained for the managers included status in or outside the top Fortune 500 companies, number of years of management experience, number of years of formal schooling, salary, number of employees supervised, and level of job title. Undergraduates completed the DAT Verbal Reasoning subtest.

Responses to the test were scored by correlating ratings on each item with an index variable for group membership (1 = undergraduates, 2 = business school graduate students, 3 = business managers). Wagner and Sternberg found significant correlations between tacit knowledge and company level (.34), number of years schooling (.41), and salary (.46). For the undergraduates, the correlation between tacit knowledge scores and verbal reasoning ability was not significant (.16) and again indicated that the tacit knowledge test was not a proxy for a traditional general intelligence test.

In the second study, Wagner (1987) administered the test to 64 business managers, 25 business graduate students, and 60 Yale undergraduates. The distance scoring method, described above, was used. An expert profile was created from the responses of 13 business executives from Fortune 500 firms. The mean tacit knowledge scores were 244 for business managers, 340 for business graduate students, and 417 for undergraduates, indicating greater tacit knowledge with experience. Correlations with the criterion measures were lower than those for academic psychologists. However, a significant correlation was obtained between tacit knowledge scores and the number of years of management experience (−.30). Other correlations were in the predicted direction but not significant. There was no significant correlation between tacit knowledge scores and verbal reasoning scores. And again, the six subscales generally correlated significantly with one another, with values ranging from .2 to .5, indicating a weak general factor for tacit knowledge.

In this study, the undergraduate participants completed the tacit knowledge tests for both academic psychologists and business managers. The correlation between scores on the two tests was .58 and highly significant. Wagner concluded that not only do the subscales of the tacit knowledge test correlate within a domain, but tacit knowledge also appear to correlate across domains.

CENTER FOR CREATIVE LEADERSHIP STUDY

Further research on what later was formalized as the Tacit Knowledge Inventory for Managers (TKIM) (Wagner & Sternberg, 1991) (see Appendix A) was conducted with a sample of 45 business executives who were participants in a Leadership Development Program at the Center for Creative Leadership (Wagner & Sternberg, 1990). The purpose of the study was to validate the test against a managerial simulation and assess its discriminant validity with a variety of psychological measures. Wagner and Sternberg (1990) administered the TKIM with nine work-related scenarios, each with 10 response options. Participants also completed, as part of the program, the Shipley Institute for Living Scale, an intelligence test; the California Psychological Inventory, a self-report personality inventory; the Fundamental Interpersonal Relations Orientation-Behavior (FIRO-B), a measure of desired ways of relating to others; the Hidden Figures Test, a measure of field independence; the Myers-Briggs Type Indicator, a measure of cognitive style; the Kirton Adaptation Innovation Inventory, a measure of preference for innovation; and the Managerial Job Satisfaction Questionnaire. The participants' behavior was also assessed on two managerial simulations.

Beginning with zero-order correlations, the best predictors of managerial performance on the simulation were tacit knowledge ($r = -.61$, $p < .001$) and IQ ($r = .38$, $p < .001$). (The negative correlation for tacit knowledge reflects the deviation scoring system used, in which better performance corresponds to less deviation from the expert prototype and thus to lower scores.) The correlation between tacit knowledge and IQ was not significant ($r = -.14$, $p > .05$).

Hierarchical regression analyses were performed to examine the unique predictive value of tacit knowledge when used in conjunction with the various other intelligence and personality tests. For each hierarchical regression analysis, the unique prediction of the TKIM was represented by the change in R^2 from a restricted model to a full model. In each case, the restricted model contained a subset of all the measures, and the full model was created by adding the TKIM to the equation. A significant change in R^2 indicated that the predictive relation between tacit knowledge and the simulation performance was not accounted for by the set of predictors in the restricted model. The results are presented in Table 3.

In Table 3, the measures listed in the first column are the predictors that already had been entered in the regression prior to entering the tacit knowledge score. For example, in the first row the sole predictor used in the restricted model was IQ. The values reported in the second column show the increases in variance accounted for in perfor-

TABLE 3. Hierarchical Regression Results from the Center for Creative Leadership Study

Measures in Restricted Model	R^2 Change When Tacit Knowledge Is Added	R^2 for Full Model
1. IQ	.32***	.46***
2. 17 CPI subtests, IQ	.22**	.66*
3. 6 FIRO-B subtests, IQ	.32***	.65***
4. Field independence, IQ	.28***	.47***
5. Kirton innovation, IQ	.33***	.50***
6. 4 Myers-Briggs subtests, IQ	.35***	.56***
7. 5 Job satisfaction subtests, IQ	.32***	.57***

* $p < .05$; ** $p < .01$; *** $p < .001$.

mance when tacit knowledge was added to the prediction equation. For example, tacit knowledge accounts for an additional 32% of criterion variance that is not accounted for by IQ. The values reported in the third column indicate the total proportion of variance in performance that is accounted for by tacit knowledge and the other measures combined.

In every case, tacit knowledge accounted for a significant increase in variance. In addition, when tacit knowledge, IQ, and selected subtests from the personality inventories were combined as predictors, nearly all of the reliable variance in the criterion was accounted for. These results support the strategy of enhancing validity and utility by supplementing existing selection procedures with additional ones. They also suggest that the construct of tacit knowledge cannot readily be subsumed by the existing constructs of cognitive ability and personality represented by the other measures used in the study.

SALESPEOPLE

Two studies were conducted by Wagner, Rashotte and Sternberg (1994) with salespeople (see also Wagner, Sujan, Sujan, Rashotte, & Sternberg, 1999). The objective of the first study was to develop and validate a rule-of-thumb approach to measuring tacit knowledge. Previous studies relied on empirical scoring, using either the correlation between items and an index of group membership or the deviation from an expert profile. Wagner et al. (1994, 1999) sought to identify a more objective, expert-based scoring method based on the rules of thumb that salespeople use to optimize their performance.

Based on interviews, literature on sales, and personal experience, these investigators generated a list of rules of thumb for salespeople. The rules of thumb were divided into several categories, such as setting sales goals, handling the customer who delays, attracting new accounts, and handling the competition. In the category of attracting new accounts, examples of rules of thumb included being selective with regard to whom promotion efforts are directed and asking customers to provide leads to new accounts.

The sample consisted of two groups, a group of salespeople with an average of 14 years sales experience and a group of 50 undergraduates at Florida State University. The participants were given eight sales scenarios, with 8 to 12 response options constructed by the rules-of-thumb approach. The options included accurate representations of the rules of thumb as well as weakened or distorted versions of them. Responses were evaluated on the extent to which participants preferred the actual or distorted versions of the rules of thumb. The Tacit Knowledge Inventory for Sales (TKIS); Wagner & Sternberg, 1989) is included as Appendix B. In addition to the sales test, the undergraduates completed the DAT Verbal Reasoning test.

Participants were asked to rate the appropriateness of each strategy for addressing the problem. Points were awarded on the basis of the participant's endorsement of the actual rules of thumb. Wagner et al. (1994, 1999) found that scores on the tacit knowledge test improved with experience. The average score for salespeople was 209 versus 166 for undergraduates. The total scores for undergraduates were uncorrelated with verbal reasoning test scores.

In the second study, measures of sales performance were obtained in addition to tacit knowledge test scores. Participants included 48 life insurance salespeople with an average of 11 years sales experience and 50 undergraduates at Florida State University with no sales experience. Participants in both groups completed the TKIS, and undergraduates completed the DAT Verbal Reasoning test. In addition, the investigators obtained from the salespeople data on number of years with the company, number of years in sales, number of yearly quality awards, yearly sales volumes and premiums, college background, and business education.

Tacit knowledge again increased with experience, with the scores 165 and 206 for undergraduates and salespeople, respectively. Significant correlations were obtained between tacit knowledge scores and number of years with the company (.37), number of years in sales (.31), number of yearly quality awards (.35), and business education (.41). When local and global scores were also computed, Wagner et al. found that global tacit knowledge scores also correlated significantly with yearly sales volumes and premiums (r ranging from .26 to .37). The tacit knowledge scores again did not correlate significantly with verbal reasoning scores.

AIR FORCE RECRUITS

In a study carried out at the Human Resources Laboratory at Brooks Air Force Base under the supervision of Malcolm Ree, Eddy (1988) examined relations between the TKIM and the Armed Services Vocational Aptitude Battery (ASVAB) for a sample of 631 Air Force Recruits, 29% of whom were women and 19% of whom were members of a minority group. The ASVAB is a multiple-aptitude battery used for selection of candidates for all branches of the U.S. Armed Forces. Prior studies of the ASVAB suggest that it is a typical measure of cognitive ability, with correlations between ASVAB scores and other cognitive ability measures of about .7. Factor analytic studies of the ASVAB also suggest that it appears to measure the same verbal, quantitative, and mechanical abilities as the DATs and the same verbal and mathematical knowledge as the California Achievement Tests.

Eddy's (1988) study showed small correlations between tacit knowledge and ASVAB subtests. The median correlation was −.07, with a range of .06 to −.15. Of the 10 correlations, only two were significantly different from zero, despite the large sample size of 631 recruits. A factor analysis of all the test data, followed by oblique rotations, yielded the usual four ASVAB factors (vocational-technical information, clerical/speed, verbal ability, and mathematics) and a distinct tacit knowledge factor. The factor loading for the TKIM score on the tacit knowledge factor was .99, with a maximum loading for scores on the four ASVAB factors of only .06. On oblique rotation, the four ASVAB factors were moderately intercorrelated, but the correlations between the tacit knowledge factor and the four ASVAB factors were near zero (.08, .00, .10, .08).

An additional point about these results concerns the possibility that measures of tacit knowledge might identify potential managers from nontraditional and minority backgrounds whose practical knowledge suggests that they would be effective managers, even though their performance on traditional selection measures such as intelligence tests does not. Eddy (1988) did not report scores separately by race and sex but did report correlations between scores and dummy variables indicating race and sex. Significant correlations in the .2 to .4 range between ASVAB subtest scores and both race and sex indicate that on the ASVAB, minority group members scored more poorly than majority group members and women scored more poorly than men. Nonsignificant correlations between tacit knowledge and both race (.03) and sex (.02), however, indicate comparable levels of performance on the tacit knowledge measures between minority and majority group members and between women and men.

MANAGERS ACROSS ORGANIZATIONAL LEVELS

In a study focusing on the development of tacit knowledge over the managerial career, Williams and Sternberg (in press) constructed a measure of both a general and a level-specific tacit knowledge. They obtained nominations from superiors for managers they deemed to be outstanding and underperforming at the lower, middle, and upper levels in four high-technology manufacturing companies. This approach allowed them to delineate the specific content of tacit knowledge for each level of management (lower, middle, and upper) by examining what experts at each level knew that their poorly performing colleagues did not.

Williams and Sternberg identified specialized tacit knowledge for each of the three management levels and found that this knowledge was differentially related to success. These results were obtained by comparing responses of outstanding and underperforming managers within each management level on level-specific tacit knowledge inventories. Within the domain of intrapersonal tacit knowledge, knowledge about how to seek out, create, and enjoy challenges is substantially more important to upper-level executives than to middle- or lower-level executives. Knowledge about maintaining appropriate levels of control becomes progressively more significant at higher levels of management. Knowledge about self-motivation, self-direction, self-awareness, and personal organization is roughly comparable in importance at the lower and middle levels and somewhat more important at the upper level. Finally, knowledge about completing tasks and working effectively within the business environment is substantially more important for upper-level managers than for middle-level managers and substantially more important for middle-level managers than for lower-level managers. Within the domain of interpersonal tacit knowledge, knowledge about influencing and controlling others is essential for all managers but especially for those at the upper level. Knowledge about supporting, cooperating with, and understanding others is extremely important for upper level executives, very important for middle level executives, and somewhat important for lower-level executives.

In addition, Williams and Sternberg examined the relationship of tacit knowledge to several criteria across levels. They found that tacit knowledge was related to the following measures of managerial success: compensation ($r = .39, p < .001$), age-controlled compensation ($r = .38, p < .001$), and level of position ($r = .36, p < .001$). These correlations were computed after controlling for background and educational experience. Tacit knowledge was also moderately associated with enhanced job satisfaction ($r = .23, p < .05$).

These investigators further found that age, years of management experience, and years in current position were unrelated to tacit knowledge. The lack of a correlation of tacit knowledge with years of management experience suggests that it is not experience alone that matters, but perhaps rather what a manager learns from experience. A manager's number of years with current company was negatively related to tacit knowledge ($r = -.29, p < .01$), which perhaps indicates that ineffective managers stayed around longer than effective managers. The number of companies that a manager had worked for was positively correlated with tacit knowledge scores ($r = .35, p < .001$). Number of years of higher education was highly related to tacit knowledge ($r = .37, p < .001$), as was self-reported school performance ($r = .26, p < .01$). Similarly, college quality was related to tacit knowledge ($r = .34, p < .01$). These results, in conjunction with the independence of tacit knowledge and IQ, suggest that tacit knowledge overlaps with the portion of these measures that are not predicted by IQ.

Williams and Sternberg also performed hierarchical regression analyses to examine whether tacit knowledge contained independent information related to success that was distinct from that provided by background and experience. The pattern of results was similar across analyses. In the regression analysis predicting maximum compensation, the first variable entered in the regression equation was years of education, accounting for 19% of the variance ($p < .001$). The second variable entered was years of management experience, accounting for an additional 13% of the variance ($p < .001$). The third and final variable entered was tacit knowledge, accounting for an additional 4% of the variance ($p = .04$) and raising the total explained variance to 36%. In the regression predicting maximum compensation controlling for age, the number of years of education was entered into the equation first, accounting for 27% of the variance ($p < .001$), and tacit knowledge was entered second, explaining an additional 5% of the variance ($p = .03$). This final regression demonstrates the value of tacit knowledge to managers who are relatively successful for their age.

COLLEGE STUDENTS

Williams and Sternberg (cited in Sternberg et al., 1993) studied the tacit knowledge of college students. They asked 50 Yale undergraduates the question, "What does it take to succeed at Yale that you don't learn from textbooks?" and used the responses to develop a tacit knowledge inventory for college students. The inventory consisted of 14 situations and asked respondents to rate the quality of several options on a 1 to 9 scale. For example, one question described a student enrolled in a large introductory lecture course. The class requirements included three examinations and a final. Participants were asked to rate how characteristic of their behavior it was to spend time doing various activities, such as attending class regularly, attending optional weekly review sessions with a teaching fellow, reading assigned text chapters thoroughly, taking comprehensive class notes, and speaking with the professor after class and during office hours.

The criteria were two indices, an academic index and an adjustment index. The academic index was a composite of high school GPA, college GPA, SAT scores, and College Board achievement test scores. The adjustment index was a composite of a measure of happiness in college, a measure of self-perceived success in college, a measure of self-perceived success in using tacit knowledge, a measure of the extent of benefit each participant had experienced from acquiring tacit knowledge, and a measure of the rated closeness of the college to the participant's ideal college.

The academic and adjustment indices were not significantly correlated (−.09). Individual items of tacit knowledge correlated differently with the academic index and the adjustment index. The academic index was correlated with the perceived importance of maintaining a high GPA (.42); doing extra reading and school work not specifically assigned (.27); not attending optional weekly review sessions (.23); not skimming required reading the morning before class (.37); not preparing a brief outline of points to raise in class discussion (.31); not helping friends with their assignments (.34); not behaving consistently from situation to situation (.25); finding it uncharacteristic to accept pressure and stress as parts of life (.30); finding it uncharacteristic to stand up for oneself (.34); and finding it uncharacteristic to play a sport or exercise regularly (.45).

Items that correlated significantly with the adjustment index included beliefs that professors value a clear, direct writing style, good organization of thoughts and ideas, and creative or unusual ideas (.38); beliefs that professors value papers that bring in outside interests or material (.27); beliefs that it is sometimes important to take on too many responsibilities at once (.31); seeking advice from several faculty members in addition to one's own professors (.31); taking classes that permit occasional absences (.36); being positive and looking on the bright side of life (.42); not being intimidated (.33); being flexible (.27); maintaining a strong sense of confidence and independence (.37); not worrying unnecessarily or destructively (.31); knowing how to make oneself happy (.32); and not letting small disappointments affect one's long-term goals (.29).

Williams and Sternberg also obtained predictions of academic and adjustment indices with subsets of items from the tacit knowledge inventory. Four items (not preparing an outline of points to raise in class discussion; maintaining a high GPA; not helping friends with assignments; and not playing a varsity or intramural sport) were predictive of the academic index, with an overall R^2 of .43. Six items (believing professors value a clear, direct writing style; maintaining a strong sense of confidence and independence; standing up for oneself; sometimes taking on too many responsibilities at once; seeking advice from faculty in addition to the course instructor; and taking classes that permit occasional absences) were predictive of the adjustment index, with an overall R^2 of .63. This study showed that tacit knowledge is important not only in occupational settings but in school settings as well.

CONCLUSIONS FROM THE TACIT KNOWLEDGE RESEARCH PROGRAM

Our discussion of the findings from the tacit knowledge research will be organized around four main issues: the relationship of tacit knowledge to experience; the relationship of tacit knowledge to general intelligence; tacit knowledge as a general construct; and the relationship of tacit knowledge to performance.

Tacit Knowledge and Experience

In most of the studies that we have just reviewed, tacit knowledge was found to relate to experience, indicated either by group membership (expert versus novice) or by the number of years in one's current position.

In several studies, Sternberg and his colleagues showed that individuals with less experience in a given domain exhibit lower tacit knowledge scores (Wagner, 1987; Wagner & Sternberg, 1985; Sternberg et al., 1993). In Wagner and Sternberg (1985), for example, group differences were obtained among business managers, business graduate students, and undergraduates on 39 of the response-item ratings on a tacit knowledge test for managers; a binomial test of the probability of finding this many significant differences by chance yielded $p < .001$. Comparable results were obtained with Yale undergraduates, psychology graduate students, and psychology faculty on a tacit knowledge test for academic psychologists. In addition, Wagner (1987) found that business managers obtained the highest tacit knowledge scores, followed by business graduate students and then by undergraduates, with comparable results obtained in a study with psychology professors, psychology graduate students, and undergraduates. Wagner et al. (1994) also found that scores on a tacit knowledge test for salespeople correlated significantly with number of years of sales experience.

Williams and Sternberg (in press), however, did not find significant correlations between tacit knowledge scores and several experience-based measures, including age, years of management experience, and years in current position but they did find that the importance of specific pieces of tacit knowledge varied across organizational level. Their findings suggest that it may not be simply the amount of experience but what a manager learns from experience that matters to success.

Tacit Knowledge and General Intelligence

In proposing a new approach to measuring intelligence, it is important to show that one has not accidentally reinvented the concept of g, or so-called general ability, as measured by traditional intelligence tests. We do not dispute the relevance of general cognitive ability to performance. Schmidt and Hunter (1998) have shown that g predicts performance in a number of domains. Our aim is to show that tacit knowledge tests measure something in addition to g. In all the above studies in which participants were given a traditional measure of cognitive ability, tacit knowledge test scores correlated insignificantly with g.

The most consistently used measure of g in the above studies was the Verbal Reasoning subtest of the DAT. The absolute values of the correlations between tacit knowledge and verbal reasoning ranged from .04 and .16 with undergraduate samples (Wagner, 1987; Wagner &

Sternberg, 1985) and .14 with a sample of business executives (Wagner & Sternberg, 1990).

One potential limitation of these findings is that they were obtained with restricted samples (e.g., Yale undergraduates, business managers). However, similar support for the relationship between tacit knowledge and g was found in a more general sample of Air Force recruits studied by Eddy (1988). The correlations between scores on the TKIM and ASVAB scales were modest, and none of the four ASVAB factors correlated significantly with the tacit knowledge factor.

Tacit knowledge tests may also be a better predictor than measures of personality, cognitive style, and interpersonal orientation, as suggested by the findings from the Center for Creative Leadership study (Wagner & Sternberg, 1990). Sternberg and Grigorenko (1999) recently developed a test of common sense for the workplace (e.g., how to handle oneself in a job interview) that predicts self-ratings of common sense but not self-ratings of various kinds of academic abilities. The test also predicts supervisory ratings at a correlational level of about .4.

Finally, there is evidence that tacit knowledge may even correlate negatively with measures of academic intelligence and achievement in some environments. In a study in a rural village in Kenya, Sternberg et al. (in press) developed a test to measure children's tacit knowledge of herbal medicines used to treat various illnesses. Parasitic infections are endemic among this population, and knowledge of these medicines and how to use them is important to adaptation to the environment. This knowledge, however, is not acquired in the classroom but rather from family members and healers in the community.

The tacit knowledge test for herbal medicines consisted of brief stories describing the specific manifestations of a given illness and provided the child with options regarding how to treat the illness (Sternberg et al., in press). The tacit knowledge test, along with the Raven Colored Progressive Matrices test (Raven, 1958), the English Mill Hill Vocabulary Scale (Raven, Court, & Raven, 1992), Dholuo (home language) Vocabulary Scale, and school-based measures of English and mathematics achievement, were administered to 85 children ages 12 to 15. The tests of academic intelligence were all significantly and positively correlated with each other. Scores on the tacit knowledge test correlated in a negative direction with all of the academic intelligence tests and showed a significant negative correlation with scores on the vocabulary tests. Tacit knowledge scores also exhibited a significant negative correlation with English achievement.

Sternberg et al. concluded that practical intelligence, as manifested in tacit knowledge relevant to adaptation in daily life, may be distinct from the kind of academic intelligence associated with school success. The negative correlation between tacit knowledge scores and some of the academic intelligence measures supports the claim that expertise developed in one environment (e.g., school) may have limited application in other environments (e.g., home or community life). Thus, there is a growing body of evidence, obtained in work, school, and community settings, that suggests that tacit knowledge measures a construct distinct from general academic intelligence.

Tacit Knowledge as a General Construct

Although the kinds of informal procedural knowledge measured by tacit knowledge tests do not correlate with traditional psychometric intelligence, tacit knowledge test scores do correlate across domains. Furthermore, the structure of tacit knowledge appears to be represented best by a single general factor.

Wagner (1987) examined the structure of the tacit knowledge inventory for managers. He performed two kinds of factor analyses on the tacit knowledge scores of the business managers in his study. First, a principal components analysis yielded a first principal component that accounted for 44% of the total variance and for 76% of total variance after the correlations among scores were disattenuated for unreliability. The 44% variance accounted for by the first principal component is typical of analyses carried out on traditional cognitive ability subtests. Second, a confirmatory factor analysis suggested that a model consisting of a single general factor provided the best fit to the data. The results of both factor analyses suggested a general factor of tacit knowledge.

Similar analyses were performed on a measure of tacit knowledge for academic psychologists. As with the study of managers, the factor analytic results suggested a single factor of tacit knowledge within the domain of academic psychology. Wagner (1987) also examined the generalizability of tacit knowledge across domains by administering both tacit knowledge measures (for business managers and academic psychologists) to undergraduates in his study. He obtained a significant correlation of .58 between the two scores, suggesting that in addition to the existence of a general factor of tacit knowledge within a domain, individual differences in tacit knowledge are generalizable across domains. These findings lend support for a common factor underlying tacit knowledge, a factor that is considered to be an aspect of practical intelligence.

Tacit Knowledge and Performance

Finally, we have shown that tacit knowledge measures are predictive of performance in a number of domains, correlating in the range of .2 to .5 with measures such as rated prestige of business or institution, salary, simulation performance, and number of publications. These correlations, uncorrected for attenuation or restriction of range, compare favorably with those obtained for IQ within the range of abilities we have tested.

In studies with business managers, tacit knowledge scores correlated in the range of .2 to .4 with criteria such as salary, years of management experience, and whether or not the manager worked for a company at the top of the Fortune 500 list (Wagner, 1987; Wagner & Sternberg, 1985). Wagner and Sternberg (1990) obtained a correlation of .61 between tacit knowledge and performance on a managerial simulation and found that tacit knowledge scores explained additional variance beyond IQ and other personality and ability measures. In a study with bank branch managers, Wagner and Sternberg (1985) obtained significant correlations between tacit knowledge scores and average percentage of merit-based salary increase ($r = .48$, $p < .05$) and average performance rating for the category of generating new business for the bank ($r = .56$, $p < .05$).

Williams and Sternberg (in press) also found that tacit knowledge was related to several indicators of managerial success, including compensation, age-controlled compensation, level of position, and job satisfaction, with correlations ranging from .23 to .39.

Although much of the tacit knowledge research has involved business managers, there is evidence that tacit knowledge explains performance in other domains. In the field of academic psychology, correlations in the .4 to .5 range were found between tacit knowledge scores and criterion measures such as citation rate, number of publications, and quality of department (Wagner, 1987; Wagner & Sternberg, 1985). In studies with salespeople, Wagner et al. (1994) found correlations in the .3 to .4 range between tacit knowledge and criteria such as sales volume and sales awards received. Finally, tacit knowledge for college students was found to correlate with indices of academic performance and adjustment to college (Williams & Sternberg, cited in Sternberg et al., 1993).

In summary, the program of tacit knowledge research reviewed above shows that tacit knowledge generally increases with experience but is not simply a proxy for experience; that tacit knowledge tests measure a distinct construct from that measured by traditional abstract intelligence tests; that scores on tacit knowledge tests represent a general factor, which appears to correlate across domains; and finally, that tacit knowledge tests are predictive of performance in a number of domains and compare favorably with those obtained for IQ within the range of abilities we have tested. In chapter 9 we present in full a study to identify, measure, and validate tacit knowledge tests in a new domain, military leadership.

Practical Intelligence

An Example from the Military Workplace

In both military and civilian settings, leaders are faced with increasingly complex and dynamic environments. Advances in technology, increases in the volume of information, shorter time periods for decision making, and a reliance on fewer people are just some of the factors that contribute to this complexity. So, what does it take to be an effective leader in such environments? Consider the following story told by a leader of a U.S. Army battalion:

> I noticed that my subordinate commanders were trying so hard to be successful that they would accept missions that their units did not have the capabilities to execute. The commanders would expend a great deal of their units' effort and time to accomplish the mission without asking for help in order to demonstrate their talents as leaders. One of my commanders worked his unit overtime for two weeks to accomplish a mission. I realized that the same mission could have been accomplished in two days if the commander had requested additional resources. After that incident, I make it a point to ask all my subordinate commanders to realistically assess their units' resources before taking on a mission.

The leader in the above example learned that subordinates may go to great lengths to impress their superiors and that these efforts may impede efficiency. He learned also that it is important to ask subordinates to evaluate their resources before initiating tasks in order to minimize inefficiency. This story demonstrates our approach to understanding what distinguishes more effective from less effective leaders. We explore the knowledge that effective leaders acquire from their personal experiences about what to do to accomplish their objectives (e.g., efficient unit performance).

This chapter reviews a 6-year project to identify and measure tacit knowledge within the domain of military leadership and to apply the results to leadership development. In the previous chapter we reviewed tacit knowledge research in civilian settings, much of which was conducted with managers. The present chapter addresses leadership and, in particular, leadership in the military domain. First, we review general approaches to studying leadership. Next, we discuss the difference between leadership and management and relate the distinction to the adaptation and shaping functions of practical intelligence. Then we outline the role of tacit knowledge in understanding military leadership in particular. Finally, we present the results of our efforts to elicit tacit knowledge and to develop and validate a tacit knowledge inventory for military leaders.

APPROACHES TO UNDERSTANDING LEADERSHIP

Researchers and practitioners within civilian and military organizations have long sought an answer to the question of what it takes to be an effective leader. Numerous approaches to answering this question have been pursued over the years. Most definitions of leadership share the idea that leadership involves interpersonal influence (Bass, 1990; Yukl, 1998). Beyond this abstract notion, however, there is little agreement as to whether leadership is best understood in terms of characteristics of the leader, the processes (behaviors) used to exert interpersonal influence, the actions of followers, or some more complex function of the situation. We briefly summarize here the various approaches to studying leadership.

Trait-based Approaches

Prior to the 1940s, the emphasis in leadership research was on identifying the characteristics, or traits, of effective leaders (Bass, 1990). A review of the literature by Stogdill (1948) suggested that however many studies supported the importance of a certain trait, there were equally many studies that did not support the trait. In response to this review, many researchers decided to pursue other approaches to understanding leadership. Some investigators nevertheless continued to explore the characteristics that identify effective leaders. Over the years, trait researchers have studied motivational factors (e.g., need for achievement and need for affiliation), personality characteristics (e.g., emotional maturity and locus of control), interpersonal skills (e.g., communication and empathy), and conceptual skills (e.g., analytical ability and creativity) (Bass, 1990; Yukl, 1998).

Behavioral Approaches

During the 1950s and 1960s, the emphasis in leadership research shifted from understanding what leaders are to understanding what leaders do. Early behavioral research led to the identification of two contrasting styles of leadership, consideration and initiating structure (Fleishman, 1953; Fleishman & Harris, 1962). Consideration characterizes the degree to which leaders are supportive and exhibit concern for the welfare of their subordinates. Initiating structure characterizes the degree to which leaders define roles and structure the activities of their subordinates. These two broad classes of behaviors also have been identified as task-oriented and relations-oriented (Likert, 1967). Like trait research, behavioral research was criticized for its inconsistent findings. It was further criticized for methodological problems. For example, the same individuals (e.g., subordinates) often were reporting on leader behaviors and leadership effectiveness. Out of the limitations of behavioral research emerged a set of new theories that attempted to take into account the complex relationships between leaders and their environments. Before discussing what are collectively referred to as contingency approaches to leadership, we note that behavioral approaches have not been completely abandoned. Some researchers argue that identifying the behaviors that are common to most leadership situations adds value to understanding a complex phenomenon (Yukl, 1998).

Contingency Approaches

Contingency, or situational approaches, which dominated the field from the late 1960s to the early 1980s, seek to explain leadership outcomes in terms of the interaction between various characteristics or behaviors of leaders and a wide range of situational variables (Fiedler, 1967; Hersey & Blanchard, 1977; House, 1971; Kerr & Jermier, 1978; Yukl, 1971). Yukl's (1971) multiple-linkage model, for example, describes how situational factors such as subordinates' skill levels, the quantity and quality of resources at a leader's disposal, and group cohesiveness determine whether leadership based on initiation or consideration will be more effective.

A more recent situational model is cognitive resources theory (Fiedler, 1986; Fiedler & Garcia, 1987). The theory proposes that certain conditions (e.g., stress) alter the relationship between cognitive resources, such as intelligence and experience, and outcomes such as group performance. In testing this model, Fiedler (1995) found that intelligence is positively correlated with leadership success under conditions of low stress but that it is negatively correlated with success under conditions of high stress. Furthermore, the relationship between experience and leadership performance is greater under conditions of high stress than under conditions of low stress.

Although contingency-based research is intended to account for all the relevant variables that characterize a situation, most of the theories have been only partially tested (Yukl, 1998). There are limits on the number of variables that can be included in a study, and many of the variables have been difficult to measure. Because of the complexity of these models, it is not surprising that many of the findings regarding individual theories have been inconsistent across studies. Nevertheless, contingency theories continue to be popular with leadership researchers, but new approaches to studying leadership have emerged in the past two decades.

Transformational Approaches

A more recent approach to studying leadership is transformational leadership theory, which addresses the relationship between leaders and followers. In this theory, the role of the leader is to inspire and stimulate followers to think and perform rather than to influence their behaviors through power and rewards (Bass, 1985; Yukl, 1989). Research testing this theory suggests that leaders who exhibit charisma, inspiration, intellectual stimulation, and individualized consideration elicit more positive outcomes in terms of subordinate performance (Bass & Avolio, 1993).

The transformational approach offers one alternative approach to addressing the question of what constitutes effective leadership. However, many approaches currently are being pursued in the field of leadership, some of which focus on leadership styles, leadership skills, team leaders, and organizational culture (Bryman, 1996). It is yet to be determined whether these approaches will be more successful than previous ones in understanding leadership. We note below some of the issues that have yet to be adequately addressed in leadership research.

Limitations of Existing Approaches

Existing approaches to studying leadership have underemphasized both what leaders know about how to lead and how they gain that knowledge. Reviews of the literature confirm this observation (Bass, 1990; Hollander, 1985; Yukl & Van Fleet, 1992). The importance of knowledge acquisition to leadership, however, has been recognized by others (Argyris, 1991; U.S. Department of the Army, 1990). Argyris suggested that self-learning, or the ability to evaluate one's cognitive processes and improve on those processes, is important to successful leadership. In military organizations, experience-based learning is considered one of the three pillars of leadership development, along with institutional training and self-development (U.S. Department of the Army, 1990). The ideas of self-learning and learning from experience are consistent with our proposition that effective acquisition of tacit knowledge is important for leadership performance. They also serve to highlight an aspect of leadership that is largely neglected by existing approaches, that is, the knowledge about how to be an effective leader. For example, in taking a contingency perspective, how do leaders know whether a directive or participative leadership style is more appropriate in a given situation with a given subordinate?

Another limitation of the literature is its overemphasis on exclusively quantitative approaches (Bass, 1990; Bryman, 1996). These approaches often fail to capture the full complexity of leadership. Some researchers (e.g., Yukl, 1998) suggest a need for both qualitative and quantitative approaches to studying leadership. Our approach to studying tacit knowledge combines qualitative and quantitative methods of studying leadership. We attempt to identify context-specific knowledge about leadership, that is, knowledge about what to do in particular situations, and we attempt to quantify the possession of this knowledge so that we can assess its relationship to effective leadership.

LEADERSHIP VERSUS MANAGEMENT

The relationship between leadership and management has been debated for decades by academics and practitioners. Two alternative positions have emerged concerning this relationship: either the concepts are distinct or they are interrelated. According to the first position, management and leadership are qualitatively different concepts. Often the distinction is made between managers and leaders rather than management and leadership. For example, Zaleznik (1977) proposed that managers and leaders are different types of people in terms of their motivation, personal history, thoughts, and behaviors. Managers are problem solvers who create goals in order to maintain the stability of the organization. Leaders are visionaries who inspire workers to take part in their own and the organization's development and change. Bennis and Nanus (1985) also proposed that leaders and managers differ qualitatively in their perspectives and willingness to implement change. Managers have a narrow perspective, which is concerned with mastering routines to ensure the efficiency of daily operations. Leaders, in contrast, have a broad perspective, which allows them to assess the organization's needs, envision the future, and implement change. Kotter (1987) made a distinction between leadership and management in terms of the processes involved rather than the personalities of individuals. Management tends to be a formal, scientific, and present-oriented process whereas leadership tends to be an informal, flexible, inspirational, and future-oriented process.

There are others, however, who view leadership and management as overlapping processes that fulfill the functions or expectations of an organizational role. Mintzberg (1975), for example, suggested that one of the functions of the manager's role is to be a leader. According to this perspective, the term *manager* is a role label, whereas *leader* is a role function. Leadership is a process associated with the function of a leader. Both Yukl (1989) and Lau and Shani (1992) suggested that the functions associated with supervisory positions in organizations require the incumbent to be both a leader and a manager. Supervisors must practice both leadership and management in order to fill role requirements. Bass (1990) similarly suggested that leaders must manage and managers must lead. These researchers take the position that the terms *leader* and *manager* are interchangeable.

Military doctrine on leadership seems to take the position that management and leadership are overlapping concepts. The U.S. Army uses the term *leader* to refer to all officers in supervisory positions. Thus, the term leader provides a role label in the military context in the same way that the term *manager* provides a role label in civilian organizations. It is clear from the definition of leadership in the Army that part of the role of a leader involves performing managerial functions. Leadership is viewed as a process of exerting influence on others in order to satisfy organizational objectives. Management, on the other hand, refers to a set of expected activities or behaviors "performed by those in senior positions to acquire, direct, integrate, and allocate resources to accomplish goals and tasks" (U.S. Department of the Army, 1987a).

We agree with the position that leadership and management are functions that may be part of the same role, whether the individual's title is manager or leader; however, drawing on our definition of practical intelligence, we view these functions as serving different purposes in relation to the environment. That is, management deals with functions associated with adapting to the environment, whereas leadership involves shaping the environment. We readily see this difference in the definitions above. The management function addresses daily activities associated with efficiency and effectiveness. Leadership functions to change, or shape, the environment. Clearly, these two functions are interrelated – both are important to success. In our research, we view leadership as involving overlapping functions with management, but we consider leadership to be more than management – it involves shaping as well as adapting to the environment in order to achieve desired goals.

TACIT KNOWLEDGE IN MILITARY LEADERSHIP

The U.S. Army's definition of leadership varies slightly across organizational levels (U.S. Department of the Army 1987a, 1987b, 1990). For example, leadership at junior levels (through battalion command) is defined as "the process of influencing others to accomplish the mission by providing purpose, direction, and motivation" (U.S. Department of the Army, 1990). At the next level (brigade through corps), leadership is viewed as an influence process in which direct and indirect means are used to create conditions for the sustained success of an organization. At the highest levels, leadership is defined as obtaining the commitment of subordinates to the organization's purposes and goals, beyond that which is possible by using position power alone.

Given that the U.S. Army has devoted so much attention to defining leadership, it is not surprising that it has a comprehensive system to develop its leaders. Leadership development is based on three complementary processes: institutional training (i.e., formal schooling), self-development, and operational assignments (i.e., on-the-job learning). Implicit in this doctrine is the belief that Army leaders learn from their experience and that the lessons of job experience make a significant and independent contribution to leader development beyond that of formal training. On-the-job experiences provide opportunities for officers to learn how to apply leadership knowledge codified in doctrine and taught in the Army school system. They also provide a context for acquiring new knowledge about leadership – knowledge that may not be well supported by doctrine or formal training.

Although Army doctrine acknowledges the importance of job experience and leaders spend most of their careers in operational assignments, relatively little is known about the role of operational assignments in leadership development. That is, we have a limited understanding of the process by which Army leaders develop their leadership skills while on the job. The objective of our research was to understand the experience-based, practically relevant knowledge – in other words, tacit knowledge – that is related to successful leadership. We organize our discussion around three main questions that guided our research. First, can we identify knowledge that meets our criteria as tacit within the domain of military leadership? Second, can we develop instruments to measure the tacit knowledge of military leaders? Third, is the possession of tacit knowledge for leadership related to effective leadership performance? The methods we described in chapters 6 and 7 for identifying, measuring, and validating tacit knowledge were used to address these questions.

Identifying the Tacit Knowledge of Military Leaders

As we described in the method for eliciting tacit knowledge, we began by reviewing domain-relevant literature to identify examples of published tacit knowledge relevant to military leadership (Horvath, Williams, et al., 1994). This literature consisted of formal doctrine, trade journals, educational publications, and military memoirs. Army doctrine (e.g., field manuals) provides an overview of what leaders are expected to know. Trade journals and memoirs, which reflect the lessons learned from the experiences of military practitioners, are more likely to include knowledge that is practically relevant, procedural, and acquired under conditions of low environmental support. From this literature review we identified some initial examples of tacit knowledge and developed a preliminary framework for classifying tacit knowledge items.

The preliminary structure of tacit knowledge for military leadership, along with examples from the literature, is shown in Table 4. According to this structure, tacit knowledge exemplars may be distinguished in terms of their relevance to dealing with the self, dealing with others, or dealing with the organization. These categories correspond to knowledge that functions at the intrapersonal, interpersonal, and organizational levels, respectively. Within these functions we identify more descriptive subcategories of knowledge. Tacit knowledge about managing the self (e.g., how to manage one's time) and seeking challenges and control (e.g., how to take initiative) is categorized as intrapersonal knowledge. Tacit knowledge about influencing and controlling others (e.g., motivating subordinates), supporting and cooperating with others (e.g., taking care of soldiers), and learning from others (e.g., keeping an open mind) falls under interpersonal knowledge. And the organizational category includes knowledge about solving organizational problems (e.g., understanding the organization's culture).

TABLE 4. A Preliminary Framework of Tacit Knowledge Based on a Review of Practitioner Literature

INTRAPERSONAL TACIT KNOWLEDGE

Managing the Self

Focus on what is important rather than urgent. A leader who loses sight of his priorities may spend all his time putting out "fires" and neglect progress toward his most important goals. Effective leaders make decisions about what is important and what is not, and they allocate their time accordingly. Sometimes this means that deadlines for low-priority tasks are missed or that extra responsibility is delegated to subordinates.

Seeking Challenges and Control

Be prepared to disobey an order in extraordinary circumstances. When the need to disobey an order is both clear and critical, a leader should be prepared to do so. The decision to disobey should increase rather than decrease personal and professional risk to oneself, and a principle of *minimal divergence* should be followed. According to this principle, one seeks to diverge as little as possible from the commander's intent – even when an order must be disobeyed.

INTERPERSONAL TACIT KNOWLEDGE

Influencing and Controlling Others

Fight rumor-mongering with information. If you keep soldiers in the dark, the orders you issue will seem obscure and arbitrary. Keeping soldiers in the dark encourages rumor mongering about the mission, and this rumor mongering can harm morale and decrease readiness. Don't take a vote on what your unit will do, but explain the situation to your soldiers, explain what you expect them to do, and tell them why it is important. Be prepared to respond to questions and even objections, but make it clear that the mission is nonnegotiable.

Supporting and Cooperating with Others

When you refer a soldier to another source for help, make the call yourself. When you counsel a soldier and decide, for whatever reason, that the soldier should see someone else for further help, make the appointment then and there. This small detail can make the difference between the soldier feeling "handed off" and feeling taken care of.

Learning from Others

Get opinions from your junior leaders in writing. Ask your junior leaders to submit their opinions of the company in writing when you assume command. For example, ask them for their opinion of the three greatest strengths and the three greatest weaknesses of the company, along with suggestions for remediating the weaknesses. Asking your junior leaders to submit opinions in writing gives you early information about the strengths and weaknesses in the company. Asking for opinions in writing also tells you who in your unit can think analytically and write clearly and who needs remediation in these areas.

ORGANIZATIONAL TACIT KNOWLEDGE

Solving Organizational Problems

Don't always choose the best person or team for the job. To remediate weaknesses in your unit, get in the habit of distributing tasks in a manner that meets development as well as efficiency goals. If you always pick the best persons for the job, they are the only ones who will get any experience at the job. For example, pair an able soldier with a less able soldier and assign the job to them as a team. With any luck, the able soldier will tutor the less able soldier. This experience can be a beneficial experience for both soldiers.

This structure is preliminary and does not represent any final or conclusive categorization of tacit knowledge for military leadership. It simply provides a foundation for a more thorough exploration of tacit knowledge. As we shall now discuss, we found that face-to-face interviews provided much more substantive and incontrovertible evidence of tacit knowledge than the literature search. They also allowed us to identify knowledge that is specific to different organizational levels.

INTERVIEWS WITH ARMY LEADERS. In order to obtain more direct evidence of what Army leaders know about how to lead, we conducted interviews with incumbent officers at three organizational levels. Specifically, we were interested in understanding the tacit knowledge of leaders at the platoon, company, and battalion levels. Platoon leaders have very limited experience in Army leadership (typically 1 to 3 years) and are responsible for supervising about 25 to 45 soldiers who have relatively greater time in service. They exercise direct leadership through face-to-face interactions with their subordinates and have relatively little formal position power. Company commanders have more experience than platoon leaders and have considerably more position power. They also decide how missions will be accomplished. They lead larger organizations, typically 120 to 200 soldiers, and as a result have less direct contact with their subordinates. Battalion commanders have considerable experience in the Army, having served 16 to 20 years as officers. Their selection for command is the result of a highly competitive process, and they have considerable power and discretion in discharging the legal authority of command. They command organizations of typically 500 to 700 soldiers, making it difficult to interact with subordinates face to face.

We conducted interviews with a representative sample of 81 Army officers who were selected by their senior commanders to participate in the study (Horvath, Forsythe, et al., 1994). The sample included 30 platoon leaders, 32 company commanders, and 19 battalion commanders from three categories of military specialties (combat arms, combat support, and combat service support). We followed the interview procedures described in chapter 7.

The interviews were conducted by members of the research team working in pairs, with one member as lead interviewer and the other as notetaker. At the beginning of each interview, the researcher informed the participant of the study's purpose and assured the participant that he or she was not being evaluated. All participants were asked to relate a story about a job-related experience from which they learned something about leadership at their current organizational level. The interviewer clarified that the researchers were interested in specific examples of informal knowledge obtained while leading and not necessarily knowledge obtained from reading leadership doctrine or attending formal leadership instruction. The interviewer also specified that the researchers were not interested in purely technical knowledge, such as military tactics or supply and maintenance procedures. All participants were encouraged to express, in their own words, the leadership lessons learned in the specific situations they recalled.

During each interview, the interviewer asked follow-up questions based on the set of guidelines included in an interview protocol, as described in chapter 7. The follow-up questions probed for greater detail in the leadership stories and more elaboration of the lessons the participant derived from the situation. The officers often began by articulating general rules ("A good leader needs to know people"), but when probed, they revealed more complex, specific procedural rules (e.g., rules about how to judge people accurately for different purposes and in a variety of circumstances) based on the stories that they recalled. Periodically, the interviewer also paraphrased the participants' comments to ensure interpretive accuracy. After each interview, the notetaker prepared a written summary, attempting to capture the leadership stories and lessons learned in the participant's own words. Then the lead interviewer reviewed these summaries, and together the interviewers resolved any disagreements in the summary contents, referring to an audiotape of the interview if necessary.

Once all the interview summaries were compiled, we sought to identify and extract the examples of tacit knowledge contained within those summaries. The knowledge was designated as tacit knowledge for leadership if it was based on a personal experience; was not well supported by formal training or doctrine; expressed some form of action; and pertained to intrapersonal and interpersonal aspects of leadership rather than technical aspects of job performance. We assessed the degree of interrater agreement, that is, the extent to which the raters agreed as to whether or not a story represented tacit knowledge, by asking two raters to independently rate 18 of the 81 interview summaries. We divided the number of stories on which the raters agreed by the total number of stories independently evaluated. After resolving discrepancies over knowledge that was practically useful for leadership (since only one of the raters had military experience), the interrater agreement was determined to be 90%. In other words, the raters agreed in their classification of knowledge as tacit 9 out of 10 times.

The interview summaries rarely expressed the tacit knowledge directly. As discussed earlier, tacit knowledge, as a type of procedural knowledge, is not readily articulated. Instead, the tacit knowledge often was embedded in the stories leaders related about their personal experiences. Therefore, we sought to extract the tacit knowledge content from those stories. This process consisted of coding the stories into a simplified, standard format reflecting the procedural feature of tacit knowledge. Each piece of knowledge was rewritten into a set of antecedent conditions (IF statements), a set of consequent actions (THEN statements), a brief explanation ("BECAUSE" statement), and other logical operators (AND, OR, and ELSE). A sample coded item has been shown in Table 1.

The coded tacit knowledge items are viewed as markers for the complex, predominantly implicit mental representations, which are not directly available to conscious introspection and articulation. The items are not, strictly speaking, the tacit knowledge of the domain, but rather the best available description of that knowledge as it is employed in solving actual problems. This coding process produced 174 unique items of tacit knowledge across the three organizational levels.

The coded tacit knowledge items served two main purposes in our research. First, they served as the basis for developing instruments to measure the possession of tacit knowledge. Second, they served as products in that they provided insight about the nature and structure of tacit knowledge for leaders at different organizational levels. As products, these items were analyzed to identify more abstract categories of tacit knowledge that characterized leadership. These categories were used to elaborate the framework presented in Table 4; to characterize differences in leadership across levels; and to relate our findings to the general leadership literature.

IDENTIFYING CATEGORIES OF TACIT KNOWLEDGE. Three senior military members of the research team were asked to sort the set of 174 items into categories of their own devising. The sortings were done separately for each organizational level (Horvath, Forsythe, et al., 1994). There were no constraints on the size or number of sort categories, as long as no categories overlapped. The results of the independent sortings were used to form a set of dissimilarity matrixes, one for each level. The dissimilarity matrices were cluster-analyzed by using a joining algorithm based on the computation of euclidean distances derived from the dissimilarity matrices. Cluster analysis is a family of techniques used to uncover natural groupings in the data (Hartigan, 1975). The joining algorithm produces hierarchically organized clusters of items in the form of a tree. The hierarchical tree includes successively more inclusive clusters. The military experts interpreted the tree, labeling high-level subclusters in the tree diagram based on the content of the included items. These labeled subclusters were taken to represent categories of tacit knowledge and are shown in Table 5.

The sample sizes in Table 5 are the number of tacit knowledge items at that level on which the sortings were performed. The values in the columns indicate the proportion of the total items that are included in the

TABLE 5. Categories of Tacit Knowledge with Proportion of Items Obtained by Level

	Level		
Category	Battalion (n = 67)	Company (n = 64)	Platoon (n = 42)
Dealing with Poor Performers: solving problems; deciding when to relieve officers of their duty	.06	—	—
Managing Organizational Change: using subordinates as change agents	.04	—	—
Protecting the Organization: exhibiting loyalty; encouraging trust; protecting subordinates from unreasonable external demands	.13	—	—
Balancing Mission and Troops: resolving conflicts between orders from superiors and the welfare of subordinates	—	.08	—
Cooperating with Others: networking; developing cooperation and trust among peers	—	.06	—
Directing and Supervising Subordinates: coordinating; encouraging cooperation; organizing units; managing training assignments; encouraging subordinates to take initiative; holding subordinates accountable	—	.16	—
Establishing Credibility: showing respect and listening to more experienced soldiers; improving one's own knowledge and skills	—	—	.12
Developing Subordinates: engaging them in decision making[c]; allowing them to solve their own problems[b]; providing them with opportunities to gain experience[b]; counseling them on their mistakes[b]; helping them to identify their strengths and weaknesses[b]	.18	.06	—
Influencing the Boss: confronting superiors when you disagree with their directives[c,p]; clarifying role	—	.08	.14

(continued)

TABLE 5 *(continued)*

	Level		
Category	Battalion (n = 67)	Company (n = 64)	Platoon (n = 42)
expectations[p]; taking initiative[p]; seeking autonomy[c]			
Communicating: imparting values[b]; visioning[b]; correcting misperceptions[b]; communicating expectations[b,c]; seeking information from subordinates[c,p]; targeting messages to the appropriate level[c,p]; using the chain of command[p]	.15	.13	.13
Establishing Trust: protecting soldiers[b,c]; keeping soldiers informed[c]; seeking additional information before making decisions[c]; giving subordinates responsibility[p]; being open and honest with subordinates[p]	.07	.08	.07
Managing the Self: seeking feedback[b,c,p]; managing stress[b,c,p]; seeking social support[c]; managing emotions[b]; setting goals[c]; monitoring your performance[b,p]; reflecting on mistakes[c]; relying on internal rewards for motivation[c]	.07	.09	.19
Motivating Subordinates: providing rewards/recognition[b,c]; engaging them in decision making[b]; encouraging them to take initiative[c]; using persuasion when appropriate[c]; maintaining consistency in their lives[p]; meeting their basic needs[p]; preventing boredom[p]; recognizing their limits[p]; building their confidence[p]; providing support[p]	.09	.14	.28
Taking Care of Soldiers: providing support[b]; managing their work load[b]; making their living quarters comfortable[b]; showing concern for their well-being[b,c]; dealing with personal problems[b,c,p]; managing training demands[p]	.14	.12	.05
Unaffiliated items	.07	.00	.02

[b,c,p] Describes the tacit knowledge obtained from battalion commanders (b), company commanders (c), and platoon leaders (p).

category at each organizational level. For example, the category *Protecting the Organization* comprised 9 of the 67 total items obtained from battalion commanders, yielding a proportion of .13; in other words, 13% of the items at the battalion level related to knowledge of how to protect the organization. A blank in the table means that the category did not emerge from the cluster analysis at that level. For example, the category *Protecting the Organization* emerged at the battalion but not at the company or platoon level. In all, seven categories were unique to a single level and two were common across two levels but not across all three levels. When a category appeared in two out of the three levels, it was always in adjacent levels. Five categories were shared across all three levels. Next to each category label are brief descriptions of the content of tacit knowledge items making up that category. When the category emerged at more than one level, we have indicated which level the content description reflects.

In Table 6, we integrate the categories with the framework that emerged from our review of the practice literature (Table 4). We found that the abstract categories that emerged from the literature review accommodated fairly well the more specific categories from the interview study. For each specific tacit knowledge category, we also provide an example of a coded tacit knowledge item from the interviews. As is apparent from even these condensed examples, we obtained more convincing evidence of tacit knowledge from the interviews than from the literature review.

In comparing the results of the interviews with those of the literature review, we found two categories from the literature review that did not appear in the interviews. We did not obtain tacit knowledge that fitted the category Learning from Others; this function, however, may be distributed across other categories. For example, knowledge about how and when to elicit feedback from subordinates may fit the category Learning from Other but was grouped with knowledge about communicating. Alternatively, learning from others may not have been considered a part of leadership by our participants.

The other category that did not emerge in the interview data was Seeking Challenges and Control. Knowledge about seeking challenge and control may be expressed by other categories, such as knowledge about influencing superior officers. Alternatively, the participants may have believed that their positions already offered enough challenge and control and therefore did not express knowledge related to this category, or knowledge about seeking challenge and control may represent self-oriented goals, which we excluded from the definition of leadership provided to participants.

TABLE 6.   Tacit Knowledge for Military Leadership:
An Integrated Framework

INTRAPERSONAL TACIT KNOWLEDGE

Managing the Self

Managing the self.[b,c,p] *How to manage yourself when you are upset.* IF your subordinate's action causes you to become angry to the point where you are about to lose your composure, THEN do something (take a time-out, take deep breaths, sit down) to gain your composure before you act, BECAUSE losing your composure in front of your subordinates may hurt your credibility.

Seeking Challenges and Control[x]

INTERPERSONAL TACIT KNOWLEDGE

Influencing and Controlling Others

Motivating subordinates.[b,c,p] *How to encourage your soldiers to take initiative.* IF you want to encourage your subordinates to exercise initiative, THEN provide subordinates with your intent and give them the responsibility to develop their own plan to accomplish the mission. Involve senior noncommissioned officers in major decisions. Recognize soldiers' achievements with awards, BECAUSE giving soldiers the responsibility to plan and execute a mission allows and encourages them to exercise initiative. Also, rewarding soldiers for achievements tends to increase their motivation to take the initiative and earn future awards.

Directing and supervising subordinates.[c] *How to build a team made up of both military and civilian personnel.* IF you are a commander of a unit that has both military and civilian personnel AND IF you are having problems with perceptions of unfairness in allocation of workload and awards between civilian and military personnel, THEN use a sign-out sheet to make visible each member's location during the day, BECAUSE the sign-out sheet communicates information about each member's whereabouts during the duty day, and this may prevent misunderstanding about work allocation.

Influencing the boss.[c,p] *How to confront your boss.* IF your commander has made a decision that you do not agree with AND IF you feel a need to confront your boss about it, THEN frame your input as an approach for guidance instead of a protest. When confronting the boss, do not make evaluative statements about the decision. Instead, communicate how the decision affected you (e.g., discuss your feelings) or the unit, BECAUSE if you approach the commander in a more confrontational manner, you might cause him to become defensive and "close the loop" (e.g., close off communications with the commanding officer).

Developing subordinates.[c] *How to use participative leadership in solving problems and developing subordinate leaders.* IF you find a problem in the unit AND IF the problem pertains to a subordinate leader's area of responsibility, THEN direct the subordinate leader to solve it. After you select an alternative, let the subordinate leader execute it, BECAUSE getting subordinates involved gives them ownership of responsibility for the problem. Also, subordinate participation in the decision making process tends to increase commitment to the solution and promotes development.

Communicating.[p] *How to effectively communicate with your soldiers.* IF you want to effectively communicate with your soldiers, THEN tailor your message to fit their average educational level and look them in the eye when you deliver it. Do not use a lot of profanity or soldier slang in your message BECAUSE you think that tailoring the complexity of the message to fit the general educational level of the soldiers increases the likelihood that they will understand it. By not using profanity and slang in your messages, you maintain your leader–subordinate social distance and also reduce the risk of offending your soldiers.

Supporting and Cooperating with Others

Taking care of soldiers.[b,c,p] *How to take care of soldiers by handling their problems promptly.* IF a subordinate thinks a problem is important enough to see you after hours, THEN take immediate action on the problem and do not defer it to the next business day, BECAUSE taking immediate action on your soldiers' problems demonstrates that you care about them.

Establishing trust.[b,c,p] *How to preserve you subordinate leaders' trust and confidence in you.* IF you provide a subordinate leader with a directive AND IF your commander confronts the subordinate leader about the appropriateness of the directive AND IF you are aware of this confrontation, THEN let your commander know that you issued the directive to the subordinate leader, BECAUSE if you do not take responsibility for the directive, your subordinate leader may lose confidence in you.

Cooperating with others.[c] *How to choose between conflicting training events.* IF a training event scheduled by your battalion commander conflicts with a training event scheduled by your supported unit commander AND IF both training events have equal training value and impact on soldiers' quality of life, THEN support the training event scheduled by your battalion commander, BECAUSE doing so preserves and demonstrates your loyalty to your battalion commander.

Learning from Others[x]

ORGANIZATIONAL TACIT KNOWLEDGE

Solving Organizational Problems

Communicating.[c,b] *How to get information from your soldiers.* IF you need feedback or input from your soldiers, THEN talk to them in informal settings, for

(continued)

TABLE 6 *(continued)*

example, while eating lunch in back of a track, or arrange the furniture in your office to facilitate open communication, for example, by putting chairs in a circle, BECAUSE you receive more candid feedback from a discussion with soldiers in an informal setting in which they can feel relaxed.

How to control distortion of communications and correct misperceptions. IF you want to make sure that your guidance is communicated accurately to all levels of the organization, THEN conduct periodic sensing sessions with your soldiers to correct misperceptions, clarify your intent, and locate sources of information loss, BECAUSE you can get distortion of your intentions and guidance just by passing information through a number of nodes.

Developing subordinates.[b] *How to deal with mistakes made by your subordinates.* IF a subordinate makes a mistake AND IF you are in a public setting, THEN do not embarrass the subordinate in public and do not use coercive means to correct the mistake. Use mistakes as an opportunity to coach and develop your subordinates. Have subordinates recognize their own mistakes, and coach them to think of ways to correct the mistakes. Be sure that you give them positive feedback at the end of this development session in order to restore their confidence, BECAUSE coercion destroys initiative and does not foster development in a subordinate. Discussing mistakes in a nonthreatening environment facilitates learning and development.

Dealing with poor performers.[b] *Dealing with weak subordinate commanders.* IF you have weak company commanders who have some potential for development, THEN give them strong subordinate leaders. Never criticize them in front of the brigade commander. Set them up for success and invite the brigade commander to watch them perform, BECAUSE you always want to set your commanders up for success in front of their senior rater if they are trying, but you also have to consider the welfare of your soldiers. BUT IF you have a company commander who is dishonest or immoral or mistreats soldiers, THEN relieve that commander immediately, BECAUSE an unethical commander jeopardizes the welfare and morale of your soldiers.

Managing organizational change.[b] *How to implement change in the battalion.* IF you desire to implement change in the battalion you are in charge of, THEN focus your efforts on changing or developing company commanders and lieutenants, BECAUSE the company commanders and lieutenants are the agents who will implement change in the battalion. The battalion commander commands through the battalion's company commanders.

Protecting the organization.[b] *Deciding when to jump the chain of command.* IF you are having problems with your immediate commander AND IF you decide to seek advice from your boss' commander (jump the chain of command) on how to solve the problem, THEN be prepared for the possibility of a disruption of loyalty in your unit, BECAUSE you have modeled disloyalty and the effects of this may carry over into your own unit.

ADDITIONAL TACIT KNOWLEDGE

Establishing Credibility[p]

How to establish your credibility in a new unit. IF you are taking charge of a new unit, THEN present an image of knowing what you are doing, even if you don't. Sound off – state what you do know with authority. Don't pretend to know things; instead state what you do know with conviction. Also, study to get yourself up to speed, BECAUSE a sense of confidence builds trust with superiors and subordinates, which opens the flow of communications.

Balancing Mission and Troops[c]

When not to pass orders on as your own. IF you receive an order from above that you do not agree with because it does not seem to make sense, THEN let your key subordinates know that you do not agree with the order and that it is not your own. Tell them what you think, and tell them that their opinion about the directive should not be communicated to the soldiers. Then focus on how to make it work BECAUSE letting key subordinates know that a questionable order is not your own and what you think about it preserves your relationship with them.

[b] Obtained from battalion commanders; [c] Obtained from company commanders; [p] Obtained from platoon leaders; [x] Obtained from literature review only.

Two categories that emerged from the interviews did not fit into the earlier framework. These categories were tacit knowledge about balancing mission and troops, which was unique to company commanders, and tacit knowledge about establishing credibility, which was unique to platoon leaders. Because these categories were each unique to one level, they may not have had the same probability of emerging in the literature as categories that crossed all three levels and presumably applied to most leaders. The interview data allowed us to observe the distinctions in tacit knowledge across organizational levels. Both Tables 5 and 6 show changes in the composition of tacit knowledge as leaders ascend the organizational hierarchy. The unique categories of tacit knowledge reflect the different developmental challenges faced by leaders at each level.

DEVELOPMENTAL CHALLENGES AT EACH LEVEL. By identifying more general categories of tacit knowledge at each level, we were able to observe some similarities and differences in leadership across organizational levels. We briefly discuss how the tacit knowledge categories exemplify the unique developmental challenges of leaders at each level.

The tacit knowledge of platoon leaders reflects their limited experience and formal position power, as well as their direct form of leadership, generally through face-to-face interaction. Of the knowledge we uncovered at the platoon level, 28% was about motivating subordinates. Motivating relatively more experienced subordinates without much formal authority also raises issues of personal credibility for platoon leaders. Platoon leaders must also establish credibility with their immediate superiors if they are to protect their limited autonomy. We found that tacit knowledge about establishing credibility was unique to the platoon level. Tacit knowledge about managing the self was also more frequent at the platoon level than at the company and battalion levels, which may reflect the stress of establishing credibility and authority over more experienced soldiers.

The tacit knowledge of company commanders reflects the greater power and discretion associated with their position. At this level, we observed the emergence of tacit knowledge about directing and supervising others. Tacit knowledge about establishing credibility, however, was not as important. The role of a company commander also requires the incumbent to consider the needs of subordinates and simultaneously to coordinate with higher headquarters. This is apparent in the distinct knowledge at the company level about cooperating with others and balancing mission accomplishments with the needs of subordinates.

Finally, the tacit knowledge of battalion commanders reflects their considerable experience and authority. They also are concerned with more system-wide issues, and in line with this, we find that tacit knowledge for protecting the organization and managing organizational change is unique to battalion commanders. We also found that the tacit knowledge about communicating differed from that obtained at lower levels. Specifically, battalion commanders learned to use indirect methods and systems of communication, and these communications were oriented primarily toward conveying the organization's mission and values. Finally, knowledge about dealing with poor performers was unique to battalion commanders, which can be attributable to the greater authority and discretion they possess to deal with personnel issues.

TACIT KNOWLEDGE AND GENERAL LEADERSHIP FRAMEWORKS. Many of the categories of tacit knowledge that we identified overlap with those described by other leadership researchers (Bass & Avolio, 1993; Yukl, 1998). Although none of the existing frameworks address tacit knowledge for leadership per se, the action-oriented nature of tacit knowledge allows comparisons of its categories with behaviors identified by other researchers. We focus our comparisons mainly on the managerial practices taxonomy of Yukl (1998) and Yukl, Wall, and Lepsinger (1990) and refer to other perspectives that speak to our findings (Bass & Avolio, 1990, 1993).

Most of the 14 leader behaviors (managerial practices) identified by Yukl (1998) are represented in the tacit knowledge categories we identified. For example, the category Directing and Supervising Subordinates involves planning and organizing activities, although Yukl's description includes tasks we consider to be more characteristic of managers (e.g., resource allocation). Tacit knowledge about developing subordinates and taking care of soldiers closely match the managerial practices of developing and supporting. Other managerial practices are combined within a single tacit knowledge category. Motivating Subordinates, for example, includes the practices of motivating, rewarding, and recognizing, and Communicating includes the managerial practices of clarifying roles and objectives, informing, monitoring, and consulting.

Yukl (1998) also suggested that the relative importance of each of the managerial practices might vary across different types of managers or leaders. As noted earlier, we observed differences in the tacit knowledge that emerged at each leadership level. Some of these differences were most noticeable in moving from company level to battalion level command. The unique tacit knowledge of battalion commanders includes behaviors such as communicating a vision, helping subordinates identify strengths and weaknesses, using subordinates as change agents, and showing concern for soldiers' well being. These behaviors share similarities with those identified by Bass and Avolio (1993) as characteristic of transformational leaders. In other words, behaviors that show individualized consideration, inspire subordinates to act, stimulate followers to think critically, and establish a clear, attainable vision appear to be more representative of the tacit knowledge of leaders at higher levels of command.

Finally, three categories of tacit knowledge were not represented directly in either Yukl's (1998) or Bass and Avolio's (1993) framework.

One category is Managing the Self. This category includes behaviors that are consistent with theories of self-management and self-leadership (Manz & Sims, 1980; Markham & Markham, 1995), such as setting goals and taking initiative to accomplish them, regulating one's thoughts and emotions, and providing self-reinforcement. The other categories are Establishing Credibility and Establishing Trust. Issues of credibility are addressed by leadership approaches that focus on how leaders gain influence over their followers – in other words, how they acquire power. Increasing one's knowledge and skills is a source of expert power, while demonstrating respect is a source of referent power (French & Raven, 1959). Trust is also viewed as a source of power and is included in transformational leadership theory (Bass & Avolio, 1993). However, establishing trust is not represented as a major component in any existing approach to understanding leadership. The emergence of establishing credibility and establishing trust as separate tacit knowledge categories may indicate that these are more prominent concerns among military than among civilian leaders.

In general, we found substantial overlap in the categories of tacit knowledge that we identified and the behaviors suggested by other researchers to be characteristic of most leaders. However, some categories emerged as more prominent in our research with military leaders, and others did not apply at all levels of leadership. Although there may be common categories of leadership behaviors across settings, the relative importance and expression of these behaviors depend on the specific situation in which they are applied. These findings support our contention that the role of tacit knowledge in military leadership should be explored at each organizational level separately.

Developing a Tacit Knowledge Inventory for Military Leaders

In order to measure the possession of tacit knowledge by military leaders and to test our assertion that tacit knowledge is important to leadership performance, we developed an inventory for each organizational level based on the data obtained from our interviews. In developing each inventory, we followed the process described in chapter 7. Specifically, we sought to identify, from the body of tacit knowledge elicited in the interview study, items that were most promising for use in developing a measurement instrument (Horvath et al., 1996). By *promising*, we mean that the items represent knowledge that is characteristic of more experienced as well as more effective leaders.

The 174 tacit knowledge items collected during the interview study were used to develop a rating instrument called the Tacit Knowledge Survey (TKS). A separate TKS was constructed for leaders at the platoon, company, and battalion levels and consisted of 66, 67, and 46 items, respectively. The purpose of the TKS was not to obtain possible responses to the items but rather to obtain ratings on the quality or usefulness of the knowledge represented in each item. In order to include all the items in the TKS, we first condensed them into shorter, simpler forms. The key components of each tacit knowledge item were abstracted and any unnecessary information deleted. Military members of the research team reviewed and edited the condensed items to ensure their comprehensibility for a military audience and to preserve the intentions of the interviewees who provided the items.

The purpose of the TKS was to determine which items represented good advice about military leadership that might not be common knowledge. Each tacit knowledge item was followed by four 7-point rating scales. Specifically, leaders were asked to make the following judgments about each tacit knowledge item: (1) How good does the respondent think the advice is? (2) How commonly known does the respondent think the advice is? (3) How often do leaders at the specific level face situations such as the one described? (4) To what extent does the advice match the respondent's personal concept of leadership? A sample item from the TKS was shown earlier in Table 2.

In order to identify promising tacit knowledge items, we administered the TKS to two separate samples. The first sample consisted of leaders who represented different levels of experience (experienced or novice) at each of the three organizational levels. The leaders were asked to rate the tacit knowledge items on several dimensions. For a second sample, we obtained ratings of leadership effectiveness in addition to ratings on the tacit knowledge items. Our aim was to identify items that best discriminated between experienced and novice leaders in the first sample and between relatively more and less effective leaders in the second. We discuss the method and results of these two samples separately.

RELATIONSHIP OF TACIT KNOWLEDGE TO EXPERIENCE. The first sample consisted of 791 Army leaders enrolled in various military educational programs of the U.S. Army Training and Doctrine Command (TRADOC). During their careers, Army leaders cycle between operational assignments and enrollment in TRADOC schools. The TRADOC schools were chosen as a source of participants for two main reasons. First, they provided a ready pool of active-duty leaders at all three levels under study (platoon, company, and battalion). Second, this sample provided the opportunity to stratify leaders according to experience. Leaders were identified as either novices for the next level of command or as experienced leaders for the one they had just finished and completed a version of the TKS accordingly. This assignment to one group or the other allowed us to examine which tacit knowledge items discriminated between experienced and novice leaders.

Members of the research team randomly chose leaders to participate from class rosters. The surveys were administered in 13 different courses at nine separate locations with the help of TRADOC staff. The overall response rate was 79%.

In analyzing the data, we first examined relationships among the four rating scales of the TKS using a principal components analysis of the intercorrelations among these ratings. We were interested in what distinct information, if any, was provided by the separate rating scales. For each version of the TKS, the analysis yielded only one component with an eigenvalue greater than or equal to 1, which we interpreted to indicate a general factor of quality. We decided to use the "good" rating in subsequent analyses because it correlated highly with the other ratings and it permitted the most straightforward inference about the respondent's leadership knowledge. That is, we could readily identify items that more experienced officers rated as good. Once we determined which rating to use, we conducted discriminant analyses to identify items that distinguished between experienced and novice officers.

Discriminant analysis was used (1) to assess the overall discriminating power of the goodness ratings in the combined set of tacit knowledge items (i.e., Do the item ratings on the whole differ between experts and novices?) and (2) to identify tacit knowledge items with the highest degree of discrimination (i.e., On which items do the ratings vary most between experts and novices?). We computed a canonical discriminant function, which distinguished between experienced and novice groups for each of the levels under study. The canonical correlation coefficient based on the discriminant function was significant at each level and indicated that the overall set of tacit knowledge items discriminated well between novice and experienced leaders. We then examined the discriminating potential of the individual tacit knowledge items. We computed a structure coefficient for each item, which represented the correlation between the rating on the item and the output of the canonical discriminant function. Higher absolute values for the structure coefficients indicated greater discrimination. Tacit knowledge items with the highest structure coefficients were identified as most promising for further instrument development.

RELATIONSHIP OF TACIT KNOWLEDGE TO LEADERSHIP EFFECTIVENESS. In the second sample, we sought to identify items that related to perceived leadership effectiveness. The sample consisted of leaders assigned to active-duty army units in U.S. Army Forces Command (FORSCOM). The FORSCOM sample provided a large sample of incumbent leaders at each level under study. The TKS was administered to all available members of the chain of command in approximately 30 battalions, representing a total of 447 leaders. A battalion is composed of approximately 600 soldiers commanded by a lieutenant colonel who has an average of 17 years of experience as a commissioned officer. A typical battalion contains five companies, each with approximately 120 soldiers and commanded by a captain, with typically 5 to 8 years of commissioned service. Generally companies have three platoons, each platoon with about 40 soldiers under the leadership of a lieutenant with 1 to 3 years of commissioned service.

By using intact chains of command we were able to identify subordinates, peers, and superiors from which to obtain ratings of each leader's effectiveness. These ratings allowed us to examine the relationship between ratings on the tacit knowledge items and leadership effectiveness. Ratings were obtained by using the Leadership Effectiveness Survey (LES). The LES (shown in Table 7) asks participants to rate the effectiveness of all leaders, at the specified level, that they know in their unit. We obtained ratings from at least three perspectives: self, superior, peer and/or subordinate. For battalion commanders, we did not collect peer ratings because these leaders have limited opportunities to observe one another. We also did not obtain ratings from the subordinates of platoon leaders because operational assignments precluded them from participating.

As in the first sample, a principal components analysis suggested that one overall factor best represented rating on the TKS. For ease of interpretation, we again focused our analyses on the "good" scale ratings. For the LES, we formed high and low effectiveness groups from the top and bottom quartiles on each effectiveness measure (e.g., subordinate ratings, peer ratings). We then computed a point-biserial correlation between the goodness ratings and an index of effectiveness

---

TABLE 7. Sample Question from the Leadership Effectiveness Survey

LEADERSHIP EFFECTIVENESS RATINGS

Battalion Commander Ratings

Instructions: Think about the battalion commanders listed below who are under your command. Compared to all other battalion commanders you have known, how good (effective) is the leadership of each battalion commander? Please circle the number under the statement that best corresponds to your rating for each battalion designation.

Name	The Best	One of the Best	Better than Most	As Good as Most	Not Quite as Good as Most but Still Gets the Job Done	Well Below Most	The Worst
_____	1	2	3	4	5	6	7
_____	1	2	3	4	5	6	7
_____	1	2	3	4	5	6	7
_____	1	2	3	4	5	6	7

(high or low). The number of effectiveness ratings varied depending on the number of sources from which the ratings were obtained (subordinates, peers, superior, self) at each level. The correlational analysis generated a total of 198 correlations (66 TKS items × 3 rater sources) for battalion commanders, 268 correlations (67 TKS items × 4 rater sources) for company commanders, and 138 correlations (46 TKS items × 3 rater sources) for platoon leaders. The percentage of correlation coefficients that met conventional standards for statistical significance ($p < .05$) in the point-biserial analyses were 8% at the battalion level, 9% at the company level, and 16% at the platoon level.

The large number of statistical tests raises concern about an inflated probability of type I error, in that statistical significance may be due to chance. However, we considered this concern to be tempered by our objectives at this stage in the research. First, the correlations between individual items and rated leadership effectiveness are not intended to test a theoretical proposition about the relationship between tacit knowledge and leadership effectiveness. They are intended to suggest items that hold promise, in combination with other items, to measure tacit knowledge that relates to leadership effectiveness. Second, in comparing the relative costs of type I and type II errors, we decided that it was more important to retain items than to exclude items that might prove valuable in further instrument development. Using the data collected from these two samples, we were able to identify tacit knowledge items that were more likely to be characteristic of experienced and effective leaders.

CONSTRUCTING THE TACIT KNOWLEDGE INVENTORY. Using the set of tacit knowledge items that we obtained from the interviews, we developed three versions of the Tacit Knowledge for Military Leaders (TKML) inventory corresponding to the three organizational levels studied, namely, platoon, company, and battalion. We used two primary criteria to guide the selection of items for inclusion in the inventories. First, we selected items that were individually construct-relevant based on item statistics from the TRADOC and FORSCOM data and based on the judgments of military experts. We retained items that were more characteristic of experienced and effective leaders at each level and that the experts judged to fit the definition of tacit knowledge for military leaders. Second, we selected items that were collectively construct-relevant based on the category framework derived from the interview data. That is, we sought to include a representative sample of the tacit knowledge domain for military leaders.

Each selected tacit knowledge item was expanded into a scenario that posed a leadership problem and presented a set of 5 to 15 response options. We used the original stories collected during our interview study to create these scenarios. We tried to ensure that the scenarios represented situations that likely would be encountered by most leaders at the particular level, avoiding stories that were idiosyncratic to a particular individual. Each scenario plus response options represented a question in the tacit knowledge inventory, with each inventory containing multiple questions.

Preliminary versions of the inventory were presented to focus groups representing each organizational level. The focus group members were officers assigned to staff or faculty positions at the U.S. Military Academy (but external to the research team) who had served in leadership positions at the platoon, company, or battalion levels. The focus groups were asked to evaluate the correspondence between the inventory and the tacit knowledge construct as we defined it for them. We asked them questions such as "Does this question represent the type of problem that leaders learn to solve through experience?" and "Does this question tap knowledge of the sort that we have defined as tacit knowledge?" We also asked them to provide additional plausible response options, identify areas of confusion or lack of clarity, and identify problems of sexual, racial, ethnic, or military branch bias. After making any necessary revisions, we finalized three versions of the TKML inventory, one for each organizational level (platoon, company, and battalion). Table 8 presents a sample question taken from the TKML for company commanders. Respondents to the TKML are asked to rate the quality or advisability of each response option, using a 9 point scale ranging from "extremely bad" to "extremely good." Sample questions from the platoon, company, and battalion versions of the TKML are included in Appendix C.

TABLE 8. Sample Question from the Tacit Knowledge for Military Leaders Inventory (TKML)

TACIT KNOWLEDGE FOR MILITARY LEADERS
Company Commander Questionnaire

1	2	3	4	5	6	7	8	9
Extremely Bad		Somewhat Bad		Neither Bad nor Good		Somewhat Good		Extremely Good

You are a company commander, and your battalion commander is the type of person who seems always to "shoot the messenger" – he does not like to be surprised by bad news, and he tends to take his anger out on the person who brought him the bad news. You want to build a positive, professional relationship with your battalion commander. What should you do?

_____ Speak to your battalion commander about his behavior and share your perception of it.

_____ Attempt to keep the battalion commander "over-informed" by telling him what is occurring in your unit on a regular basis (e.g., daily or every other day).

_____ Speak to the sergeant major and see if he or she is willing to try to influence the battalion commander.

_____ Keep the battalion commander informed only on important issues, but don't bring up issues you don't have to discuss with him.

_____ When you bring a problem to your battalion commander, bring a solution at the same time.

_____ Disregard the battalion commander's behavior. Continue to bring him news as you normally would.

_____ Tell your battalion commander all of the good news you can, but try to shield him from hearing the bad news.

_____ Tell the battalion commander as little as possible; deal with problems on your own if at all possible.

Validating the Tacit Knowledge Inventory for Military Leaders

The next stage of our research involved conducting a preliminary construct validation of the TKML. We sought evidence of the convergent validity of the TKML with the criterion of leadership effectiveness. We sought evidence of discriminant validity in the relationship of the TKML to measures of verbal ability and tacit knowledge for managers. In addition, we sought evidence that the TKML explains variance in leadership effectiveness above and beyond measures of general cognitive ability and tacit knowledge for managers. We discuss the methods used to conduct our validation study and the results we obtained for leaders at the platoon, company, and battalion levels (Hedlund et al., 1998).

VALIDATION SAMPLE. We administered the TKML, along with the other validation measures that we will describe in the next section, to officers from 44 battalions stationed at six Army posts around the United States. The number of battalions sampled at each post ranged from 4 to 10. By sampling intact battalions, we were able to administer the tacit knowledge inventory at all three levels of interest (battalion, company, and platoon) and simultaneously to obtain judgments of leadership effectiveness from multiple sources. We obtained complete data for 368 platoon leaders, 163 company commanders, and 31 battalion commanders. In addition, we obtained ratings of leadership effectiveness from the superior officers of battalion commanders (i.e., brigade commanders), who themselves did not serve as participants.

VALIDATION MEASURES. In addition to the TKML, we administered measures of verbal ability, experience, and tacit knowledge for managers, and we obtained ratings of leadership effectiveness for all participants.

The Concept Mastery Test (CMT) (Terman, 1950) is a measure of general verbal ability and was administered to provide evidence of discriminant validity. It consists of two sections, synonym–antonym problems and verbal analogy problems. We included a measure of verbal ability in order to show that the TKML measures more than verbal reasoning ability and also that the TKML can add to the prediction of leadership effectiveness beyond a traditional measure of general cognitive ability. The CMT was scored by using an answer key, and the number of correct responses was summed for synonym–antonym and analogy problems separately.

The Tacit Knowledge Inventory for Managers (TKIM) (Wagner & Sternberg, 1991), which was designed to measure the experience-based knowledge of civilian managers and which we have discussed in chapter 8, also was administered to further establish the discriminant validity of the TKML. Including a measure of tacit knowledge for managers would enable us to show that despite any potential overlap in the knowledge of managers and leaders, the TKML represents domain-specific knowledge that is more relevant to understanding effective leadership than is the TKIM.

Like the TKML, the TKIM is a type of situational judgment test in which respondents rate the quality of response options. The TKIM has been validated in earlier research and has been found to be a significant predictor of managerial success (Wagner, 1987; Wagner & Sternberg, 1990). Responses to the TKIM were scored on the basis of an expert profile consisting of the mean responses of 13 business executives from Fortune 500 firms (Wagner, 1987). The total score on the TKIM reflects the squared deviations of each response from the expert mean, summed across all response options within questions. Because a smaller deviation represents greater tacit knowledge, we reflected the TKIM scores by subtracting each score from the maximum value in order to ease interpretation. In the analyses, a higher value represents a better TKIM score.

The definition of tacit knowledge suggests that it is knowledge gained through experience. Although experience does not guarantee learning, we do expect that leaders with more experience will be more likely to have acquired tacit knowledge. We asked participants to report the number of months they have been in their current position in order to assess the relationship between job experience and tacit knowledge.

Finally, to establish convergent validity, we included a measure of leadership performance. We expected that TKML scores would correlate significantly with leadership effectiveness and that they would explain variance in effectiveness not accounted for by our other measures. The LES, described in the previous section on developing the TKIM and illustrated in Table 7, consisted of single-item measures that asked respondents to rate other leaders on their interpersonal, task-oriented, and overall effectiveness using a 7-point scale.

Some researchers have found that ratings from multiple sources can represent significant and meaningful sources of variation about perceptions of performance (Salam, Cox, & Sims, 1997). We therefore sought ratings from multiple sources based on a 360-degree approach to performance feedback (Church & Bracken, 1997; Tornow, 1993). Our purpose in using this procedure was to explore different perspectives of leadership effectiveness from different sources.

We asked all officers in the battalion (immediate superiors, peers in the unit, and subordinate officers) to provide ratings. For battalion commanders we were unable to obtain peer ratings because of their limited contact with fellow battalion commanders, and for platoon leaders we did not obtain subordinate ratings owing to the unavailability of noncommissioned officers to participate in the study. When feasible, we obtained multiple ratings of effectiveness from each source. For those cases in which multiple ratings were obtained (e.g., from subordinates and peers), a mean ratings was computed for each of the effectiveness dimensions (overall, task, and interpersonal). For the data analysis, ratings on the LES were reverse-coded so that higher ratings corresponded to greater perceived effectiveness.

SCORING OF THE TKML. Scoring of the TKML, like scoring of most situational judgment tests (Chan & Schmitt, 1998; Motowidlo et al., 1990), typically relies on expert opinions. The questions pose problem situations that can lead to different interpretations and solutions. The appropriate interpretation and solution depend on one's knowledge of how to solve the problem, knowledge presumably gained through experience. Therefore, an appropriate standard for judging the quality of responses is a group of experienced and successful practitioners.

To serve as the expert samples, we chose highly select groups of officers at each level who had recently demonstrated outstanding performance, as defined by the army's performance evaluation, promotion, and selection system. We administered the TKML to 59 expert battalion commanders, 29 expert company commanders, and 50 expert platoon leaders. From the expert data we constructed expert profiles that included the mean and standard deviation of the experts' ratings for each response option within a question. The level of agreement among the experts was considered acceptable, with the standard deviations among experts generally falling between 1 and 2 on a 9-point scale.

We assessed the proximity of each participant's ratings to those of the experts by computing the squared deviation of the participant's response on each option from the expert mean. These squared distances were then summed across all response options within a question.

We performed two corrections on these squared distances. First, we were concerned that for some options respondents might be penalized for being far from the experts in their ratings when the experts themselves disagreed as to the appropriate response. Because of this concern, we wanted those options about which the experts agreed less to receive less weight in the measurement of leaders' tacit knowledge. Therefore, we weighed the squared distances by the reciprocal of the standard deviation among experts.

Second, the squared distances were adjusted for different rating styles on the part of respondents (use of scale-range and response bias), which could produce artificially larger distances. We computed an overall score for each respondent that reflected the squared distances summed across all questions. Then, the overall score was divided by the average standard deviation in the respondent's ratings across response options within questions. In order to maintain consistency across variables, we reflected the final TKML scores by subtracting each score from the maximum score, so that a higher score on the TKML represented more expertlike responses and therefore greater tacit knowledge.

INTERNAL CONSISTENCY OF THE TKML. Because we had three different versions of the TKML, one for each level under study, we analyzed the data separately by level following the same general procedures. First, we wanted to ensure that the TKML was a reliable measure of tacit knowledge. Tacit knowledge inventories, like most SJTs, are different from traditional knowledge tests in that the item stems consist of poorly defined, complex problem situations (Legree, 1995). Each problem can be considered to be multidimensional in nature, drawing on a combination of knowledge, skills, and abilities (Chan & Schmitt, 1998). Across the inventory, the questions may measure diverse areas of knowledge, of which some may be acquired by the individual and some may not. The complexities of the tacit knowledge inventory reduce the likelihood of obtaining high levels of internal consistency. Therefore, we do not expect to find the same level of reliability as with traditional knowledge or ability tests.

We computed coefficient α values for each version of the TKML. We also examined item-total correlations to identify questions that exhibited poor fit with the rest of the inventory. We examined more closely questions that had item-total correlations less than .15 and removed those questions that we determined did not fit the conceptual definition of tacit knowledge or appeared to be too narrow in focus (e.g., pertaining to a particular specialty such as chemical weapons).

The initial versions of the TKML for platoon leaders, company commanders, and battalion commanders all had α values below .80. At the platoon level we removed one question that correlated poorly with the overall inventory and was determined to be too narrow in its focus; the final version consisted of 15 questions ($\alpha = .69$). At the company level we removed two questions that correlated poorly with the overall inventory and on further review did not adequately meet our criteria as tacit knowledge; the final version consisted of 18 questions ($\alpha = .76$). At the battalion level we removed five questions that exhibited low item-total correlations and were subsequently evaluated to be too narrow in focus or to represent common knowledge (and thus not tacit knowledge); the final version of the TKML for battalion commanders consisted of 11 questions ($\alpha = .66$). Although these reliabilities are below those found for traditional knowledge and ability tests, they are in the typical range of .5 to .8 for SJTs (Legree, 1995). Because our obtained reliabilities fell within this range, we considered them to be promising with regard to the internal consistency of our instruments.

LEADERSHIP EFFECTIVENESS RATINGS. In the next step we explored the relationship among LES ratings on the three dimensions of leadership (task, interpersonal, and overall) and from multiple sources (subordinates, peers, superiors). We expected that different rater sources would vary in their perceptions of leadership effectiveness and that raters would distinguish between task and interpersonal aspects of leadership. For example, consider a leader who goes out drinking with his soldiers every Friday night. His subordinates may think he is a good leader, but his superiors may feel he has no authority or credibility with his soldiers. We examined the intercorrelations among rater sources and rating dimensions. The correlation matrix produced is similar to that used in multitrait-multimethod (MTMM) analysis (Campbell & Fiske, 1959). However, the multitrait-multimethod approach is traditionally intended to rule out the effects of method variance, whereas we looked to confirm it. We expected to find higher correlations within a single rater source (e.g., subordinates) across dimensions (e.g., overall and interpersonal leadership) than between different rater sources (e.g., subordinates and peers) on a single dimension (e.g., interpersonal leadership).

The number of sources that provided ratings of leadership effectiveness varied across levels. Platoon leaders were rated by one supervisor and, on average, two peers. Company commanders were rated, on average, by two subordinates, three peers, and one superior. Battalion commanders were rated by three subordinates, on average, and one superior. At all levels, we consistently found higher intercorrelations within rater sources across dimensions (e.g., peer ratings of task and interpersonal leadership) than across rater sources on a single dimension (e.g., supervisor and peer ratings of interpersonal leadership). The average intercorrelations within rater source were .76 for platoon leaders, .77 for company commanders, and .63 for battalion commanders. The average correlations across rater sources were .32 for platoon leaders, .27 for company commanders, and −.12 for battalion commanders. In other words, there appears to be some variability in the ratings a leader received from different sources. The intercorrelations between task and interpersonal ratings also were lower than the correlations of either task or interpersonal ratings with overall ratings of leadership effectiveness. These correlations suggest that raters discriminated somewhat between task and interpersonal leadership effectiveness. Of greater interest than the intercorrelations among ratings, however, was the relationships between these ratings and scores on the TKML.

EVIDENCE OF DISCRIMINANT VALIDITY. In order to assess both the convergent and the discriminant validity of the TKML, we conducted correlational analyses among all the study variables (TKML, TKIM, CMT, experience, and LES ratings). At all three levels, experience, as measured by months in current position, did not correlate significantly with TKML. This finding is consistent with our earlier argument that the amount of experience one has does not guarantee the occurrence of effective learning from that experience. In the military, this finding may be complicated by the rapid progression of effective leaders through the organization's hierarchy, particularly at the levels we addressed. Thus, we might expect a negative or even curvilinear relationship between experience and tacit knowledge in that leaders who remain in their current position beyond a certain tenure (e.g., 1 year) may not have developed the level of proficiency required for promotion. Therefore, time-based measures of experience may not be as informative as measures of what has been learned during that time.

TKML scores correlated moderately with CMT (verbal ability) scores at the platoon level ($r = .18$ with analogy scores, $p < .01$) and company level ($r = .25$ with analogy scores, $p < .01$). At the battalion level, this relationship was not significant. The finding of a significant relationship between TKML and verbal ability differs from previous research on tacit knowledge (Sternberg et al., 1995). However, it is consistent with a body of research that reveals a moderate association between leadership and intelligence as measured by conventional ability tests (Bass, 1990). Although there may be some association between verbal reasoning ability and TKML scores, the TKML clearly is not simply another cognitive ability test.

TKML scores correlated with TKIM scores at the platoon level ($r = .36$, $p < .01$) and company level ($r = .32$, $p < .01$). At the battalion level, the relationship was not significant. The correlation between TKML and TKIM scores suggests some overlap, which is to be expected, in the knowledge of managers and leaders. Military leaders may engage in activities similar to those of civilian managers (e.g., resource allocation, subordinate development), which allow them to recognize and respond to comparable situations presented in the context of management. This correlation may also reflect an underlying ability to acquire and use tacit knowledge that generalizes across performance domains, which is considered an important aspect of practical intelligence (Sternberg, 1997a). Again, the magnitude of this correlation does not indicate that the TKML and TKIM are measuring the same construct.

EVIDENCE OF CONVERGENT VALIDITY. Next, we examined the relationships of the various predictors, individually and in combination, to leadership effectiveness. The number of criteria varied across levels as a function of the number of sources who provided ratings. We included ratings on all three dimensions – interpersonal, task, and overall leadership – in our analyses.

Experience did not correlate significantly with leadership effectiveness ratings at any of the three levels. At the platoon level, CMT scores only correlated significantly with ratings of task-oriented leadership by superiors ($r = .16$, $p < .05$). At the company level, CMT scores correlated significantly with subordinate ratings on all three dimensions of leadership effectiveness (r's from $-.17$ to $-.22$, $p < .05$) and with peer ratings of overall and interpersonal effectiveness ($r = -.18$ and $-.20$, respectively, $p < .05$). However, the direction of these correlations suggested that higher CMT scores were associated with lower effectiveness ratings. At the battalion level, there were no significant correlations between CMT scores and LES ratings. Finally, in terms of TKIM scores, we found a significant correlation with leadership effectiveness only at the battalion level. Subordinates rated battalion commanders who scored higher on the TKIM as more effective on task-related leadership ($r = .36$, $p < .05$). This finding is consistent with army doctrine and with our earlier findings that indicate that part of the battalion commander's role involves managing a complex system.

At all three levels, we obtained evidence of convergent validity of the TKML with LES ratings. The pattern of these relationships varied across rater sources and across levels. At the platoon level, higher TKML scores correlated significantly with higher effectiveness ratings by superiors on all three leadership dimensions (r's of .14 to .20, $p < .05$). At the company level, higher TKML scores correlated significantly with higher effectiveness ratings by peers for overall and task leadership (r's of .19 and .20 respectively, $p < .05$). At the battalion level, higher TKML scores correlated significantly with higher ratings of overall effectiveness by superiors ($r = .42$, $p < .05$).

In light of the pattern of relationships that emerged across levels, we considered the possibility that the inventory may represent multiple dimensions of tacit knowledge that pertain to different aspects of leadership and that these aspects may vary in their relevance to the leadership perceptions of different constituents. For example, tacit knowledge items that pertain to subordinate relations may be most relevant to subordinates' perceptions of leadership effectiveness. In an earlier stage of our research, we identified a category framework that guided the selection of tacit knowledge items included in the instrument. In these categories we observed different knowledge that pertained to relations with subordinates, superiors, and peers.

Using a principal components factor analysis, we explored the structure of the TKML to identify potential subsets of items that may provide additional prediction of leadership effectiveness. At the platoon level, the principal components factor analysis did not reveal any readily interpretable multiple factors. We concluded that the overall TKML score for platoon leaders best represented the data.

At the company level, the initial solution from the principal components analysis suggested the possibility of multiple factors. An oblique rotation was conducted on the initial solution to ease interpretation of the factors. An examination of the factor pattern matrices revealed two interpretable factors, one representing tacit knowledge about "dealing with the boss" (seven questions, $\alpha = .61$), and another representing tacit knowledge for "motivating and developing subordinates" (five questions, $\alpha = .60$). The two interpretable factors were consistent with categories shown in Table 5.

We constructed subscale scores using the questions that loaded on each factor and examined their relationship to leadership effectiveness. Subscale scores representing tacit knowledge about managing the boss correlated significantly with ratings of overall effectiveness by superiors ($r = .17$, $p < .05$). Subscale scores representing tacit knowledge for motivating and developing subordinates correlated significantly with ratings of task effectiveness by subordinates ($r = .15$, $p < .05$). A principal components analysis was not performed at the battalion level because of small sample size.

In the final step of our analyses, we conducted hierarchical regression analyses to assess the extent to which the TKML adds predictive validity beyond CMT and TKIM scores. Hierarchical regressions were only performed for LES ratings that were significantly correlated with TKML scores in the prior analyses. In each hierarchical regression, we entered scores on the two CMT scales and the TKIM in the first step, followed by scores on the TKML in the second step. For ratings of platoon leaders by their superiors, TKML scores provided a significant increment in prediction above scores on the CMT and the TKIM combined (ΔR^2 from .02 to .04, $p < .05$).

For company commanders, TKML scores provided a significant increment in prediction of effectiveness ratings by peers above CMT and TKIM scores, even when these latter variables contributed a significant prediction to the first step of the regression analysis (ΔR^2 from .03 to .06, $p < .05$). In addition, the TKML subscale scores representing tacit knowledge about managing the boss provided significant incremental prediction of superior ratings of overall effectiveness beyond CMT and TKIM scores ($\Delta R^2 = .06$, $p < .05$). Subscale TKML scores representing tacit knowledge for motivating and developing subordinates provided a significant incremental prediction of subordinate ratings of task effectiveness beyond CMT and TKIM scores ($\Delta R^2 = .03$, $p < .05$).

The limited number of raters (fewer than 31) who rated the battalion commanders precluded us from testing the incremental validity of the TKML using hierarchical regression analysis. However, the pattern of correlations suggested that the TKML might be a better predictor of leadership effectiveness than the CMT – in fact, it suggested that the CMT did not correlate significantly with any of the effectiveness ratings. We proceeded to test the hypothesis that the TKML is a better predictor of LES than the CMT by using a t-test of the difference between two dependent correlations (Cohen & Cohen, 1983). We did not find a significant difference between the two correlations (TKML – LES and

CMT – LES; t = .98, nonsignificant). Again, the ability to test the significance of this difference likely was limited by our sample size.

The Role of Tacit Knowledge in Military Leadership

Researchers have explored numerous factors believed to explain effective leadership. These factors include traits such as cognitive abilities and personality (Fiedler, 1995), behaviors such as consideration and initiating structure (Yukl, 1971), and the inspiration and stimulation of followers (Bass & Avolio, 1993). Most researchers acknowledge that the situation plays an important role in determining what traits or behaviors will be most effective. Attempts to identify the various contingencies affecting leadership performance have at times become overwhelming. The tacit knowledge approach addresses many of these issues from the perspective of what leader know about how to lead effectively. It focuses on what the leader learns from experience with specific situations about what is and what is not effective in those types of situations. Leaders differ, however, in their ability to learn from experience and to apply existing knowledge to new situations. Because individuals differ in their acquisition and use of tacit knowledge, it is a potentially useful way to understand what distinguishes leaders who are more successful from those who are less successful. It also suggests new avenues for developing more effective leaders.

Tacit knowledge is knowledge, acquired primarily through personal experience, about what to do in particular situations to achieve one's goals. Although tacit knowledge, like any personal attribute, can be studied in terms of broad, abstract categories that generalize across settings, it is best understood in relation to specific, personally experienced situations. By identifying the specific content of tacit knowledge, we obtained a more detailed understanding of the types of situations leaders encounter at each organizational level and the kinds of actions that are more and less effective in those situations.

Our research set out to address three main questions: (1) Can we identify tacit knowledge for military leadership?; (2) Can we measure the tacit knowledge of military leaders?; and (3) Does possessing tacit knowledge explain individual differences in leadership effectiveness that are not accounted for by traditional intelligence tests or tacit knowledge for managers? Over the course of the 6-year project that we have described in this chapter, we provided affirmative answers to each of these questions. We summarize and discuss the implications of our findings for leadership here and will address the broader applications of this research in chapter 10.

THE INTERVIEWS. We began our research by reviewing the literature pertaining to leadership, both in general and with specific regard to the military domain. The military literature provided us with some insight about the types of things that are formally taught and widely recognized and the type of knowledge that might be characterized as tacit. Because we were interested in the latter, we sought a more direct source for learning about the tacit knowledge of leaders – job incumbents. We interviewed leaders to find out what they learned from their experiences about how to be an effective leader. We found that the stories leaders shared often contained knowledge that met our criteria for being tacit. That is, the knowledge appeared to be acquired with little support from other sources, it was procedural in structure, and it pertained to the individual's personal goals.

The stories obtained from the interviews were quite varied, thus confirming the personal relevance of tacit knowledge. The content of the knowledge also varied by organizational level, supporting our contention that tacit knowledge is domain-specific. We proceeded to analyze the stories further in order to assess the common issues that emerged in leaders' tacit knowledge and also to ensure that items chosen for later instrument development represented adequately the domain of tacit knowledge for military leaders.

Although each item of tacit knowledge obtained from the interviews was unique in its content, common themes appeared across these stories, which reflected the similarity of situations encountered by those who held similar positions. Among company commanders, for instance, we obtained several stories about how to encourage subordinates to take initiative. We also found some common themes in the content of tacit knowledge across leadership levels, such as how to establish trust and how to develop subordinates. However, there were several categories of tacit knowledge that were unique to a particular level. For example, tacit knowledge about establishing credibility was unique to platoon leaders, whereas tacit knowledge about dealing with poor performers was unique to battalion commanders.

INSTRUMENT DEVELOPMENT. In the next stage of the tacit knowledge research, we sought to identify a subset of tacit knowledge items that were most characteristic of experienced and effective leaders. In other words, we wanted to find out what more experienced and effective leaders considered to be good tacit knowledge. We compiled all the tacit knowledge items in the form of a survey, which asked respondents to rate the quality of each item. The survey was administered to two separate samples. In one sample, leaders were designated as more or less experienced, and in the other sample, they were rated in terms of their effectiveness. This step allowed us to narrow down the pool of items to those that best distinguished between more and less experienced and more and less effective leaders.

The results of the interview and content validation studies provided the foundation for the development and validation of the TKML. The purpose of developing a measurement instrument was to assess, in new samples of leaders, the acquisition and use of tacit knowledge in solving leadership problems. In order to develop the scenarios and response options for the tacit knowledge inventory, we relied on material from the original interview summaries, item statistics from the TKS study, and suggestions from military experts. These steps ensured the content representativeness and construct relevance of the tacit knowledge items we chose to include in the inventory. From the selected items, we developed a set of situation descriptions along with multiple response options for each leadership level, resulting in three versions of the TKML inventory.

VALIDATION STUDY. In the final stage of our research, we subjected the TKML to a rigorous construct validation. We included measures of verbal ability, experience, and tacit knowledge for managers, along with leadership effectiveness ratings, in order to obtain evidence of discriminant and convergent validity.

At all three military levels, leaders who scored higher on the TKML were rated as more effective by their superiors. For platoon leaders and battalion commanders, we found that the overall score on the TKML correlated with effectiveness ratings, while for company commanders it was the subscale score on questions dealing with managing the boss that correlated with superiors' ratings. The finding that leaders with higher TKML scores were rated as more effective by their superiors is consistent with the method used to score the TKML. Responses to the TKML were scored in terms of their proximity to expert ratings, and leaders were designated as experts by their superiors. Therefore, responses that resemble those of the experts more closely are likely to be associated with positive perceptions of effectiveness by superiors.

At the company level, we obtained ratings from peers, superiors, and subordinates and found associations between TKML scores and leadership effectiveness for all three sources of raters. Leaders who obtained a higher overall score on the TKML were rated as more effective by their peers. Those who obtained a higher score on the TKML subscale dealing with motivating and developing subordinates were rated as more effective by their subordinates. Finally, leaders who scored higher on the TKML subscale dealing with managing the boss were rated as more effective by their superiors. These results were consistent with our characterization of the challenges associated with leadership at the company level. The company commander is caught in the middle and must learn how to motivate and develop subordinates, cooperate with peers, and simultaneously perform as part of a larger complex organization (a battalion). The tacit knowledge that pertains to each of these issues appears to be most relevant to the perceptions of constituents who are most likely to be affected by them.

Although we obtained significant correlations of the TKML with leadership effectiveness ratings, the question still remained as to the relative contribution of the TKML in understanding leadership. Using hierarchical regression analyses, we examined the incremental validity of the TKML over a conventional ability test, the CMT, and over the TKIM. For each case in which the zero-order correlation between TKML and effectiveness ratings was significant, we found that TKML scores accounted for a significant increment of TKML over TKIM scores, which provides further support for the domain specificity of tacit knowledge.

Considering all the data that we gathered, we have shown that military leaders do exhibit knowledge that fits our definition as tacit, that tacit knowledge can be measured with some degree of reliability, and that possessing tacit knowledge is relevant to understanding leadership effectiveness.

IMPLICATIONS FOR UNDERSTANDING LEADERSHIP. In addition to providing a better understanding of military leadership, our findings also offer insights about leadership in general. At an abstract level, we can identify what types of behaviors are characteristic of effective leaders. These behaviors include motivating and developing subordinates, communicating, recognizing and rewarding, and establishing trust. The relevance and manifestation of these behaviors, however, depend on the context. Knowledge of general rules, such as a good leader motivates his or her subordinates, has limited value if the leader does not know how to apply those rules to action. Tacit knowledge about motivating subordinates, for example, may specify how to give responsibility to soldiers and reward them for accomplishments in order to encourage them to take initiative. The distinction between familiarity with general rules and knowledge of how to implement those rules is confirmed by our findings that domain-specific tacit knowledge of military leaders correlated with leadership effective ratings (with one exception at the battalion level), whereas tacit knowledge for managers did not. Although the broad, abstract categories of behaviors or tacit knowledge may be useful for understanding the similarities and differences across leaders, the tacit knowledge about what to do in a given situation may be more relevant for understanding effective leadership.

IMPLICATIONS FOR LEADERSHIP DEVELOPMENT. A number of products were generated in the process of identifying and assessing tacit knowledge. These included leadership stories and advice, coded tacit knowledge items and a category framework, and the TKML and its associated response data. All these products have potential value for developing effective leaders. Although the specific products from this research are applicable primarily to military leaders, the type of products and their potential use can apply to any domain in which tacit knowledge is studied. Therefore, we briefly describe these products here.

Transcripts of the interviews contain the stories that leaders shared about their experiences. These stories represent potentially rich sources of insight about the everyday lives of army leaders. In contrast to published knowledge, these stories have the advantages of being drawn from a broader sample of leaders, representing knowledge that is likely to be more current, and being intentionally selected for their tacit content. The stories can be organized on the basis of the category framework to allow leaders to select stories that represent particular developmental challenges.

The stories can be viewed as cases pertaining to leadership. More junior leaders, for example, can read about the experiences of other leaders in their current position. They might read about a situation similar to one that they have faced and compare the solutions and outcomes of the two. In more formalized settings, students could be asked to review certain cases and evaluate the situation described, the course of action taken, and the consequences of that action.

The category framework developed by our military experts is another product of the tacit knowledge research. It offers a structure for organizing and interpreting the tacit knowledge of military leaders and suggests areas of leadership development in which tacit knowledge may play an important role. The category framework provides a "meta-story" about leadership. It offers an overview of what leaders need to know to be effective and shows how the knowledge demands change as one ascends the organizational hierarchy. The categories also represent aspects of leadership that may not necessarily be covered by military doctrine or learned through formal training.

One can argue reasonably that the most effective way to acquire tacit knowledge is through one's own experiences. However, not everyone is exposed to the same situations, and not everyone may recognize important developmental opportunities. The category framework may provide some guidance to leaders and their mentors about the key areas of development in which experience-based learning appears to play an important role. Mentors or coaches can help identify relevant experiences and even create the opportunities to develop the knowledge. The category framework also serves to organize all the knowledge collected, both in story and question form, so that users have a way to select information that is most relevant to the issues they face and the areas of leadership that they wish to develop.

Finally, the TKML and its associated data are the main product of our work. The inventory is intended to assess the acquisition and use of tacit knowledge, but it may also provide a source for in-depth case analysis or self-assessment. Each inventory question consists of both a situation description and multiple response options. It contains much of the same information that exists in a leadership story but presents the information in a different format.

For each version of the inventory, we have response data from an expert sample. The expert profile summarizes the ratings given by experts to each response option, providing an indication of the level (i.e., how good or bad is the response option considered) and variability of experts' responses (i.e., how much do the experts agree in their ratings). These data can be used to score one's responses or to evaluate the expert opinions regarding each option. The data can be presented as the percentage of experts who rated each response option as good, bad, or neither good nor bad, allowing users to identify readily the expert solutions to the problem. These data could even be used to create expert rules of thumb about how to handle various situations.

The response data from leaders in our validation study of the TKML can be linked with effectiveness ratings in order to examine the response patterns of leaders who are viewed as more or less effective. An examination of these data may provide insight into the complexities of leadership. Leaders may observe that there may be no right answer or one best answer that applies in a situation. The best answer may depend on how the action is perceived. For example, a leader who endorses the option "Ignore a directive from your commanding officer in order to protect your soldiers" may be considered highly effective by his subordinates, but his endorsement of this option may be associated with a low effectiveness rating from his superior.

All of the above products are potentially useful for sharing the tacit knowledge that we have unveiled with other military leaders. They allow leaders to experience vicariously some of the important lessons of leadership and to assess their own level of tacit knowledge. The products can be applied to formalized classroom instruction, self-development, and on-the-job learning. In chapter 10, we consider some of the applications of the tacit knowledge work to training and development in general.

CHAPTER 10

Practical Implications

The ultimate goal of tacit knowledge research is to improve our understanding of what it takes to be a successful performer in a particular domain. We have addressed a number of performance domains thus far, with our most recent effort involving military leaders. From each of these efforts we gain increased support for the importance of tacit knowledge as well as new insights about the construct itself. The value of this work also lies in its potential applications to various real-world issues. We organize our discussion of the practical implications around three main applications: identification, development, and assessment.

IDENTIFICATION

One of the primary goals guiding much of our tacit knowledge research has been to identify what distinguishes individuals who are more successful from those who are less successful in a particular performance domain. In many domains, it may be extremely important to identify individuals who have acquired tacit knowledge about how to perform various tasks. If one needs a ride to the hospital during a snowstorm, one will be more likely to ask a friend from Vermont than a friend from Texas, assuming that the friends have equal driving records. This decision is based on the assumption that the friend from Vermont has learned something about driving in the snow from personal experience in such situations.

In a less extreme example, if a military organization wants to promote its best leaders to top levels of command, it will want to identify which individuals have the requisite knowledge, skills, and abilities. Often in such organizations, individuals already have been selected on the basis of some type of intelligence test and perhaps some formal knowledge test. Consequently, the variation among individuals on these measures may be minimal. The variation in performance, however, often appears to be quite large, a variation that can be attributed, in part, to the acquisition of tacit, experience-based knowledge. In other words, tacit knowledge accounts for some of the developed expertise that is acquired through actual everyday experiences.

Tacit Knowledge Tests

Measuring individual differences in the possession of tacit knowledge can be accomplished by using the types of tests we have described in this book. Tacit knowledge tests assess the amount of tacit knowledge one has acquired and one's ability to apply that knowledge to solving problems that are characteristic of those faced by individuals in the domain.

In chapter 7, we presented a methodology for developing tacit knowledge tests that can be applied to almost any performance domain. Identifying the tacit knowledge of a domain relies on a review of relevant literature and interviews with domain experts. In developing a tacit knowledge test, clear criteria are established regarding what is to be classified as tacit knowledge and what is not. Experts are relied upon throughout the process to ensure that the items continue to meet these criteria. Additional steps may be included to select items with the highest probability of measuring tacit knowledge that is characteristic of experience and of successful individuals in the domain. Of course, before a test is used to identify individuals who have more or less tacit knowledge, it should be subjected to a rigorous construct validation. It should be shown that higher test scores are indicative of better performance.

We already have developed tacit knowledge tests for several performance domains, including business management, sales, and military leadership. These tests have been demonstrated to have promising construct validity. The methods for developing tacit knowledge tests also can be applied to new domains, such as policing, patient care, and teamwork.

Tacit Knowledge Acquisition Skills

A second approach to identifying individuals who have the practical abilities to succeed in a domain is to assess their propensity to acquire and use tacit knowledge, or more generally, their ability to solve problems of a practical nature.

Seven metacognitive skills, or metacomponents, as mentioned in chapter 3, are considered important in problem solving (Sternberg, 1985a, 1986). These metacomponents help one plan what to do, monitor things as they are being done, and evaluate things after they are done. Examples of metacomponents are recognizing the existence of a problem, defining the nature of the problem, deciding on a strategy for solving the problem, monitoring the solution of the problem, and evaluating the solution after the problem is solved.

Sternberg (1985a, 1997a) also has proposed three cognitive processes, described in chapter 6, that underlie the acquisition of tacit knowledge. These are selective encoding, selective combination, and selective comparison.

The three processes of selective encoding, selective combination, and selective comparison are not viewed as independent processes. Instead, they are used interactively to maximize learning. An individual may be confronted with an overwhelming amount of information in a given situation and must decide not only what information to attend to, but also how to make sense of it. In order to determine how to deal with the situation, the individual must also be able to rely, to some extent, on prior knowledge related to the situation in order to respond in a timely and appropriate manner.

We often can identify these processes in action in the stories that individuals relate about their practical experiences. The following story told by a military leader about influencing subordinates' behaviors helps to illustrate these processes.

> I had a boss who routinely stayed at the office until 1900 hours each evening. The subordinates on down also stayed until after 1900 when they saw their superior's light go out. One day when I was on duty, I stopped in the superior's office and saw him with his feet on the desk, reading a newspaper and watching the news on TV. Since I had a good rapport with the superior, I asked what he was doing. He said, "I have six kids at home. This is my chance to unwind from the day and catch up on the news." I took him in my jeep and showed him that all the subordinate officers were still at work because he was still at work. He explained his behavior at the subsequent staff meeting and told the officers to close shop and go home at a reasonable time.

First, the battalion commander notices that everyone stays until after 1900 hours. He also notices that the boss's light is turned off at the same time (selective encoding). He associates the two occurrences and arrives at the conclusion that all the subordinates wait until the boss goes home before they leave (selective combination). Next, he observes that his boss has his feet up, is reading a newspaper, and is watching television (selective encoding). He recognizes that these activities together suggest that his boss is no longer working (selective combination) and, based on his past interaction with the boss (selective comparison), he decides to ask him about his behavior. He has learned through this process that a superior's behavior can have a substantial influence on subordinates.

The relevance of these three cognitive processes (selective encoding, selective combination, and selective comparison) to success is supported by the literature on expert–novice differences. Research on expertise suggests that experts take more time to analyze new problems before solving them than do novices; perceive large, meaningful patterns of information more readily than do novices; and are able to draw on prior knowledge in their domain better than are novices (Chi, Glaser, & Farr, 1988; Sternberg, 1996). Furthermore, when faced with unfamiliar problems, expert problem solvers search for and recognize previously overlooked relevant information (selective encoding), ways of combining information (selective combination), and connections between prior knowledge and the problem situation (selective comparison) (Davidson & Sternberg, 1998).

We are currently working on developing tests of these processes in the domains of military leadership and business management. The tests present rich, in-depth case studies, along the lines of a written in-basket test, and ask individuals to solve the problem presented in those cases. The examinees either are given a single prompt, asking them to develop a solution to the problem, or a set of question prompts directly targeting the use of metacognitive and knowledge acquisition skills. Responses are scored according to how well the individuals exhibit each of the processes in solving the problem as well as on the quality of their solutions. These scores can be compared with the performance on a traditional tacit knowledge test to assess whether individuals with more tacit knowledge exhibit more effective use of problem solving and knowledge acquisition skills. An abbreviated example question is shown in Table 9.

DEVELOPMENT

In addition to identifying individuals who either possess the requisite knowledge or show some propensity to acquire tacit knowledge, we can

---

TABLE 9. Prototype Question for Assessing Tacit Knowledge Acquisition Skills

TACIT KNOWLEDGE ACQUISITION SKILLS FOR MANAGEMENT

You are an executive vice president in the marketing division of Sherman Electronics, a company that sells audio and video supplies. You have been with the company since finishing college, having spent 13 years in a managerial role in human resources. After completing a weekend executive MBA program 2 years ago, you were offered and accepted a position as vice president of marketing at Sherman. You are responsible primarily for improving Sherman's market share and competitiveness. Sherman has been losing market share for its products steadily over the past 5 years. Sherman's strength in the past has been introducing new products before its competition, but now its product line seems to be three steps behind the leaders in a rapidly changing market. Since your position was previously in human resources, your knowledge of the latest audio and video products and technology is limited. You have a very busy schedule but cannot afford to lose your job if you or the company perform poorly.

Format A:

Write a response that describes what you would do in this situation and why.

Format B:

Answer the following questions with regard to the situation described above:

1. What do you see as the problem in this situation? *(problem recognition and definition)*
2. What would you do to address this problem? *(strategy formulation)*
3. What information did you use to formulate your strategy for addressing this problem *(information representation)*
   a. that is in the information provided above? *(selective encoding)*
   b. that you know from your past experience with this kind of situation? *(selective comparison)*
   c. Please rate on a 1 (low) to 3 (high) scale the importance of each of the pieces of information in items a and b above. *(selective combination)*
4. What additional human and/or material resources would you need, if any, to address this problem? *(resource allocation)*
5. How would you know if your proposed strategy is succeeding? *(strategy monitoring and evaluation)*

---

focus our efforts on developing people's tacit knowledge. That is, we can focus on enhancing performance by increasing the amount of tacit knowledge that an individual possesses. These efforts may involve directly teaching the lessons learned by more experienced and successful practitioners or may involve helping individuals to develop the skills needed to learn more effectively from their own experiences (Wagner, 1997).

In any domain, knowledge can be transmitted via "push" or "pull." By push, we mean that knowledge is delivered in a structured format from one source (e.g., instructor or training manual) to another (e.g., student or trainee). Knowledge of this form is typically preprocessed for the learner. It is in a form that can be readily communicated. Traditional classroom instruction relies on the push form of transmitting knowledge because it helps ensure that a standard set of knowledge is conveyed. In contrast, pull means that learners draw the knowledge from the environment as it is needed and have to process the information for themselves. We address these two methods, push and pull, in relation to the development of tacit knowledge.

Enhancing Tacit Knowledge Acquisition

One of the products of research on tacit knowledge is a body of knowledge that, for the most part, has been undervalued relative to its importance to success. This body of knowledge can be incorporated into training and development initiatives in order to share the lessons of experience with others. The tacit knowledge that is uncovered may be shared directly with others (e.g., by reading a story about someone's experience), or it may be used to help guide individuals to the types of situations that are conducive to acquiring relevant tacit knowledge. In considering these initiatives, we distinguish between formalized training programs, which typically have specified time frames and take place away from the actual performance setting; developmental activities, which typically occur in conjunction with actual performance; and self-development activities, which are performed by individuals on their own.

TRAINING PROGRAMS. Training programs range from short-term workshops to courses in formal institutional settings such as universities or training centers. Many organizations rely on formal training programs to improve the knowledge and skills of their employees. The importance of formal training is also demonstrated by the requirements of many employers that their employees have certain level of formal education. Most training programs are designed to improve generic knowledge and skills. The content of these programs typically is based on a body of widely recognized and accepted knowledge. However, these programs also may be used to facilitate the acquisition of the less openly conveyed tacit knowledge that is characteristic of successful performers in a domain.

There is reason to believe that incorporating tacit knowledge into training programs can enhance their effectiveness. Prescriptions for designing effective training programs include approaches such as building on a trainee's prior knowledge, using relevant and concrete examples, helping trainees to interpret their experiences, providing opportunities to apply general principles, and providing feedback (Campbell, 1988; Howell & Cooke, 1989). The tacit knowledge uncovered in a domain can provide a way of meeting many of these objectives.

Specific instances of tacit knowledge can be used to follow up on more general principles with concrete examples. The stories shared by experts can help individuals to reflect on their own experiences. The tacit knowledge can also provide opportunities to practice applying the lessons and receiving feedback. For example, individuals could be asked to solve a problem from a tacit knowledge inventory and then use the data from an expert response profile to evaluate their responses.

Various training methods have been used to impart the knowledge and skills of a domain. These methods include lectures, group discussions, cases, behavioral role modeling, and simulations. We briefly consider how tacit knowledge can be applied in using these different methods.

The lessons of experience can be taught directly by instructors to their students. Rules of thumb may be generated by using the tacit knowledge scenarios along with the responses of experts. For example, in a situation in which a boss has given his subordinate an unreasonable task to complete, the experts might agree that a good alternative is to let the boss know that the task requires resources beyond the subordinate's means. The experts might also agree that a poor alternative is to struggle with the task to show the boss that one is willing to work hard. This information can be used to form rules of thumb about how to handle an unreasonable request from a boss. Such rules of thumb can be taught explicitly to those with less experience in a domain.

The potential to teach tacit knowledge was demonstrated in a program of research with children (Gardner, Krechevsky, Sternberg, & Okagaki, 1994; Sternberg, Okagaki, & Jackson, 1990). The project, called the Practical Intelligence for Schools Project, involved a joint collaboration between researchers at Yale and Harvard, with the Harvard team led by Howard Gardner (Williams et al., 1996). The goal of this program was to teach children practical school-survival skills, such as how to study for different types of tests, how to allocate time in doing homework, how to decide what things can and cannot be said to teachers, and figuring out how to get along with classmates. Research on the effectiveness of this program has found that it improves performance in reading, writing, homework assignments, and test taking (Sternberg et al., 1990).

Because tacit knowledge is characterized as context-specific knowledge, that is, it includes information about aspects of particular situations and appropriate action to take in those situations, it may be conveyed more appropriately through the rich stories that individuals express about the lessons they have learned. Cases describe events that occur over an extended period of time or in a specific incident. Cases are commonly used as a method of teaching analytical skills, but they also can help to develop practical problem-solving skills. The cases from tacit knowledge research may be particularly useful because they represent situations that successful individuals considered important to their development. Individuals can be asked to evaluate the cases individually or in groups. They can assess the situation, evaluate the course of action taken, and assess the consequences of the action. They can consider what they might have done differently in the situation and what alternative outcomes might have resulted.

The tacit knowledge scenarios can also be developed into behavioral role-playing scenarios or simulations. Behavioral role modeling is a method of training in which trainees observe an individual demonstrating target behaviors and then are given an opportunity to practice the target behaviors. Feedback generally is provided by a trainer, by other trainees, or by having the trainee examine a videotape of his or her behavior. Behavioral role modeling is most effective for training concrete behaviors and thus has potential for developing tacit, procedural knowledge. The tacit knowledge scenarios could be presented, perhaps on videotape, to trainees, who subsequently would be presented with a new situation, similar to that in the videotape, and asked to role-play how they would respond to the situation. Some reviews of the training literature suggest that behavioral role modeling is one of the most effective methods for developing practical behaviors (Burke & Day, 1986; Latham, 1988).

Finally, incorporation of tacit knowledge into training programs can be taken a step further by developing simulations of actual work situations. Simulations are similar to cases in that trainees may have to solve a presented problem, but in simulations the stimuli are designed to be more realistic and the individual is more accountable for his or her action. The advantage of simulations over actual experiences is that feedback can be provided immediately. For example, Reichert and Dorner (1988) constructed a cold storage depot simulation in which participants could employ up to 100 interventions in an effort to keep the depot operating after an automated control system had purportedly failed. Participants could be told immediately whether or not their chosen strategy was effective. In reality, the consequences of one's actions may not be known for some time.

The products of tacit knowledge research again are useful because they suggest situations that can provide added value in a simulation. Additionally, simulated exercises may help individuals to acquire their own tacit knowledge. That is, in working through the simulation, individuals may learn what strategies are more or less effective in what types of situations. There is increasing evidence that simulations are effective for developing practical competencies (Keys & Wolfe, 1990; Thornton & Cleveland, 1990).

DEVELOPMENTAL ACTIVITIES. Perhaps more effective than any of the training methods describe above for increasing tacit knowledge is actual on-the-job experience. Managers report, for instance, that much of what they really need in order to know to do their jobs they learned from experience (Wagner & Sternberg, 1985). In fact, learning from experience is one of the defining features of tacit knowledge. Studies of the origin of important practical knowledge and skills of managers indicate that learning from experience plays a greater role than does formal training (Davies & Easterby-Smith, 1984; McCall, Lombardo, & Morrison, 1988). Learning from experience is facilitated when the situations are diverse and challenging and provide feedback. Learning from experience also can be facilitated through special assignments, job rotation programs, formal mentoring, and systematic after-action reviews (Druckman, Singer, & Van Cott, 1997).

Individuals can also improve their tacit knowledge through self-development activities. These activities can take a form similar to formal training activities, such as reading textbooks, completing self-assessment tools, and engaging in simulations. Alternatively, the activities may be aimed at facilitating experiential learning. For example, individuals may seek out opportunities on their own to obtain new experiences. They may focus more attention on situations that are relatively novel as potential sources of development.

Developing the Practical Abilities to Acquire Tacit Knowledge

Even when efforts are used to facilitate the learning experience, some individuals may acquire tacit knowledge more effectively than others. We already discussed several processes believed to underlie the successful acquisition of tacit knowledge. In addition to identifying these processes through testing, it may be possible to develop methods of promoting the development and use of these skills.

By understanding why some individuals learn more effectively from their experiences than others, we can teach people to be more sensitive to the lessons of experience. Individuals, for example, can be given strategies to help them selectively encode, selectively combine, and selectively compare information. Teaching these strategies could entail providing examples in which the relevant information is highlighted, showing charts or figures that illustrate how the information is combined, and explaining how the new information is related to prior knowledge. Individuals could also be given question prompts to practice using in solving new and unfamiliar problems.

In a study by Okagaki, Sternberg, and Wagner (cited in Sternberg et al., 1993), participants were given different cues to help them acquire tacit knowledge. The participants were assigned to one of five conditions, two control and three experimental conditions. In all conditions, the participants were given a pretest and a posttest of the tacit knowledge test for salespeople. In addition, in some conditions participants completed a tacit knowledge acquisition task in which they took the role of a personnel manager whose job was to read the transcripts of three job interviews and evaluate the candidates for a sales position in the company.

In the first control group, participants completed the pre- and posttests without intervention. In the second control group, participants were given a tacit knowledge acquisition task without any cues. In the first experimental group, participants were given the task with cues to help them selectively encode. Specifically, relevant information was highlighted and a relevant rule of thumb provided. In the second experimental group, participants were given the task with cues to aid selective combination. Relevant information was highlighted, a rule of thumb provided, and a note-taking sheet given to help participants combine the information. In the third experimental group, participants were given the acquisition task with selective comparison cues. Again, relevant information was highlighted and a rule of thumb provided, but in addition, participants were given an evaluation of the situation made by a previous salesperson.

The researchers found that for participants who completed the acquisition task, those in the control group (with no cues) performed the worst in terms of their accuracy in identifying relevant information from the transcripts (Sternberg, Wagner, & Okagaki, 1993). Among the experimental groups, the selective combination group performed the best. In terms of pretest–posttest difference scores on the tacit knowledge test, the control group with no task performed the worst. In the groups with the acquisition task, the selective encoding and selective combination groups showed the most gain in test scores. The selective comparison cueing did not have an effect on scores. These findings suggest that prompting individuals to selectively encode and selectively combine information can enhance the acquisition of tacit knowledge.

ASSESSMENT

In addition to identification and development, tacit knowledge can be used as a basis for assessing one's level of developed expertise. In other words, tacit knowledge may be a useful indicator of the level of performance one has achieved.

Performance criteria are used to make salary and promotion decisions, to provide feedback and foster development, and to assess the effectiveness of selection and training efforts. Performance criteria include performance appraisal ratings, production rates, turnover and absences, job level and salary, performance on work sample tests, and job knowledge tests (Borman, 1991).

Performance ratings are the most commonly employed and the most researched method of assessment (Ilgen, Barnes-Farrell, & McKellin, 1993; Landy & Farr, 1980). Typically, another source (e.g., peers, supervisors, subordinates) rates an individual's performance, although self-ratings are sometimes used, on dimensions ranging from overall effectiveness to specific behavioral incidents (e.g., wearing loose clothing when operating a lathe). The behaviorally anchored rating scale (BARS), for example, asks the rater to compare observed behaviors with behavioral anchors on a rating scale (Bernardin & Smith, 1981). Of course, ratings are problematic whatever their format because they rely on the judgment of other people, some of whom may have limited contact with the person being rated (e.g., supervisors), have limited experience making performance evaluations (e.g., subordinates and peers), or have biases in the way they view others or themselves.

Objective criteria, such as absences, salary, sales, or production rates, also may be used to assess performance. Although they do not suffer many of the perceptual biases associated with ratings, there may be biases in terms of what these measures indicate. For example, someone who is absent because of illness may make up for lost time by working overtime. Likewise, salary may depend on one's tenure with the organization or on market values, not necessarily on merit. Objective criteria also typically assess a very limited aspect of performance, such as the number of publications rather than the quality of those works.

Work sample tests assess performance on a subset of the actual tasks the individual performs as part of the job. This method of assessing performance also has limitations, primarily because it assesses maximal rather than typical performance. That is, work sample tests measure what an individual can do rather than what that person will do. Work sample tests, however, do provide opportunities to observe performance directly, which may be particularly useful when potential raters do not have such opportunities, as, for example, in assessing the performance of a field technician. Work sample tests are more commonly employed in assessing the effectiveness of training than in assessing job performance (Borman, 1991).

Job knowledge tests typically assess the technical, task-oriented aspects of performance (e.g., how to perform a safety check on a piece of machinery). Like work sample tests, they are more commonly used to assess training effectiveness, and generally they are viewed as measures of maximal rather than typical performance.

Unlike traditional knowledge tests, tacit knowledge tests are more characteristic of typical than of maximal performance measures. There is no one right answer to a question, but there may in fact be multiple good responses. Tacit knowledge tests measure procedural rather than declarative knowledge, and in particular, procedural knowledge of a tacit nature. As such, they measure what an individual considers to be the best action to take in a given situation, not just his or her abstract knowledge of general rules and procedures. Tacit knowledge tests also measure more than task proficiency – they assess one's interpersonal and intrapersonal effectiveness as well.

Unlike performance ratings, which may be based on a limited set of observations, tacit knowledge tests measure an individual's response to a variety of situations that are representative of the performance domain. Some researchers have considered situational judgment tests, which are similar in format and development to tacit knowledge tests, to be low-fidelity simulations (Motowidlo et al., 1990). In this sense, tacit knowledge tests may be viewed as small-scale work sample tests. That is, tacit knowledge tests assess how an individual may respond in a set of real-world situations.

Borman (1991) suggested that a performance criterion should assess one or more important performance requirements and, in combination with other criteria, should provide comprehensive coverage of the performance domain. We agree with Borman (1991) that no single measure is likely to fully capture the performance domain, but tacit knowledge tests measure an important aspect of performance – that is, experience-based, practical knowledge. In combination with other measures (e.g., supervisor ratings), tacit knowledge tests may provide a more comprehensive assessment of an individual's performance. Of course, research is needed to determine the value of tacit knowledge tests in assessing performance.

SUMMARY

The research we have reviewed in the preceding chapters supports the value of tacit knowledge for purposes related to identification, development, and assessment. Tacit knowledge tests have been shown to distinguish effectively individuals who are more successful from those who are less successful in a variety of domains. Currently, we are working also to identify individual differences in the skills that support the acquisition of tacit knowledge. This important aspect of performance can also be improved through training and development initiatives. The tacit knowledge in a domain can be brought to light through interviews with domain experts and shared with those with less experience. The tacit knowledge can be taught directly or can be used to develop valuable training tools, such as behavioral role modeling scenarios and simulations, that have a clear basis in actual performance. Alternatively, efforts can be made to facilitate learning from experience. Knowledge that is acquired on one's own likely will have greater relevance to one's personal goals and be applicable to the situations one encounters. The use of job rotation, special assignments, action reviews, and the like offers additional support to make sure that individuals are exposed to critical learning experiences and that they learn effectively from those experiences. Of course, these support systems may not be readily available in all situations, and there may be some individuals who still do not effectively learn the lessons of experience. Therefore, understanding and promoting the use of skills that support the acquisition of tacit knowledge, which we discussed earlier, may offer a promising direction for developing one aspect of practical intelligence. Finally, tacit knowledge may add a new dimension in the assessment of performance. It provides an indication of the amount of practical expertise one has developed, and thus how successful one is in one's performance domain.

CHAPTER 11

Conclusions

Over 25 years ago, McClelland (1973) questioned the validity of cognitive ability testing for predicting real-world criteria such as job performance, arguing in favor of competency tests that would more closely
reflect job performance itself. Subsequent reviews of the literature on
the predictive validity of intelligence tests suggest that McClelland
may have been pessimistic about their validity. Individual differences
in intelligence test performance account for, on average, between 4%
and 25% of the variance in real-world criteria such as job performance
(Barrett & Depinet, 1991; Hunter & Hunter, 1984; Schmidt & Hunter,
1998; Wigdor & Garner, 1982). Nevertheless, these findings indicate
that between 75% and 96% of the variance in real-world criteria such as
job performance cannot be accounted for by individual differences in
intelligence test scores. The emerging literature on practical intelligence and similar constructs, such as social and emotional intelligence,
is a belated response to McClelland's call for new methods to assess
practical abilities. The literature and research reviewed in this volume
provide several sources of evidence to support a distinction between
academic and practical intelligence.

First, the distinction between academic and practical intelligence is
entrenched in the conception of intelligence held by laypeople and
researchers alike. In addition to evidence provided by studies of
implicit theories of intelligence (Sternberg et al., 1981), analyses of
researchers' descriptions of the nature of intelligence suggest a prominent role for practical intelligence. Seventy years ago, the editors of the
Journal of Educational Psychology convened a symposium at which
prominent psychological theorists of the day were asked to describe
what they imagined intelligence to be and what they considered the
most crucial next steps in research. In a replication, Sternberg and

Detterman (1986) posed the same questions to contemporary prominent theorists. An analysis of the responses of both cohorts of intelligence theorists revealed concerns about practical aspects of intelligence
(Sternberg & Berg, 1986). For example, among the 42 crucial next steps
that were mentioned by one or more theorists from either cohort,
studying real-life manifestations of intelligence was among the most
frequently mentioned next steps of both the contemporary researchers
and the original respondents. A distinction between academic and
practical aspects of intelligence also is supported by older adults' perception of age-related changes in their ability to think and solve problems (Williams, Denney, & Schadler, 1983). Three-fourths of the older
adults sampled believed that their ability to solve practical problems
increased over the years, despite the fact that performance on academic
tasks begins to decline on completion of formal schooling.

A second source of evidence to support a distinction between academic and practical intelligence is provided by studies in which participants were assessed on both academic and practical tasks. These
studies consistently find little or no correlation between performance
on the two kinds of tasks. The results of IQ tests and similar measures
have been found to be unrelated to the order-filling performance of
milk processing plant workers (Scribner, 1986); the degree to which
racetrack handicappers employ a complex and effective algorithm
(Ceci & Liker, 1986, 1988); the complexity of strategies used in computer-simulated roles such as city manager (Dörner & Kreuzig, 1983;
Dörner et al., 1983); or the accuracy with which grocery shoppers identified quantities that provided the best value (Lave et al., 1984;
Murtaugh, 1985). This research has shown that the performance of both
children and adults is susceptible to the context in which abilities are
measured. When problems are presented in a familiar context, whether
that context is school or work, individuals appear more intelligent
(Carraher et al., 1985; Roazzi, 1987).

A third source of support for the importance of practical abilities
comes from theories of managerial performance. Rational theories that
are based on conventional notions of how people solve problems
(Kepner & Tregoe, 1965; Plunkett & Hale, 1982) do not accurately represent the problem solving of experienced and successful managers.
These observations led theorists to describe managerial problem solving as nonlinear, convoluted, and action-oriented (McCall & Kaplan,
1985; Mintzberg et al., 1976). Furthermore, knowledge of how to solve
problems can be characterized as tacit, and it may only enter into con-

scious awareness through reflection (Schön, 1983). The recognition that rational models of managerial problem solving do not explain the behavior of successful practitioners suggests that alternative approaches are needed to identify the practical abilities underlying performance.

Finally, the research on tacit knowledge described throughout this volume offers an approach to understanding practical intelligence. Over the course of studies with academic psychologists (Wagner, 1987; Wagner & Sternberg, 1985), business managers (Wagner & Sternberg, 1990), salespersons (Wagner et al., 1994), U.S. Air Force recruits (Eddy, 1988), and military leaders (Hedlund et al., 1999), we have found that tacit knowledge offers insight into the practical abilities associated with success.

Several conclusions can be drawn from this program of research. First, these studies showed that tacit knowledge exists in the stories successful practitioners share about the lessons they learned in the process of performing their respective roles. These stories provide rich insights about the practically oriented knowledge that practitioners are often unaware that they have acquired. Second, we showed that tacit knowledge can be measured through instruments that take into account the procedural and context-specific nature of tacit knowledge. Third, using such instruments, we have found that individuals who exhibit the ability to acquire and use tacit knowledge are more effective in their respective performance domains. Fourth, tacit knowledge helps to explain some of the additional variance in performance that is not accounted for by measures of general cognitive ability. Fifth, although the acquisition of tacit knowledge may be influenced, to some extent, by g and by amount of experience, tacit knowledge inventories are not simply new measures of these constructs. Finally, tacit knowledge generally appears to be a singular construct within domains, but the content of tacit knowledge varies across domains. In other words, tacit knowledge appears to reflect a single underlying ability, which we label practical intelligence. But this underlying ability is not sufficient for performing well on domain-specific tacit knowledge tests. Experience in a particular domain is important in the acquisition of tacit knowledge.

On the basis of consistent findings that tacit knowledge contributes to our understanding performance in a variety of domains, we discussed a number of potential ways to promote the acquisition and use of tacit knowledge. Numerous insights and products are obtained through the process of studying tacit knowledge. The categories of tacit knowledge within a domain, for example, offer insight into the experiences that provide important developmental opportunities. The products, such as the stories and the inventory questions, can be used to share the tacit knowledge with other practitioners. The tacit knowledge research also suggests that training activities, such as case studies and simulations, may be valuable ways to impart experience-based tacit knowledge and to provide opportunities to acquire new practical knowledge. Although these approaches may encourage the acquisition and use of tacit knowledge in rapidly changing, complex environments, it may be more effective in the long run to identify and develop ways to help individuals to learn better from their everyday experiences.

Up to this point, our research efforts have been targeted primarily at understanding and measuring practical intelligence. For the present and foreseeable future, we believe that the most viable approach to increasing the variance accounted for in real-world criteria such as job performance is to supplement existing intelligence and aptitude tests with selection of additional measures based on new constructs such as practical intelligence. Although we are excited by the promise of a new generation of measures of practical intelligence, we are the first to admit that existing evidence for the new measures does not yet match that available for traditional cognitive-academic ability tests. However, a substantial amount of evidence indicates that performance on measures of practical intelligence is related to a wide variety of criterion measures of real-world performance but is relatively unrelated to traditional measures of academic intelligence. Consequently, use of both kinds of measures explains more variance in performance than reliance on either kind alone. Intelligence is not only academic but also practical.

References

Ackerman, P. (1987). Individual differences in skill learning: An integration of psychometric and information processing perspectives. *Psychological Bulletin, 102,* 3–17.

Ackerman, P. (1994). Intelligence, attention, and learning: Maximal and typical performance. In D. K. Detterman (Ed.), *Current topics in human intelligence: Theories of intelligence* (Vol. 4, pp. 1–27). Norwood, NJ: Ablex.

Ackerman, P. L., & Heggestad, E. D. (1997). Intelligence, personality, and interests: Evidence for overlapping traits. *Psychological Bulletin, 121,* 219–245.

Albert, K. J. (Ed.) (1980). *Handbook of business problem solving.* New York: McGraw-Hill.

Aldwin, C. M., Sutton, K. J., Chiara, G., & Spiro, A. (1996). Age differences in stress, coping, and appraisal: Findings from the normative aging study. *Journal of Gerontology: Psychological Sciences, 51B,* 178–188.

Anastasi, A., & Urbina, S. (1997). *Psychological testing* (7th ed.). Upper Saddle River, NJ: Prentice-Hall.

Anderson, J. R. (1983). *The architecture of cognition.* Cambridge, MA: Harvard University Press.

Anderson, J. R. (1986). Knowledge compilation: The general learning mechanism. In R. S. Michalski, J. G. Carbonell, & T. M. Mitchell (Eds.), *Machine learning: An artificial intelligence approach.* Los Altos, CA: Kaufman.

Anderson, J. R. (1987). Skill acquisition: Compilation of weak-method problem solutions. *Psychological Review, 94,* 192–210.

Anderson, J. R. (1993). *Rules of the mind.* Hillsdale, NJ: Erlbaum.

Archer, D. (1980). *How to expand your social intelligence quotient.* New York: M. Evans.

Archer, D., & Akert, R. M. (1980). The encoding of meaning: A test of three theories of social interaction. *Sociological Inquiry, 50,* 393–419.

Argyris, C. (1991). Teaching smart people how to learn. *Harvard Business Review, 69,* 99–109.

Arlin, P. K. (1990). Wisdom: The art of problem finding. In R. J. Sternberg (Ed.), *Wisdom: Its nature, origins, and development* (pp. 230–243). New York: Cambridge University Press.

Bäckman, L., & Dixon, R. A. (1992). Psychological compensation: A theoretical framework. *Psychological Bulletin, 112,* 259–283.

Baltes, P. B. (1987). Theoretical propositions of life-span developmental psychology: On the dynamics between growth and decline. *Developmental Psychology, 23,* 611–626.

Baltes, P. B. (1993). The aging mind: Potentials and limits. *The Gerontologist, 33,* 580–594.

Baltes, P. B. (1997). On the incomplete architecture of human ontogeny. *American Psychologist, 52,* 366–380.

Baltes P. B. (in press). *Wisdom: The orchestration of mind and virtue.* Boston: Blackwell.

Baltes, P. B., & Baltes, M. M. (1990). Psychological perspectives on successful aging: A model of selective optimization with compensation. In P. B. Baltes & M. M. Baltes (Eds.), *Successful aging: Perspectives from the behavioral sciences* (pp. 1–34). Cambridge, U.K.: Cambridge University Press.

Baltes, P. B., Dittmann-Kohli, F., & Dixon, R. A. (1984). New perspectives on the development of intelligence in adulthood: Toward a dual-process conception and a model of selective optimization with compensation. In P. B. Baltes & O. G. Brim (Eds.), *Life-span development and behavior* (Vol 6., pp. 33–76). New York: Academic Press.

Baltes, P. B., & Lindenberger, U. (1988). On the range of cognitive plasticity in old age as a function of experience: 15 years of intervention research. *Behavior Therapy, 19,* 282–300.

Baltes, P. B., & Smith, J. (1987, August). *Toward a psychology of wisdom and its ontogenesis.* Paper presented at the Ninety-Fifth Annual Convention of the American Psychological Association, New York.

Baltes, P. B., & Smith, J. (1990). Toward a psychology of wisdom and its ontogenesis. In R. J. Sternberg (Ed.), *Wisdom: Its nature, origins, and development* (pp. 87–120). New York: Cambridge University Press.

Baltes, P. B., Smith, J., & Staudinger, U. (1992). Wisdom and successful aging. In T. B. Sonderegger (Ed.), *Psychology and aging* (pp. 123–167). Lincoln, NE: University of Nebraska Press.

Baltes, P. B., Sowarka, D., & Kliegl, R. (1989). Cognitive training research on fluid intelligence in old age: What can older adults achieve by themselves? *Psychology and Aging, 4,* 217–221.

Baltes, P. B., & Staudinger, U. M. (1993). The search for a psychology of wisdom. *Current Directions in Psychological Science, 2,* 75–80.

Baltes, P. B., Staudinger, U. M., Maercker, A., & Smith, J. (1995). People nominated as wise: A comparative study of wisdom-related knowledge. *Psychology and Aging, 10,* 155–166.

Baltes, P. B., & Willis, S. L. (1982). Plasticity and enhancement of intellectual functioning in old age: Penn State's Adult Development and Enrichment Project (ADEPT). In F. I. M. Clark & S. E. Trehub (Eds.), *Aging and cognitive processes* (pp. 353–389). New York: Plenum.

Band, E. B., & Weisz, J. R. (1988). How to feel better when it feels bad: Children's perspective on coping with everyday stress. *Developmental Psychology, 24,* 247–253.

Bandura, A. (1986). *Social foundations of thought and action.* Englewood Cliffs, NJ: Prentice-Hall.

Barker, R. G. (Ed.) (1978). *Habitats, environments, and human behavior.* San Francisco: Jossey-Bass.

Barnard, C. I. (1938). *The functions of the executive.* Cambridge, MA: Harvard University Press.

Barnard, C. I. (1968). *The functions of the executive.* Cambridge, MA: Harvard University Press.

Barnes, M. L., & Sternberg, R. J. (1989). Social intelligence and decoding of non-verbal clues. *Intelligence, 13,* 263–287.

Bar-On, R. (1997). *The Emotional Quotient Inventory (EQI): Technical Manual.* Toronto: Multi-Health Systems.

Barrett, G. V., & Depinet, R. L. (1991). A reconsideration of testing for competence rather than for intelligence. *American Psychologist, 46,* 1012–1024.

Barrett, G. V., Mihal, W. L., Panek, P. E., Sterns, H. L., & Alexander, R. A. (1977). Information processing skills predictive of accident involvement for younger and older commercial drivers. *Industrial Gerontology, 4,* 173–182.

Barrett, G. V., & Watkins, S. K., (1986). Word familiarity and cardiovascular health as determinants of age-related recall differences. *Journal of Gerontology, 41,* 222–224.

Bass, B. M. (1985). *Leadership and performance beyond expectations.* New York: Free Press.

Bass, B. M. (1990). *Bass and Stogdill's handbook of leadership: Theory, research, and managerial applications.* New York: Free Press.

Bass, B. M., & Avolio, B. J. (1990). The implications of transactional and transformational leadership for individual, team, and organizational development. In W. Pasmore & R. W. Woodman (Eds.), *Research in organizational change and development* (Vol. 4). Greenwich, CT: JAI Press.

Bass, B. M., & Avolio, B. J. (1993). Transformation leadership: A response to critiques. In M. M. Chemers & R. Ayman (Eds.), *Leadership theory and research* (pp. 49–80). San Diego: Academic Press.

Basseches, J. (1984). *Dialectical thinking and adult development.* Norwood, NJ: Ablex.

Bastick, T. (1982). *Intuition: How we think and act.* New York: John Wiley & Sons Inc.

Beck, A. T., Epstein, N., Brown, G., & Steer, R. A. (1988). An inventory for measuring clinical anxiety: Psychometric properties. *Journal of Consulting and Clinical Psychology, 56,* 893–897.

Beck, A. T., Ward, C. H., Mendelson, M., Mock, J., & Erbaugh, J. (1961). An inventory for measuring depression. *Archives of General Psychiatry, 4,* 561–571.

Belmont, J. N., & Butterfield, E. C. (1969). The relations of short-term memory to development and intelligence. In L. Lipsitt & H. Reese (Eds.), *Advances in child development and behavior* (Vol. 4, pp. 30–83). New York: Academic Press.

Bennett, G. K., Seashore, H. G., & Wesman, A. G. (1974). *The Differential Aptitude Tests* (Form T). New York: The Psychological Corporation.

Bennis, W., & Nanus, B. (1985). *Leaders: The strategies for taking charge.* New York: Harper & Row.

Berg, C. A. (1989). Knowledge of strategies for dealing with everyday problems from childhood through adolescence. *Developmental Psychology, 25,* 607–618.

Berg, C. A. (1992). Perspectives for viewing intellectual development through-out the life course. In R. J. Sternberg & C. A. Berg (Eds.), *Intellectual Development* (pp. 1–15). New York: Cambridge University Press.

Berg, C. A. (in press). The development of adult intelligence. In R. J. Sternberg (Ed.), *Handbook of intelligence*. New York: Cambridge University Press.

Berg, C. A., & Calderone, K. (1994). The role of problem interpretations in understanding the development of everyday problem solving. In R. J. Sternberg & R. K. Wagner (Eds.), *Mind in context* (pp. 105–132). New York: Cambridge University Press.

Berg, C. A., Calderone, K. & Gunderson, M. (1990, November). *Strategies young and old adults use to solve their own everyday problems.* Paper presented at the meeting of the Gerontological Society, Boston, MA.

Berg, C. A., Hertzog, C., & Hunt, E. (1982). Age differences in the speed of mental rotation. *Developmental Psychology, 18,* 95–107.

Berg, C. A., & Klaczynski, P. (1996). Practical intelligence and problem solving: Searching for perspective. In F. Blanchard-Fields & T. M. Hess (Eds.), *Perspectives on cognition in adulthood and aging* (pp. 323–357). New York: McGraw-Hill.

Berg, C. A., Klaczynski, P., Calderone, K. S., & Strough, J. (1994). Adult age differences in cognitive strategies: Adaptive or deficient. In J. Sinnott (Ed.), *Interdisciplinary handbook of adult lifespan learning* (pp. 371–388). Westport, CT: Greenwood Press.

Berg, C. A., & Sternberg, R. J. (1985). A triarchic theory of intellectual development during adulthood. *Developmental Review, 5,* 334–370.

Berg, C. A., Strough, J., Calderone, K., Sansone, C., & Weir, C. (1998). The role of problem definitions in understanding age and context effects on strategies for solving everyday problems. *Psychology and Aging, 13,* 29–44.

Bernadin, H. J., & Smith, P. C. (1981). A clarification of some issues regarding the development and use of behaviorally anchored rating scales (BARS). *Journal of Applied Psychology, 65,* 458–463.

Berry, J. W. (1974). Radical cultural relativism and the concept of intelligence. In J. W. Berry & P. R. Dasen (Eds.), *Culture and cognition: Readings in cross-cultural psychology* (pp. 225–229). London: Methuen.

Berry, J. W. (1984). Towards a universal psychology of cognitive competence. In P. S. Fry (Ed.), *Changing conceptions of intelligence and intellectual functioning* (pp. 35–61). Amsterdam: North-Holland.

Berry, J. W., & Irvine, S. H. (1986). Bricolage: Savages do it daily. In R. J. Sternberg & R. K. Wagner (Eds.), *Practical intelligence: Nature and origins of competence in the everyday world* (pp. 271–306). New York: Cambridge University Press.

Bickhard, M. H. (1978). The nature of developmental stage. *Human Development, 21,* 217–233.

Binet, A., & Simon, T. (1905). Méthodes nouvelles pour le diagnostic du niveau intellectuel des anormaux. *L'Année psychologique, 11,* 191–336.

Binet, A., & Simon, T. (1916). *The development of intelligence in children.* Baltimore: Williams & Wilkins. (Originally published in 1905).

Birren, J. E., & Fisher, L. M. (1990). The elements of wisdom: Overview and integration. In R. J. Sternberg (Ed.), *Wisdom: Its nature, origins, and development* (pp. 317–332). New York: Cambridge University Press.

Blanchard-Fields, F. (1986). Reasoning and social dilemmas varying in emotional saliency: An adult developmental perspective. *Psychology and Aging, 1,* 325–333.

Blanchard-Fields, F. (1994). Age differences in causal attributions from an adult developmental perspective. *Journal of Gerontology: Psychological Sciences, 49,* 43–51.

Blanchard-Fields, F., Jahnke, H. C., & Camp, C. (1995). Age differences in problem-solving style: The role of emotional salience. *Psychology & Aging, 10,* 173–180.

Blanchard-Fields, F., & Norris, L. (1994). Causal attributions from adolescence through adulthood: Age differences, ego level, and generalized response style. *Aging Neuropsychology & Cognition, 1,* 67–86.

Bloom, B. S. (Ed.) (1985). *Developing talent in young people.* New York: Ballantine.

Bogen, J. E. (1975). Some educational aspects of hemispheric specialization. *UCLA Educator, 17,* 24–32.

Borman, W. C. (1991). Job behavior, performance, and effectiveness. In M. D. Dunnette & L. M. Hough (Eds.), *Handbook of industrial and organizational psychology* (Vol. 2, pp. 271–326). Palo Alto, CA: Consulting Psychologists Press, Inc.

Bowers, K. S., Regehr, G., Balthazard, C., & Parker, K. (1990). Intuition in the context of discovery. *Cognitive Psychology, 22,* 72–110.

Boyatzis, R. E. (1982). *The competent manager.* New York: John Wiley & Sons Inc.

Brand, C. (1996). *The g factor: General intelligence and its implications.* Chichester, England: John Wiley & Sons Inc.

Brandtstaedter, J., & Greve, W. (1994). The aging self: Stabilizing and protective processes. *Developmental Review, 14,* 52–80.

Bray, D. W. (1982). The Assessment Center and the study of lives. *American Psychologist, 37,* 180–189.

Broadbent, D. E., & Aston, B. (1978). Human control of a simulated economic system. *Ergonomics, 21,* 1035–1043.

Broadbent, D. E., Fitzgerald, P., & Broadbent, M. H. P. (1986). Implicit and explicit knowledge in the control of complex systems. *British Journal of Psychology, 77,* 33–50.

Broca, P. P. (1861). Nouvelle observation d'aphemie produite par une lésion de la moitié postérieure des deuxième et troisième circonvolutions frontales gauches. *Bulletins de la Societé Anatomique de Paris, 36,* 398–407.

Bronfenbrenner, U., & Ceci, S. J. (1994). Nature-nurture reconceptualized in developmental perspective: A bioecological model. *Psychological Review, 101,* 568–586.

Brown, A. L. (1975). The development of memory: Knowing, knowing about knowing, and knowing how to know. In H. W. Reese (Ed.), *Advances in child development and behavior* (Vol. 10, pp. 103–152). New York: Academic Press.

Brown, L. T., & Anthony, R. G. (1990). Continuing the search for social intelligence. *Personality and Individual Differences, 11,* 463–470.

Bruner, J. S., Shapiro, D., & Tagiuri, R. (1958). The meaning of traits in isolation and in combination. In R. Tagiuri & I. Petrollo (Eds.), *Person perception and interpersonal behavior* (pp. 277–288). Stanford, CA: Stanford University Press.

Bryman, A. (1996). Leadership in organizations. In S. R. Clegg & C. Hardy (Eds.), *Handbook of organization studies* (pp. 276–292). London: Sage Publications, Inc.

Burke, M. J., & Day, R. R. (1986). A cumulative study of the effectiveness of managerial training. *Journal of Applied Psychology, 71,* 232–246.

Campbell, D. T, & Fiske, D. W. (1959). Convergent and discriminant validation by the multitrait-multimethod matrix. *Psychological Bulletin, 56,* 81–105.

Campbell, J. P. (1988). Training design for performance improvement. In J. P. Campbell, R. J. Campbell, et al. (Eds.), *Productivity in organizations* (pp. 177–216). San Francisco: Jossey-Bass.

Cantor, N. (1978). *Prototypicality and personality judgments.* Unpublished doctoral dissertation, Stanford University.

Cantor, N. (1990). From thought to behavior: "Having" and "doing" in the study of personality and cognition. *American Psychologist, 45,* 735–750.

Cantor, N., & Harlow, R. (1994). Social intelligence and personality: Flexible life-task pursuit. In R. J. Sternberg & P. Ruzgis (Eds.), *Personality and intelligence* (pp. 137–168). Cambridge, U.K.: Cambridge University Press.

Cantor, N., & Kihlstrom, J. F. (1987). *Personality and social intelligence.* Englewood Cliffs, NJ: Prentice-Hall.

Cantor, N., & Kihlstrom, J. F. (1989). Social intelligence and cognitive assessments of personality. In R. S. Wyer & T. K. Srull (Eds.), *Advances in Social Cognition* (Vol. 2, pp. 1–59). Hillsdale, NJ: Erlbaum.

Cantor, N., Norem, J. K., Niedenthal, P. M., Langston, C. A., & Brower, A. M. (1987). Life tasks, self-concept ideals, and cognitive strategies in a life transition. *Journal of Personality and Social Psychology, 53,* 1178–1191.

Carraher, T. N., Carraher, D., & Schliemann, A. D. (1985). Mathematics in the streets and in schools. *British Journal of Developmental Psychology, 3,* 21–29.

Carroll, J. B. (1993). *Human cognitive abilities: A survey of factor-analytic studies.* New York: Cambridge University Press.

Caruso, D. R., & Mayer, J. D. (1997). *A quick scale of empathy.* Unpublished manuscript.

Cattell, J. M. (1890). Mental tests and measurements. *Mind, 15,* 373–380.

Cattell, R. B. (1940). A culture free intelligence test. *Journal of Educational Psychology, 31,* 161–180.

Cattell, R. B. (1971). *Abilities: Their structure, growth and action.* Boston: Houghton Mifflin.

Cattell, R. B., & Cattell, H. E. P. (1963). *Test of g: Culture Fair, Scale 3.* Champaign, IL: Institute for Personality and Ability Testing.

Cattell, R. B., & Cattell, H. E. P. (1973). *Measuring intelligence with the Culture Fair Tests.* Champaign, IL: Institute for Personality and Ability Testing.

Ceci, S. J. (1990). *On intelligence ... more or less: A bio-ecological treatise on intellectual development.* Englewood Cliffs, NJ: Prentice-Hall.

Ceci, S. J., & Bronfenbrenner, U. (1985). Don't forget to take the cupcakes out of the oven: Strategic time-monitoring, prospective memory and context. *Child Development, 56,* 175–190.

Ceci, S. J., & Liker, J. (1986). Academic and nonacademic intelligence: An experimental separation. In R. J. Sternberg & R. K. Wagner (Eds.), *Practical intelligence: Nature and origins of competence in the everyday world* (pp. 119–142). New York: Cambridge University Press.

Ceci, S. J., & Liker, J. (1988). Stalking the IQ-expertise relationship: When the critics go fishing. *Journal of Experimental Psychology: General, 117,* 96–100.

Ceci, S. J., & Roazzi, A. (1994). The effects of context on cognition: Postcards from Brazil. In R. J. Sternberg & R. K. Wagner (Eds.), *Mind in context: Interactionist perspectives on human intelligence* (pp. 74–101). New York: Cambridge University Press.

Ceci, S. J., & Ruiz, A. (1991). Cognitive complexity and generality: A case study. In R. Hoffman (Ed.), *The psychology of expertise.* New York: Springer-Verlag.

Chan, D., & Schmitt, N. (1998). Video-based versus paper-and-pencil method of assessment in situational judgment tests: Subgroup differences in test performance and face validity perceptions. *Journal of Applied Psychology, 82,* 143–159.

Chapin, F. S. (1942). Preliminary standardization of a social impact scale. *American Sociological Review, 7,* 214–225.

Chapin, F. S. (1967). *The Social Insight Test.* Palo Alto, CA: Consulting Psychologists Press.

Charness, N. (1979). Components of skill in bridge. *Canadian Journal of Psychology, 33,* 1–16.

Charness, N. (1981). Search in chess: Age and skill differences. *Journal of Experimental Psychology: Human Perception and Performance, 7,* 467–476.

Charness, N. (1991). Expertise in chess: The balance between knowledge and search. In K. A. Ericsson & J. Smith (Eds.), *Toward a general theory of expertise* (pp. 39–63). New York: Cambridge University Press.

Charness, N., & Bieman-Coplan, S. (1994). The learning perspective: Adulthood. In R. J. Sternberg & C. A. Berg (Eds.), *Intellectual Development* (pp. 301–327). New York: Cambridge University Press.

Charness, N., & Bosman, E. A. (1990). Expertise and aging: Life in the lab. In T. M. Hess (Ed.), *Aging and cognition: Knowledge organization and utilization* (pp. 343–385). Amsterdam: Elsevier Science.

Charness, N., & Bosman, E. A. (1995). Compensation through environmental modification. In R. A. Dixon & L. Baeckman (Eds.), *Compensating for psychological deficits and declines: Managing losses and promoting gains.* (pp. 147–168). Mahwah, NJ: Erlbaum.

Charness, N., Krampe, R., & Mayr, U. (1996). The role of practice and coaching in entrepreneurial skill domains: An international comparison of life-span chess skill acquisition. In K. A. Ericsson (Ed.), *The road to excellence* (pp. 51–80). Hillsdale, NJ: Erlbaum.

Chase, W. G., & Ericsson, K. A. (1982). Skill and working memory. In G. H. Bower (Ed.), *The psychology of learning and motivation* (Vol. 16, pp. 1–58). New York: Academic Press.

Chase, W. G., & Simon, H. A. (1973). The mind's eye in chess. In W. G. Chase (Ed.), *Visual information processing* (pp. 215–281). New York: Academic Press.

Chen, M. J. (1994). Chinese and Australian concepts of intelligence. *Psychological Developmental Sociology, 6,* 101–117.

Chen, S. A., & Michael, W. B. (1993). First-order and higher-order factors of creative social intelligence within Guilford's structure-of-intellect model: A reanalysis of a Guilford data base. *Educational & Psychological Measurement, 53,* 619–641.

Chi, M. T. H., & Ceci, S. J. (1987). Content knowledge: Its role, representation, and restructuring in memory development. In H. W. Reese (Ed.), *Advances in child development and behavior* (Vol. 20, pp. 91–142). Orlando: Academic Press.

Chi, M. T. H., Glaser, R., & Farr, M. J. (1988). *The nature of expertise.* Hillsdale, NJ: Erlbaum.

Church, A. H., & Bracken, D. W. (1997). Advancing the state of the art of 360-degree feedback: Guest editors' comments on the research and practice of multirater assessment methods. *Group & Organization Management, 22,* 149–161.

Cohen, M. (1996). Preschoolers' practical thinking and problem solving: The acquisition of an optimal solution strategy. *Cognitive Development, 11,* 357–373.

Cohen, J., & Cohen, P. (1983). *Applied multiple regression/correlation analysis for the behavioral sciences* (2nd ed.). Hillsdale, NJ: Erlbaum.

Colonia-Willner, R. (1998). Practical intelligence at work: Relationship between aging and cognitive efficiency among managers in a bank environment. *Psychology and Aging, 13,* 45–57.

Cornelius, S. W. (1984). Classic pattern of intellectual aging: Test familiarity, difficulty, and performance. *Journal of Gerontology, 39,* 201–206.

Cornelius, S. W., & Caspi, A. (1987). Everyday problem solving in adulthood and old age. *Psychology and Aging, 2,* 144–153.

Cosier, R. A., & Aplin, J. C. (1982). Intuition and decision making: Some empirical evidence. *Psychological Reports, 51,* 275–281.

Cronbach, L. J. (1957). The two disciplines of scientific psychology. *American Psychologist, 12,* 671–684.

Csikszentmihalyi, M. (1996). *Creativity.* New York: Harper Collins.

Das, J. P., & Naglieri, J. A. (1997). *Das-Naglieri cognitive assessment system.* Chicago: Riverside Publishing.

Dasen, P. (1984). The cross-cultural study of intelligence: Piaget and the Baoule. *International Journal of Psychology, 19,* 407–434.

Davidson, J. E., & Sternberg, R. J. (1984). The role of insight in intellectual giftedness. *Gifted Child Quarterly, 28,* 58–64.

Davidson, J. E., & Sternberg, R. J. (1998). Smart problem solving: How metacognition helps. In D. J. Hacker, A. C. Graesser, & J. Dunlosky (Eds.), *Metacognition in educational theory and practice* (pp. 47–68). Mahwah, NJ: Erlbaum.

Davies, J., & Easterby-Smith, M. (1984). Learning and developing from managerial work experiences. *Journal of Management Studies, 2,* 169–183.

Davies, M., Stankov, L., & Roberts, R. D. (1998). Emotional intelligence: In search of an elusive construct. *Journal of Personality and Social Psychology, 75,* 989–1015.

Deary, I., & Stough, C. (1996). Intelligence and inspection time: Achievements, prospects, and problems. *American Psychologist, 51,* 599–608.

De Groot, A. (1978). *Thought and choice in chess.* The Hague: Mouton. (Original work published 1946.)

Denney, N. W. (1979). Problem solving in late life: Intervention research. In P. B. Baltes & O. G. Brim (Eds.), *Life-span development and behavior* (Vol. 2, pp. 37–66). New York: Academic Press.

Denney, N. W. (1982). Aging and cognitive changes. In B. B. Wolman (Ed.), *Handbook of developmental psychology* (pp. 807–827). Englewood Cliffs, NJ: Prentice-Hall.

Denney, N. W. (1989). Everyday problem solving: Methodological issues, research findings, and a model. In I. W. Poon, D. C. Rubin, & B. A. Wilson

(Eds.), *Everyday cognition in adulthood and late life* (pp. 330–351). New York: Cambridge University Press.

Denney, N. W., & Palmer, A. M. (1981). Adult age differences on traditional and practical problem-solving measures. *Journal of Gerontology, 36,* 323–328.

Denney, N. W., & Pearce, K. A. (1989). A developmental study of practical problem solving in adults. *Psychology and Aging, 4,* 438–442.

Denney, N. W., Pearce, K. A., & Palmer, A. M. (1982). A developmental study of adults' performance on traditional and practical problem-solving tasks. *Experimental Aging Research, 8,* 115–118.

Dittmann-Kohli, F., & Baltes, P. B. (1990). Towards a neofunctionalist conception of adult intellectual development: Wisdom as a prototypical case of intellectual growth. In C. N. Alexander, & E. J. Langer (Eds.), *Higher stages of human development: Perspectives on adult growth* (pp. 54–78). New York: Oxford University Press.

Dixon, R. A. (1994). Contextual approaches to adult intellectual development. In R. J. Sternberg & C. A. Berg (Eds.), *Intellectual development* (pp. 350–380). New York: Cambridge University Press.

Dixon, R. A., & Baltes, P. B. (1986). Toward life-span research on the functions and pragmatics of intelligence. In R. J. Sternberg & R. K. Wagner (Eds.), *Practical intelligence: Nature and origins of competence in the everyday world* (pp. 203–235). New York: Cambridge University Press.

Dodge, K. A., Pettit, G. S., McClaskey, C. L., & Brown, M. M. (1986). Social competence in children. *Monographs of the Society for Research in Child Development, 51,* 1–85.

Dörner, D., & Kreuzig, H. (1983). Problemlösefähigkeit und Intelligenz. *Psychologische Rundschaus, 34,* 185–192.

Dörner, D., Kreuzig, H., Reither, F., & Staudel, T. (1983). *Lohhausen: Vom Umgang mit Unbestimmtheit und Komplexität.* Bern: Huber.

Druckman, D., Singer, J. E., & Van Cott, H. (Eds.) (1997). *Enhancing organizational performance.* Washington: National Academy Press.

Eddy, A. S. (1988). *The relationship between the Tacit Knowledge Inventory for Managers and the Armed Services Vocational Aptitude Battery.* Unpublished master's thesis, St. Mary's University, San Antonio, TX.

Egan, D. E., & Schwartz, B. J. (1979). Chunking in recall of symbolic drawings. *Memory and Cognition, 7,* 149–158.

Engle, R. W., & Bukstel, L. (1978). Memory processes among bridge players of differing expertise. *American Journal of Psychology, 91,* 673–679.

Ericsson, K. A. (1996). The acquisition of expert performance. In K. A. Ericsson (Ed.), *The road to excellence* (pp. 1–50). Hillsdale, NJ: Erlbaum.

Ericsson, K. A., Krampe, R. T., & Tesch-Römer, C. (1993). The role of deliberate practice in the acquisition of expert performance. *Psychological Review, 100,* 363–406.

Ericsson, K. A., & Smith, J. (1991). Empirical study of expertise: Prospects and limits. In K. A. Ericsson & J. A. Smith (Eds.), *Toward a general theory of expertise* (pp. 1–38). New York: Cambridge University Press.

Farah, M. J. (1988). Is visual imagery really visual? Overlooked evidence from neuropsychology. *Psychological Review, 95,* 307–317.

234 *Practical Intelligence in Everyday Life*

Feuerstein, R. (1979). *The Dynamic Assessment of Retarded Performers: The Learning Potential Assessment Device Theory, Instruments, and Techniques.* Baltimore: University Park Press.

Feuerstein, R., Rand, Y., Haywood, H. C., Hoffman, M., & Jensen, M. (1985). *The learning potential assessment device (LPAD): Examiner's Manual.* Jerusalem, Israel: Hadassah-Wizo-Canada Research Institute.

Fiedler, F. E. (1967). *A theory of leadership effectiveness.* New York: McGraw-Hill.

Fiedler, F. E. (1986). The contribution of cognitive resources to leadership performance. *Journal of Applied Social Psychology, 16,* 532–548.

Fiedler, F. E. (1995). Cognitive resources and leadership performance. *Applied Psychology: An International Review, 44,* 5–28.

Fiedler, F. E., & Garcia, J. E. (1987). *New approaches to leadership: Cognitive resources and organizational performance.* New York: John Wiley & Sons Inc.

Finke, R. A., Ward, T. B., & Smith, S. M. (1992). *Creative cognition: Theory, research, and applications.* Boston: MIT Press.

Flanagan, J. C. (1954). The critical incident technique. *Psychological Bulletin, 51,* 327–358.

Flavell, J. H. (1970). Developmental studies of mediated memory. In H. W. Reese & L. P. Lipsitt (Eds.), *Advances in child development and child behavior* (Vol. 5, pp. 181–211). New York: Academic Press.

Fleeson, W., & Cantor, N. (1995). Goal relevance and the affective experience of daily life: Ruling out situation explanation. *Motivation and Emotion, 19,* 25–57.

Fleishman, E. A. (1953). The description of supervisory behavior. *Personnel Psychology, 37,* 1–6.

Fleishman, E. A., & Harris, E. F. (1962). Patterns of leadership behavior related to employee grievances and turnover. *Personnel Psychology, 15,* 43–56.

Folkman, S., Lazarus, R. S., Pimley, S., & Novacek, J. (1987). Age differences in stress and coping processes. *Psychology and Aging, 2,* 171–184.

Ford, D. H. (1987). *Humans as self-constructing living systems: A developmental perspective on behavior and personality.* Hillsdale, NJ: Erlbaum.

Ford, D. H. (1994). *Humans as self-constructing living systems: A developmental perspective on behavior and personality* (2nd ed.). State College, PA: Ideals.

Ford, M. E. (1982). Social cognition and social competence in adolescence. *Developmental Psychology, 18,* 323–340.

Ford, M. E. (1986). For all practical purposes: Criteria for defining and evaluating practical intelligence. In R. J. Sternberg & R. K. Wagner (Eds.), *Practical intelligence: Nature and origins of competence in the everyday world* (pp. 183–200). New York: Cambridge University Press.

Ford, M. E., & Ford, D. H. (1987). *Humans as self-constructing living systems: Putting the framework to work.* Hillsdale, NJ: Erlbaum.

Ford, M. E., & Maher, M. A. (1998). Self-awareness and social intelligence. In M. D. Ferrari & R. J. Sternberg (Eds.), *Self-awareness: Its nature and development* (pp 191–218). New York: Guilford Press.

Ford, M. E., & Tisak, M. S. (1983). A further search for social intelligence. *Journal of Educational Psychology, 75,* 196–206.

Frederiksen, N. (1966). Validation of a simulation technique. *Organizational Behavior and Human Performance, 1,* 87–109.

Frederiksen, N. (1986). Toward a broader conception of human intelligence. *American Psychology, 41,* 445–452.

Frederiksen, N., Carlson, S., & Ward, W. C. (1984). The place of social intelligence in a taxonomy of cognitive abilities. *Intelligence, 8,* 315–337.

Frederiksen, N., Jensen, O., & Beaton, A. E. (1972). *Prediction of organizational behavior.* New York: Pergamon Press.

Frederiksen, N., Saunders, D. R., & Wand, B. (1957). The in-basket test. *Psychological Monographs, 71.*

Freeman, N. H., Lewis, C., & Doherty, M. J. (1991). Preschoolers' grasp of a desire for knowledge in false-belief prediction: Practical intelligence and verbal report. *British Journal of Developmental Psychology, 9,* 139–157.

French, J., & Raven, B. H. (1959). The bases of social power. In D. Cartwright (Ed.), *Studies of social power.* Ann Arbor, MI: Institute for Social Research.

Galton, F. (1883). *Inquiry into human faculty and its development.* London: Macmillan.

Gardiner, J. M. (1988). Functional aspects of recollective experience. *Memory and Cognition, 16,* 309–313.

Gardner, H. (1983). *Frames of mind: The theory of multiple intelligences.* New York: Basic.

Gardner, H. (1993). Seven creators of the modern era. In J. Brockman (Ed.), *Creativity* (pp. 28–47). New York: Simon & Schuster.

Gardner, H. (1998). Are there additional intelligences? The case for naturalist, spiritual, and existential intelligences. In J. Kane (Ed.), *Education, information, and transformation.* Englewood Cliffs, NJ: Prentice-Hall.

Gardner, H. (1999). Who owns intelligence? *The Atlantic Monthly, 283,* 67–76.

Gardner, H., Krechevsky, M., Sternberg, R. J., & Okagaki, L. (1994). Intelligence in context: Enhancing students' practical intelligence for school. In K. McGilly (Ed.), *Classroom lessons: Integrating cognitive theory and classroom practice* (pp. 105–127). Cambridge, MA: Bradford Books.

Gazzaniga, M. S. (1985). *The social brain: Discovering the networks of the mind.* New York: Basic Books.

Getzels, J., & Csikszentmihalyi, M. (1976). *The creative vision: A longitudinal study of problem-finding in art.* New York: John Wiley & Sons Inc.-Interscience.

Gill, R., & Keats, D. M. (1980). Elements of intellectual competence: Judgments by Australian and Malay university students. *Journal of Cross-Cultural Psychology, 11,* 233–243.

Goldberg, P. (1983). *The intuitive edge. Understanding and developing intuition.* Los Angeles: Jeremy P. Tarcher, Inc.

Goleman, D. (1995). *Emotional intelligence.* New York: Bantam Books.

Goodnow, J. J. (1986). Some lifelong everyday forms of intelligence behavior: Organizing and reorganizing. In R. J. Sternberg & R. K. Wagner (Eds.), *Practical Intelligence* (pp. 31–50). New York: Cambridge University Press.

Gough, H. G. (1966). Appraisal of social maturity by means of the CPI. *Journal of Abnormal Psychology, 71,* 189–195.

Greenspan, S. (1981). Defining childhood social competence: A proposed working model. In B. K. Keogh (Ed.), *Advances in special education* (Vol. 3, pp. 1–39). Greenwich, CT: JAI Press.

Greenspan, S., & Driscoll, J. (1997). The role of intelligence in a broad model of personal competence. In D. P. Flanagan & J. L. Genshaft (Eds.), *Contemporary intellectual assessment: Theories, tests, and issues* (pp. 131–150). New York: Guilford Press.

Greenspan, S., & Granfield, J. M. (1992). Reconsidering the construct of mental retardation: Implications of a model of social competence. *American Journal on Mental Retardation, 96*, 442–453.

Grigorenko, E. L., Geissler, P. W., Prince, R., Okatcha, F., Nokes, C., Kenny, D. A., Bundy, D. A., & Sternberg, R. J. (in press). The organization of Luo conceptions of intelligence: A study of implicit theories in a Kenyan village. *International Journal of Behavioral Development.*

Grigorenko, E. L., & Sternberg, R. J. (1998). Dynamic testing. *Psychological Bulletin, 124*, 75–11.

Grigorenko, E. L., & Sternberg, R. J. (in press). Analytical, creative, and practical intelligence as predictors of self-reported adaptive functioning: A case study in Russia. *Intelligence.*

Grigorenko, E. L., Sternberg, R. J., & Ehrman, M. (1999). A theory-based approach to the measurement of second-language learning ability: The CANAL-S theory and test. Unpublished manuscript.

Groen, G. J., & Patel, V. L. (1988). The relationship between comprehension and reasoning in medical expertise. In M. T. H. Chi, R. Glaser, & M. Farr (Eds.), *The nature of expertise.* Hillsdale, NJ: Erlbaum.

Guilford, J. P. (1967). *The nature of human intelligence.* New York: McGraw-Hill.

Guilford, J. P. (1982). Cognitive psychology's ambiguities: Some suggested remedies. *Psychological Review, 89*, 48–59.

Gustafsson, J. E. (1988). Hierarchical models of individual differences in cognitive abilities. In R. J. Sternberg (Ed.), *Advances in the psychology of human intelligence* (pp. 35–71). Hillsdale, NJ: Erlbaum.

Haier, R. J., Nuechterlein, K. H., Hazlett, E., Wu, J. C., Pack, J., Browning, H. L., & Buchsbaum, M. S. (1988). Cortical glucose metabolic rate correlates of abstract reasoning and attention studied with positron emission tomography. *Intelligence, 12*, 199–217.

Haier, R. J., Siegel, B., Tang, C., Abel, L., & Buchsbaum, M. S. (1992). Intelligence and changes in regional cerebral glucose metabolic rate following learning. *Intelligence, 16*, 415–426.

Halberstadt, A. G., & Hall, J. A. (1980). Who's getting the message?: Children's nonverbal skills and their evaluation by teachers. *Developmental Psychology, 16*, 564–573.

Harter, S. (1983). Developmental prospectives on the self-system. In P. H. Mussen (Ed.), *Handbook of child psychology* (Vol. 4). New York, John Wiley & Sons Inc.

Hartigan, J. A. (1975). *Clustering algorithms.* New York: John Wiley & Sons Inc.

Hartley, A. A. (1989). The cognitive etiology of problem solving. In L. W. Poon, D. C. Rubin, & B. A. Wilson (Eds.), *Everyday cognition in adulthood and late life* (pp. 300–329). New York: Cambridge University Press.

Havinghurst, R. (1972). *Developmental tasks and education.* New York: Van Nostrand.

Hayes-Roth, F., Waterman, D. A., & Lenat, D. B. (1983). An overview of an expert system. In F. Hayes-Roth, D. A. Watterman, & D. B. Lenat (Eds.), *Building expert systems*. Reading, MA: Addison-Wesley.

Hayslip, B., Jr. (1989a). Alternative mechanisms for improvements in fluid ability performance among older adults. *Psychology and Aging, 4*, 122–124.

Hayslip, B., Jr. (1989b). Fluid ability training with aged people: A past with a future? *Educational Gerontology, 15*, 573–595.

Hebb, D. O. (1949). *The organization of behavior: A neuropsychological theory*. New York: John Wiley & Sons Inc.

Heckhausen, J., & Schulz, R. (1995). A life-span theory of control. *Psychological Review, 102*, 284–304.

Hedlund, J., Forsythe, G. B., Horvath, J. A., Williams, W. M., Snook, S., Dennis, M., & Sternberg, R. J. (1999). Practical intelligence: The role of tacit knowledge in understanding leadership. Manuscript submitted for publication.

Hedlund, J., Horvath, J. A., Forsythe, G. B., Snook, S., Williams, W. M., Bullis, R. C., Dennis, M., & Sternberg, R. J. (1998). *Tacit Knowledge in Military Leadership: Evidence of Construct Validity* (Tech. Rep. 1080). Alexandria, VA: U.S. Army Research Institute for the Behavioral and Social Sciences.

Hendricks, M., Guilford, J. P., & Hoepfner, R. (1969) Measuring creative social intelligence. *Reports from the Psychological Laboratory, University of Southern California*, No. 42.

Hendrickson, A. E., & Hendrickson, D. E. (1980). The biological basis for individual differences in intelligence. *Personality & Individual Differences, 1*, 3–33.

Hersey, P., & Blanchard, K. H. (1977). *The management of organizational behavior* (3rd ed.). Englewood Cliffs, NJ: Prentice-Hall.

Hoffman, R. R. (Ed.). (1992). *The psychology of expertise: Cognitive research and empirical AI*. New York: Springer-Verlag.

Hofland, B. F., Willis, S. L., & Baltes, P. B. (1981). Fluid intelligence performance in the elderly: Intraindividual variability and conditions of assessment. *Journal of Educational Psychology, 73*, 573–586.

Hogan, R. (1969). Development of an empathy scale. *Journal of Consulting & Clinical Psychology, 33*, 307–316.

Holland, J. H., Holyoak, K. J., Nisbett, R. E., & Thagard, P. R. (1986). *Induction: Processes of inference, learning, and discovery*. Cambridge, MA: MIT Press.

Hollander, E. P. (1985). Leadership and power. In G. Lindzey & E. Aronson (Eds.), *Handbook of social psychology*. New York: Random House.

Horn, J. L. (1982). The theory of fluid and crystallized intelligence in relation to concepts of cognitive psychology and aging in adulthood. In F. I. M. Craik & A. Trehum (Eds.), *Aging and cognitive processes* (pp. 237–278). New York: Plenum.

Horn, J. L. (1994). Theory of fluid and crystallized intelligence. In R. J. Sternberg (Ed.), *The encyclopedia of human intelligence* (Vol. 1, pp. 443–451). New York: Macmillan.

Horn, J. L., & Cattell, R. B. (1966). Refinement and test of the theory of fluid and crystallized intelligence. *Journal of Educational Psychology, 57*, 253–270.

Horvath, J. A., Forsythe, G. B., Sweeney, P. J., McNally, J. A., Wattendorf, J., Williams, W. M., & Sternberg, R. J. (1994). *Tacit knowledge in military leadership: Evidence from officer interviews* (Tech. Rep. No. 1018). Alexandria, VA: U.S. Army Research Institute for the Behavioral and Social Sciences.

Horvath, J. A., Sternberg, R. J., Forsythe, G. B., Sweeney, P. J., Bullis, R. C., Williams, W. M., & Dennis, M. (1996). *Tacit knowledge in military leadership: Supporting instrument development* (Tech. Rep. No. 1042). Alexandria, VA: U.S. Army Research Institute for the Behavioral and Social Sciences.

Horvath, J. A., Williams, W. M., Forsythe, G. B., Sweeney, P. J., Sternberg, R. J., McNally, J. A., & Wattendorf, J. (1994). *Tacit knowledge in military leadership: A review of the literature* (Tech. Rep. No. 1017). Alexandria, VA: U.S. Army Research Institute for the Behavioral and Social Sciences.

House, R. J. (1971). A path-goal theory of leadership effectiveness. *Administrative Science Quarterly, 16*, 321–339.

Howell, W. C., & Cooke, N. J. (1989). Training the human information processor: A review of cognitive models. In I. L. Goldstein (Ed.), *Training and development in organizations* (pp. 121–182). San Francisco: Jossey-Bass.

Hoyer, W. J., Labouvie, G. V., & Baltes, P. B. (1973). Modification of response and speed deficits and intellectual performance in the elderly. *Human Development, 16*, 233–242.

Hunt, T. (1928). The measurement of social intelligence. *Journal of Applied Psychology, 12*, 317–334.

Hunt, E. B. (1978). Mechanics of verbal ability. *Psychological Review, 85*, 109–130.

Hunt, E., Frost, N., & Lunneborg, C. (1973). Individual differences in cognition: A new approach to intelligence. In G. Bower (Ed.), *The psychology of learning and motivation* (Vol. 7, pp. 87–122). New York: Academic Press.

Hunt, E. B., Lunneborg, C., & Lewis, J. (1975). What does it mean to be high verbal? *Cognitive Psychology, 7*, 194–227.

Hunter, J. E., & Hunter, R. F. (1984). Validity and utility of alternative predictors of job performance. *Psychological Bulletin, 96*, 72–98.

Ilgen, D. R., Barnes-Farrell, J. L., & McKellin, D. B. (1993). Performance appraisal process research in the 1980s: What has it contributed to appraisals in use? *Organizational Behavior and Human Decision Processes, 54*, 321–368.

Isenberg, D. J. (1984). How senior managers think. *Harvard Business Review, 62*, 81–90.

Isenberg, D. J. (1986). Thinking and managing: A verbal protocol analysis of managerial problem solving. *Academy of Management Journal, 4*, 75–778.

Jacoby, L. L. (1983). Perceptual enhancement: Persistent effects of an experience. *Journal of Experimental Psychology: Learning, Memory, and Cognition, 9*, 21–38.

Jensen, A. R. (1980). *Bias in mental testing.* New York: Free Press.

Jensen, A. R. (1982). Reaction time and psychometric g. In H. J. Eysenck (Ed.), *A model for intelligence.* Heidelberg: Springer-Verlag.

Jensen, A. R. (1993). Test validity: g versus "tacit knowledge." *Current Directions in Psychological Science, 1*, 9–10.

Jensen, A. R. (1997). The puzzle of nongenetic variance. In R. J. Sternberg & E. L. Grigorenko (Eds.), *Intelligence, heredity, and environment* (pp. 42–88). New York: Cambridge University Press.

Jensen, A. R. (1998). *The g factor: The science of mental ability.* Westport, CT: Praeger/Greenwood.

Jones, K., & Day, J. D. (1997). Discrimination of two aspects of cognitive-social intelligence from academic intelligence. *Journal of Educational Psychology, 89,* 486–497.

Kanfer, R., & Ackerman, P. L. (1989). Motivation and cognitive abilities: An integrative aptitude–treatment interaction approach to skill acquisition. *Journal of Applied Psychology, 74,* 657–690.

Karmiloff-Smith, A. (1988). The child is a theorist not an inductivist. *Mind and Language, 3,* 183–196.

Kaufman, A. S., & Kaufman, N. L. (1993). *Kaufman Adolescent and Adult Intelligence Test.* Circle Pines, MN: American Guidance Service.

Keating, D. K. (1978). A search for social intelligence. *Journal of Educational Psychology, 70,* 218–233.

Kepner, C. H., & Tregoe, B. B. (1965). *The rational manager: A systematic approach to problem solving and decision making.* New York: McGraw-Hill.

Kerr, S., & Jermier, J. M. (1978). Substitutes for leadership: Their meaning and measurement. *Organizational Behavior and Human Performance, 22,* 375–403.

Keys, B., & Wolfe, J. (1990). The role of management games and simulations in education and research. *Journal of Management, 16,* 307–336.

Kihlstrom, J. F., & Cantor, N. (in press). Social intelligence. In R. J. Sternberg (Ed.), *Handbook of intelligence,* (2nd ed.). Cambridge, U.K.: Cambridge University Press.

Kitchener, K. S. (1983). Cognition, metacognition, and epistemic cognition: A three-level model of cognitive processing. *Human Development, 4,* 222–232.

Kitchener, K. S. (1986). Formal reasoning in adults: A review and critique. In R. A. Mines & K. S. Kitchener (Eds.), *Adult cognitive development.* New York: Praeger.

Kitchener, K. S., & Brenner, H. G. (1990). Wisdom and reflective judgment: Knowing in the face of uncertainty. In R. J. Sternberg (Ed.), *Wisdom: Its nature, origins, and development* (pp. 212–229). New York: Cambridge University Press.

Kitchener, K. S., & Kitchener, R. F. (1981). The development of natural rationality: Can formal operations account for it? In J. Meacham & N. R. Santilli (Eds.), *Social development in youth: Structure and content.* Basel: Karger.

Klaczynski, P. A., Laipple, J. S., & Jurden, F. H. (1992). Educational context differences in practical problem solving during adolescence. *Merrill-Palmer Quarterly, 38,* 417–438.

Kohlberg, L. (1963). The development of children's orientations toward a moral order: I. Sequence in the development of moral thought. *Vita Humana, 6,* 11–33.

Kohn, M. L., & Schooler, C. (Eds.) (1983). *Work and personality.* Norwood, NJ: Ablex.

Kosmitzki, C., & John, O. P. (1993). The implicit use of explicit conceptions of social intelligence. *Personality and Individual Differences, 15,* 11–23.

Kotter, J. (1987). *The leadership factor.* New York: Free Press.

Kramer, D. A. (1990). Conceptualizing wisdom: The primacy of affect-cognition relations. In R. J. Sternberg (Ed.), *Wisdom: Its nature, origins, and development* (pp. 279–313). New York: Cambridge University Press.

Kreitler, S., & Kreitler, H. (1987). Conceptions and processes of planning: The developmental perspective. In S. L. Friedman & E. K. Scholnick (Eds.), *Blueprints for thinking: The role of planning in cognitive development* (pp. 205–272). Cambridge, U.K.: Cambridge University Press.

Kuhn, D., Pennington, N., & Leadbeater, B. (1983). Adult thinking in developmental perspective. In P. B. Baltes & O. G. Brim (Eds.), *Life-span development and behavior* (Vol. 5). New York: Academic Press.

Laboratory of Comparative Human Cognition (1982). Culture and intelligence. In R. J. Sternberg (Ed.), *Handbook of human intelligence* (pp. 642–719). New York: Cambridge University Press.

Labouvie-Vief, G. (1980). Beyond formal operations: Uses and limits of pure logic in life span development. *Human Development, 23,* 141–161.

Labouvie-Vief, G. (1982). Dynamic development and mature autonomy. *Human Development, 25,* 161–191.

Labouvie-Vief, G. (1990). Wisdom as integrated thought: Historical and developmental perspectives. In R. J. Sternberg (Ed.), *Wisdom: Its nature, origins, and development* (pp. 52–83). New York: Cambridge University Press.

Labouvie-Vief, G. (1992). A Neo-Piagetian perspective on adult cognitive development. In R. J. Sternberg & C. A. Berg (Eds.), *Intellectual development* (pp. 197–228). New York: Cambridge University Press.

Laipple, J. S. (1992). Problem-solving in young and old adulthood: The role of task interpretation. *Dissertation Abstracts International, 53(1-B),* 582.

Landy, F. J., & Farr, J. (1980). Performance ratings. *Psychological Bulletin, 87,* 72–107.

Latham, G. P. (1988). Human resource training and development. *Annual Review of Psychology, 39,* 545–582.

Lau, J., & Shani, A. (1992). *Behavior in organizations: An experimental approach* (5th ed.). Homewood, IL: Irwin.

Lave, J. (1988). *Cognition in practice: Mind mathematics and culture in everyday life.* New York: Cambridge University Press.

Lave, J., Murtaugh, M., & de la Roche, O. (1984). The dialectic of arithmetic in grocery shopping. In B. Rogoff & J. Lace (Eds.), *Everyday cognition: Its development in social context* (pp. 67–94). Cambridge, MA: Harvard University Press.

Lazarus, R. S., & Folkman, S. (1984). *Stress, appraisal, and coping.* New York: Springer.

Legree, P. J. (1995). Evidence for an oblique social intelligence factor established with a Likert-based testing procedure. *Intelligence, 21,* 247–266.

Lesgold, A., Rubinson, H. Feltovich, P., Glaser, R., Klopfer, D., & Wang, Y. (1985). *Expertise in a complex skill: Diagnosing X-ray pictures.* Pittsburgh: Learning Research and Development Center, University of Pittsburgh Technical Report.

Levy, J. (1974). Psychobiological implications of bilateral asymmetry. In S. Dimond & S. Beaumont (Eds.), *Hemispheric function in the human brain.* New York: Halstead.

Likert, R. (1967). *The human organization: Its management and value.* New York: McGraw-Hill.

Loehlin, J. C. (1989). Partitioning environmental and genetic contributions to behavioral development. *American Psychologist, 44,* 1285–1292.

Loewen, E. R., Shaw, J. R., & Craik, F. I. M. (1990). Age differences in components of metamemory. *Experimental Aging Research, 16,* 43–48.

Luria, A. R. (1973). *The working brain.* New York: Basic Books.

Luria, A. R. (1976). *Cognitive development: Its cultural and social foundations.* Cambridge, MA: Harvard University Press.

Luria, A. R. (1980). *Higher cortical functions in man* (2nd ed.). New York: Basic Books.

Manz, C. C., & Sims, H. P. Jr. (1980). Self-management as a substitute for leadership: A social learning theory perspective. *Academy of Management Review, 5,* 361–367.

Markham, S. E., & Markham, I. S. (1995). Self-management and self-leadership reexamined: A levels-of-analysis perspective. *Leadership Quarterly, 6,* 343–359.

Marlowe, H. A. (1986). Social intelligence: Evidence for multidimensionality and construct independence. *Journal of Educational Psychology, 78,* 52–58.

Mayer, J. D., Caruso, D., & Salovey, P. (in press). Emotional intelligence meets traditional standards for an intelligence test. *Intelligence.*

Mayer, J. D., & Greeno, J. G. (1972). Structural differences between learning outcomes produced by different instructional methods. *Journal of Educational Psychology, 63,* 165–173.

Mayer, J. D., & Salovey, P. (1993). The intelligence of emotional intelligence. *Intelligence, 17,* 433–442.

Mayer, J. D., & Salovey, P. (1997). What is emotional intelligence? In P. Salovey & D. Sluyter (Eds.), *Emotional development and emotional intelligence: Implications for educators* (pp. 3–31). New York: Basic Books.

Mayer, J. D., Salovey, P., & Caruso, D. (in press). Competing models of emotional intelligence. In R. J. Sternberg (Ed.), *Handbook of intelligence* (2nd ed.). Cambridge, U.K.: Cambridge University Press.

McCall, M. W., & Kaplan, R. E. (1985). *Whatever it takes: Decision makers at work.* Englewood Cliffs, NJ: Prentice-Hall.

McCall, M. W., Lombardo, M. M., & Morrison, A. (1988). *The lessons of experience.* Lexington, MA: Lexington Books.

McCarthy, G., & Donchin, E. (1981). A metric for thought: A comparison of P300 latency and reaction time. *Science, 211,* 77–79.

McClelland, D. C. (1973). Testing for competence rather than for "intelligence." *American Psychologist, 28,* 1–14.

McClelland, D. C. (1976). *A guide to job competency assessment.* Boston: McBer.

McClelland, J. L., & Rumelhart, D. C. (Eds.) (1988). *Explorations in parallel distributed processing: A handbook of models, programs, and exercises.* Cambridge, MA: MIT Press.

Meacham, J. (1990). The loss of wisdom. In R. J. Sternberg (Ed.), *Wisdom: Its nature, origins, and development* (pp. 181–211). New York: Cambridge University Press.

Meacham, J. A., & Emont, N. C. (1989). The interpersonal basis of everyday problem solving. In J. D. Sinnott (Ed.), *Everyday problem solving* (pp. 7–23). New York: Praeger.

Messick, S. (1995). Validity of psychological assessment: Validation of inferences from persons' responses and performances as scientific inquiry into score meaning. *American Psychologist, 50,* 741–750.

Miller, K. A., & Kohn, M. L. (1983). The reciprocal effects on job conditions and the intellectuality of leisure-time activities. In M. L. Kohn & C. Schooler (Eds.), *Work and personality* (pp. 217–241). Norwood, NJ: Ablex.

Minsky, M. (1968). *Semantic information processing*. Cambridge, MA: MIT Press.

Mintzberg, H. (1973). *The nature of managerial work*. New York: Harper & Row.

Mintzberg, H. (1975). The manager's job: Folklore and fact. *Harvard Business Review, 4*, 49–61.

Mintzberg, H., Raisinhani, D., & Theoret, A. (1976). The structure of "unstructured" decision processes. *Administration Science Quarterly, 21*, 246–275.

Mischel, W. (1984). Convergences and challenges in the search for consistency. *American Psychologist, 39*, 351–364.

Moss, F. A., & Hunt, T. (1927) Are you socially intelligent? *Scientific American, 137*, 108–110.

Moss, F. A., Hunt, T., Omwake, K. T., & Woodward, L. G. (1949). *Social Intelligence Test, George Washington University Series*. Washington, D.C.: Center for Psychological Services, George Washington University.

Motowidlo, S. J., Dunnette, M. D., & Carter, G. W. (1990). An alternative selection procedure: The low-fidelity simulation. *Journal of Applied Psychology, 75*, 640–647.

Murtaugh, M. (1985). The practice of arithmetic by American grocery shoppers. *Anthropology and Education Quarterly, 16*, 186–192.

Naus, M. J., & Ornstein, P. A. (1983). Development of memory strategies: Analysis, questions and issues. In M. T. M. Chi (Ed.), *Trends in memory development research: Contributions to human development* (Vol. 9, pp. 1–30). Basel: Karger.

Neely, A. S., & Backman, L. (1993). Long-term maintenance of gains from memory training in older adults: Two $3^1/_2$-year follow-up studies. *Journal of Gerontology, 48*, 233–237.

Neisser, U. (1976). General, academic, and artificial intelligence. In L. Resnick (Ed.), *Human intelligence: Perspectives on its theory and measurement* (pp. 179–189). Norwood, NJ: Ablex.

Neisser, U. (1979). The concept of intelligence. In R. J. Sternberg & D. K. Detterman (Eds.), *Human intelligence: Perspectives on its theory and measurement* (pp. 179–189). Norwood, NJ: Ablex.

Nelson, M. J., & Lamke, T. A. (1973). *The Henmon-Nelson test of mental ability*. Boston: Houghton Mifflin.

Nettlebeck, T. (1982). Inspection time: An index for intelligence. *Quarterly Journal of Experimental Psychology, 34*, 299–312.

Neugarten, B. L., Moore, J. W., & Lowe, J. C. (1968). Age norms, age constraints, and adult socialization. In B. L. Neugarten (Ed.), *Middle age and aging* (pp. 22–28). Chicago: University of Chicago Press.

Newell, A. (1990). *Unified theories of cognition*. Cambridge, MA: Harvard University Press.

Newell, A., & Simon, H. A. (1972). *Human problem solving*. Englewood Cliffs, NJ: Prentice-Hall.

Nunally, J. C. (1970). *Introduction to psychological measurement*. New York: McGraw-Hill.

Nuñes, T. (1994). Street intelligence. In R. J. Sternberg (Ed.), *Encyclopedia of human intelligence* (pp. 1045–1049). New York: Macmillan.

Nuñes, T., Schliemann, A. D., & Carraher, D. W. (1993). *Street mathematics and school mathematics*. New York: Cambridge University Press.

Nutt, P. C. (1989). *Making tough decisions: Tactics for improving managerial decision making.* San Francisco: Jossey-Bass.

Okagaki, L., & Sternberg, R. J. (1993). Parental beliefs and children's school performance. *Child Development, 64(1),* 36–56.

Oltman, P. K., Raskin, F., & Witkin, H. A. (1971). *Group Embedded Figures Test.* Palo Alto, CA: Consulting Psychologists Press.

Orwoll, L., & Perlmutter, M. (1990). The study of wise persons: Integrating a personality perspective. In R. J. Sternberg (Ed.), *Wisdom: Its nature, origins, and development* (pp. 160–177). New York: Cambridge University Press.

O'Sullivan, M., & Guilford, J. P. (1976). *Four factor tests of social intelligence (behavioral cognition): Manual of instructions and interpretations.* Orange, CA: Sheridan Psychological Services.

O'Sullivan, M., Guilford, J. P., & deMille, R. (1965). The measurement of social intelligence. *Reports from the Psychological Laboratory, University of Southern California,* No. 34.

Pascual-Leone, J. (1990). An essay on wisdom: Toward organismic processes that make it possible. In R. J. Sternberg (Ed.), *Wisdom: Its nature, origins, and development* (pp. 244–278). New York: Cambridge University Press.

Patel, V. L., & Groen, G. J. (1991). The general and specific nature of medical expertise: A critical look. In K. A. Ericsson & J. Smith (Eds.), *Toward a general theory of expertise* (pp. 93–125). Hillsdale, NJ: Erlbaum.

Perret-Clermont, A. N. (1980). *Social interaction and cognitive development in children.* London: Academic Press.

Peters, T. J., & Waterman, R. H. (1982). *In search of excellence.* New York: Harper & Row.

Piaget, J. (1972). *The psychology of intelligence.* Totowa, NJ: Littlefield Adams.

Plomin, R. (1997). Identifying genes for cognitive abilities and disabilities. In Sternberg, R. J., & Grigorenko, E. L. (Eds.), *Intelligence, heredity and environment* (pp. 89–104). New York: Cambridge University Press.

Plomin, R., & McClearn, G. E. (Eds.) (1993). *Nature, nurture, and psychology.* Washington, DC: American Psychological Association.

Plunkett, L. C., & Hale, G. A. (1982). *The proactive manager.* New York: John Wiley & Sons Inc.

Polanyi, M. (1966). *The tacit dimensions.* Garden City, NY: Doubleday.

Polanyi, M. (1976). Tacit knowledge. In M. Marx & F. Goodson (Eds.), *Theories in contemporary psychology* (pp. 330–344). New York: Macmillan.

Posner, M. I., & Mitchell, R. F. (1967). Chronometric analysis of classification. *Psychological Review, 74,* 392–409.

Pressley, M., Forrest-Presley, D. L., Elliot-Faust, D., & Miller, G. (1985). Children's use of cognitive strategies: How to teach strategies, and what to do if they can't be taught. In M. Pressley & C. J. Brainers (Eds.), *Cognitive learning and memory in children: Progress in cognitive development research* (pp. 1–47). New York: Springer.

Raven, J. C. (1958). *Guide to using the Coloured Progressive Matrices.* London: H. K. Lewis & Co.

Raven, J. C., Court, J. H., & Raven, J. (1992). *Manual for Raven's Progressive Matrices and Mill Hill Vocabulary Scales.* Oxford: Oxford Psychologists Press.

Ray, M., & Myers, R. (1989). Practical intuition. In W. H. Agor (Ed.), *Intuition in organizations: Leading and managing productively* (pp. 142–156). Newbury Park, CA: Sage.

Reber, A. S. (1967). Implicit learning of artificial grammars. *Journal of Verbal Learning and Verbal Behavior, 6,* 317–327.

Reber, A. S. (1969). Transfer of syntactic structure in synthetic languages. *Journal of Experimental Psychology, 81,* 115–119.

Reber, A. S. (1989). Implict learning and tacit knowledge. *Journal of Experimental Psychology: General, 118,* 219–235.

Reber, A. S., & Millward, R. B. (1968). Event observation in probability learning. *Journal of Experimental Psychology, 77,* 317–327.

Ree, M. J., & Earles, J. A. (1993). g is to psychology what carbon is to chemistry: A reply to Sternberg and Wagner, McClelland, and Calfee. *Current Directions in Psychological Science, 1,* 11–12.

Reed, T. E., & Jensen, A. R. (1992). Conduction velocity in a brain nerve pathway of normal adults correlates with intelligence level. *Intelligence, 16,* 259–272.

Reichert, U., & Dorner, D. (1988). Heurismen beim Umgang mit einem "einfachen" dynamischen System [Heuristics in the control of a "simple" dynamic system]. *Sprache & Kognition, 7,* 12–24.

Reitman, J. (1976). Skilled perception in GO: Deducing memory structures from interresponse times. *Cognitive Psychology, 8,* 336–356.

Rest, J. (1975). Longitudinal study of the Defining Issues Test of moral judgement: A strategy for analyzing development change. *Developmental Psychology, 11,* 738–748.

Riegel, K. F. (1973). Dialectical operations: The final period of cognitive development. *Human Development, 16,* 346–370.

Riggio, R. E. (1986). Assessment of basic social skills. *Journal of Personality and Social Psychology, 51,* 649–660.

Riggio, R. E. (1989). *Manual for the Social Skills Inventory.* Palo Alto, CA: Consulting Psychologists Press.

Riggio, R. E., Messamer, J., & Throckmorton, B. (1991). Social and academic intelligence: Conceptually distinct but overlapping constructs. *Personality and Individual Differences, 12,* 695–702.

Roazzi, A. (1987). Effects of context on cognitive development. In J. F. Cruz & R. A. Goncalves (Eds.), *Psicologia e Eduçao: Investigaçao e intervençao.* Porto: Associacao dos Psicologos Portugueses.

Rockenstein, Z. (1988). Intuitive processes in executive decision making. *Journal of Creative Behavior, 22,* 77–84.

Rogoff, B. (1982). Integrating context and cognitive development. In M. E. Lamb & A. L. Brown (Eds.), *Advances in development psychology* (Vol. 2, pp. 125–169). Hillsdale, NJ: Erlbaum.

Rogoff, B., Gauvain, M., & Gardner, W. (1987). Children's adjustment of plans to circumstances. In S. L. Friedman, E. K., Scholnick, & R. R. Cocking (Eds.), *Blueprints for thinking* (pp. 303–320). New York: Cambridge University Press.

Rogoff, B., & Lave, J. (Eds.) (1984). *Everyday cognition: Its development in social context.* Cambridge, MA: Harvard University Press.

Rosenthal, R. (Ed.) (1979). *Skill in nonverbal communication: Individual differences.* Cambridge, MA: Oelgeschlager, Gunn, & Hain.

Rosenthal, R., Hall, J. A., DiMatteo, M. R., Rogers, P. L., & Archer, D. (1979). *Sensitivity to nonverbal communication: The PONS test.* Baltimore: Johns Hopkins University Press.

Ross, L. D. (1977). The intuitive psychologist and his shortcomings: Distortions in the attribution process. In L. Berkowitz (Ed.), *Advances in experimental social psychology* (Vol. 10). New York: Academic Press.

Salam, S., Cox, J. F., & Sims, H. P. (1997). In the eye of the beholder: How leadership relates to 360-degree performance ratings. *Group & Organization Management, 22,* 185–209.

Salovey, P., & Mayer, J. D. (1990). Emotional intelligence. *Imagination, cognition, and personality, 9,* 185–211.

Salovey, P., & Mayer, J. D. (1994). Some final thoughts about personality and intelligence. In R. J. Sternberg & P. Ruzgis (Eds.), *Personality and intelligence* (pp. 303–318). Cambridge, U.K.: Cambridge University Press.

Salthouse, T. A. (1984). Effects of age and skill in typing. *Journal of Experimental Psychology: General, 113,* 345–371.

Salthouse, T. A. (1991). *Theoretical perspectives on cognitive aging.* Hillsdale, NJ: Erlbaum.

Salthouse, T. A. (1998). Relation of successive percentiles of reaction time distributions to cognitive variables and adult age. *Intelligence, 26,* 153–166.

Salthouse, T. A., & Somberg, B. L. (1982). Skilled performance: The effects of adult age and experience on elementary processes. *Journal of Experimental Psychology: General, 111,* 176–207.

Sansone, C., & Berg, C. A. (1993). Adapting to the environment across the life span: Different process or different inputs? *International Journal of Behavioral Development, 16,* 215–241.

Scarr, S. (1997). Behavior-genetic and socialization theories of intelligence: Truce and reconciliation. In R. J. Sternberg & E. L. Grigorenko (Eds.), *Intelligence, heredity and environment* (pp. 3–41). New York: Cambridge University Press.

Schacter, D. L. (1987). Implicit memory: History and current status. *Journal of Experimental Psychology, 13,* 501–518.

Schafer, E. W. P. (1982). Neural adaptability: A biological determinant of behavioral intelligence. *International Journal of Neuroscience, 17,* 183–91.

Schaie, K. W. (1977/1978). Toward a stage theory of adult cognitive development. *International Journal of Aging and Human Development, 8,* 129–138.

Schaie, K. W. (1986). Beyond calendar definitions of age, time, and cohort: The general developmental model revisited. *Developmental Review, 6,* 252–277.

Schaie, K. W. (1988). Variability in cognitive functioning in the elderly: Implications for societal participation. In A. D. Woodhead, M. A. Bender, & R. C. Leonard (Eds.), *Phenotypic variation in populations: Relevance to risk assessment* (pp. 191–212). New York: Plenum.

Schaie, K. W. (1989). The hazards of cognitive aging. *Gerontologist, 29,* 484–493.

Schaie, K. W. (1994). The course of adult development. *American Psychologist, 49,* 304–313.

Schaie, K. W. (1996). *Intellectual development in adulthood: The Seattle Longitudinal Study.* New York: Cambridge University Press.

Schaie, K. W., & Willis, S. L. (1986). Can decline in adult intellectual functioning be reversed? *Developmental Psychology, 22,* 223–232.

Schank, R. C. (1972). Conceptual dependency: A theory of natural language understanding. *Cognitive Psychology, 3,* 552–631.

Schank, R. C. (1990). *Tell me a story: A new look at real and artificial memory.* New York: Scribner.

Schank, R., & Abelson, R. P. (1977). *Scripts, plans, goals, and understanding: An inquiry into human knowledge structures.* Hillsdale, NJ: Erlbaum.

Schmidt, F. L., & Hunter, J. E. (1993). Tacit knowledge, practical intelligence, general mental ability, and job knowledge. *Current Directions in Psychological Science, 1,* 8–9.

Schmidt, F. L., & Hunter, J. E. (1998). The validity and utility of selection methods in personnel psychology: Practical and theoretical implications of 85 years of research findings. *Psychological Bulletin, 124,* 262–274.

Schön, D. A. (1983). *The reflective practitioner: How professionals think in action.* New York: Basic Books.

Schooler, C. (1984). Psychological effects of complex environments during the life span: A review and theory. *Intelligence, 8,* 259–281.

Schooler, C. (in press). The intellectual effects of the demands of the work environment. In R. J. Sternberg & E. L. Grigorenko (Eds.) *Environmental effects on intellectual functioning.* Mahwah, NJ: Erlbaum.

Schutte, N. S., Malouff, J. M., Hall, L. E., Haggerty, D. J., Cooper, J. T., Golden, C. J., & Dornheim, L. (1998). Development and validation of a measure of emotional intelligence. *Personality and Individual Differences, 25,* 167–177.

Scribner, S. (1984). Studying working intelligence. In B. Rogoff & J. Lave (Eds.), *Everyday cognition: Its development in social context* (pp. 9–40). Cambridge, MA: Harvard University Press.

Scribner, S. (1986). Thinking in action: Some characteristics of practical thought. In R. J. Sternberg & R. K. Wagner (Eds.), *Practical intelligence: Nature and origins of competence in the everyday world* (pp. 13–30). New York: Cambridge University Press.

Scribner, S., & Cole, M. (1981). *The psychology of literacy.* Cambridge, MA: Harvard University Press.

Serpell, R. (1982). Measures of perception, skills, and intelligence. In W. W. Hartup (Ed.), *Review of Child Development Research.* Chicago: University of Chicago Press.

Shiffrin, R. M. (1996). Laboratory experimentation on the genesis of expertise. In K. A. Ericsson (Ed.), *The road to excellence* (pp. 337–345). Mahwah, NJ: Erlbaum.

Shipley, W. C. (1940). A self-administering scale for measuring intellectual impairment and deterioration. *Journal of Psychology, 9,* 371–377.

Shirley, D. A., & Langan-Fox, J. (1996). Intuition: A review of the literature. *Psychological Reports, 79,* 563–684.

Siegler, R. S., & Richards, D. D. (1982). The development of intelligence. In R. J. Sternberg (Ed.), *Handbook of human intelligence.* New York: Cambridge University Press.

Simon, H. A., & Chase, W. G. (1973). Skill in chess. *American Scientist, 61,* 391–403.

Simon, H. A., & Gilmartin, K. (1973). A simulation of memory for chess positions. *Cognitive Psychology, 8,* 165–190.

Simonton, D. K. (1980). Intuition process and analysis: A predictive and explanatory model. *Genetic Psychology Monographs, 102,* 3–60.

Simonton, K. A. (1996). Creative expertise: A life-span developmental perspective. In K. A. Ericsson (Ed.), *The road to excellence* (pp. 227–253). Mahwah, NJ: Erlbaum.

Sinnott, J. D. (1989). A model for solution of ill-structured problems: Implications for everyday and abstract problem solving. In J. D. Sinnott (Ed.), *Everyday problem solving: Theory and applications* (pp. 72–99). New York: Praeger.

Smith, J., & Baltes, P. B. (1990). Wisdom-related knowledge: Age/cohort differences in response to life-planning problems. *Developmental Psychology, 26,* 494–505.

Smith, J., Staudinger, U. M., & Baltes, P. B. (1994). Occupational settings facilitating wisdom-related knowledge: The sample case of clinical psychologists. *Journal of Consulting and Clinical Psychology, 62,* 989–999.

Smith, P. C., & Kendall, L. M. (1963). Retranslation of expectations: An approach to the construction of unambiguous anchors for rating scales. *Journal of Applied Psychology, 47,* 149–155.

Snow, R. E., & Lohman, D. F. (1984). Toward a theory of cognitive aptitude for learning from instruction. *Journal of Educational Psychology, 76,* 347–376.

Snyder, M. (1974). Self-monitoring of expressive behavior. *Journal of Personality and Social Psychology, 30,* 526–537.

Spearman, C. E. (1904). `General intelligence' objectively determined and measured. *American Journal of Psychology, 15,* 201–293.

Spearman, C. (1923). *The nature of `intelligence' and the principles of cognition* (2nd ed.). London: Macmillan. (1923 edition reprinted in 1973 by Arno Press, New York).

Spearman, C. (1927). *The abilities of man.* London: Macmillan.

Sperry, R. W. (1961). Cerebral organization and behavior. *Science, 133,* 1749–1757.

Staudinger, U. M., & Baltes, P. M. (1996). Interactive minds: A facilitative setting for wisdom-related performance? *Journal of Personality and Social Psychology, 71,* 746–762.

Staudinger, U. M., Lopez, D. F., & Baltes, P. B. (1997). The psychometric location of wisdom-related performance: Intelligence, personality, and more? *Personality & Social Psychology Bulletin, 23,* 1200–1214.

Staudinger, U. M., Smith, J., & Baltes, P. B. (1992). Wisdom-related knowledge in life review task: Age differences and the role of professional specialization. *Psychology and Aging, 7,* 271–281.

Sternberg, R. J. (1977). *Intelligence, information processing, and analogical reasoning: The componential analysis of human abilities.* Hillsdale, NJ: Erlbaum.

Sternberg, R. J., (1981). Intelligence and nonentrenchment. *Journal of Educational Psychology, 73,* 1–16.

Sternberg, R. J. (1983). Components of human intelligence. *Cognition, 15,* 1–48.

Sternberg, R. J. (1985a). *Beyond IQ: A triarchic theory of human intelligence.* New York: Cambridge University Press.

Sternberg, R. J. (1985b). *Human abilities: An information-processing approach.* San Francisco: Freeman.

Sternberg, R. J. (1986). *Intelligence applied: Understanding and increasing your intellectual skills.* San Diego: Harcourt Brace Jovanovich.

Sternberg, R. J. (1987). Most vocabulary is learned from context. In M. G. McKeown & M. E. Curtis (Eds.), *The nature of vocabulary acquisition* (pp. 89–105). Hillsdale, NJ: Erlbaum.

Sternberg, R. J. (1988). *The triarchic mind: A new theory of human intelligence.* New York: Viking.

Sternberg, R. J. (1990a). *Metaphors of mind: Conceptions of the nature of intelligence.* New York: Cambridge University Press.

Sternberg, R. J. (1990b). Wisdom and its relations to intelligence and creativity. In R. J. Sternberg (Ed.), *Wisdom: Its nature, origins, and development* (pp. 142–159). New York: Cambridge University Press.

Sternberg, R. J. (1991a). Theory-based testing of intellectual abilities: Rationale for the Triarchic Abilities Test. In H. Rowe (Ed.), *Intelligence: Reconceptualization and measurement* (pp. 183–202). Hillsdale, NJ: Erlbaum.

Sternberg, R. J. (1991b). Triarchic abilities test. In D. Dickinson (Ed.), *Creating the future: Perspectives on educational change* (pp. 76–81). Aston Clinton, Buckinghamshire, UK: Accelerated Learning Systems.

Sternberg, R. J. (1993). *Sternberg Triarchic Abilities Test.* Unpublished test.

Sternberg, R. J. (1994a). Cognitive conceptions of expertise. *International Journal of Expert Systems: Research and Applications, 7* (1), 1–12.

Sternberg, R. J. (1994b). Intelligence. In R. J. Sternberg (Ed.), *Handbook of perception and cognition: Thinking and problem solving* (pp. 263–288). San Diego: Academic Press.

Sternberg, R. J. (1994c). Tacit knowledge and job success. In N. Anderson & P. Herriot (Eds.), *Assessment and selection in organizations* (pp. 27–39). New York: John Wiley & Sons Inc.

Sternberg, R. J. (1995a). Expertise in complex problem solving: A comparison of alternative conceptions. In P. A. Frensch & J. Funke (Eds.), *Complex problem solving: European perspectives* (pp. 295–321). Hillsdale, NJ: Erlbaum.

Sternberg, R. J. (1995b). *In search of the human mind.* Orlando: Harcourt Brace College Publishers.

Sternberg, R. J. (1995c). Theory and measurement of tacit knowledge as part of practical intelligence. *Zeitschrift fur Psychologie, 203,* 319–333.

Sternberg, R. J. (1996). Costs of expertise. In K. A. Ericsson (Ed.), *The road to excellence.* Mahwah, NJ: Erlbaum.

Sternberg, R. J. (1997a). *Successful intelligence.* New York: Plume.

Sternberg, R. J. (1997b). Tacit knowledge and job success. In N. Anderson & P. Herriot (Eds), *International handbook of selection and assessment* (pp. 201–213). New York: John Wiley & Sons Inc.

Sternberg, R. J. (1998a). Abilities as forms of developing expertise. *Educational Researcher, 27,* 11–20.

Sternberg, R. J. (1998b). A balance theory of wisdom. *Review of General Psychology, 2,* 347–365.

Sternberg, R. J. (1998c). Successful intelligence: An expanded approach to understanding intelligence. In K. Pribram (Ed.), *Brain and Values: Is a biological science of values possible* (pp. 1–21). Mahwah, NJ: Erlbaum.

Sternberg, R. J. (1999a). A propulsion model of types of creative contributions. *Review of General Psychology, 3,* 83–100.

Sternberg, R. J. (1999b). Schools should nurture wisdom. In B. Z. Presessen (Ed.), *Teaching for Intelligence I: A Collection of articles* (pp 55–82). Arlington, Heights: Ill Skylight.

Sternberg, R. J. (Ed.) (in press, a) *Handbook of Intelligence.* New York: Cambridge University Press.

Sternberg, R. J. (in press, b). Intelligence as developing expertise. *Contemporary Educational Psychology.*

Sternberg, R. J. (in press, c). The theory of successful intelligence. *Review of General Psychology.*

Sternberg, R. J., & Ben-Zeev, T. (in press). *Complex cognition: The psychology of human thought.* New York: Oxford University Press.

Sternberg, R. J., & Berg, C. A. (1986). Quantitative integration: Definitions of intelligence: A comparison of the 1921 and 1986 symposia. In R. J. Sternberg & D. K. Detterman (Eds.), *What is intelligence? Contemporary viewpoints on its nature and definition* (pp. 155–162). Norwood, NJ: Ablex.

Sternberg, R. J., & Berg, C. A. (1992). *Intellectual development.* New York: Cambridge University Press.

Sternberg, R. J., & Clinkenbeard, P. R. (1995). A triarchic model of identifying, teaching, and assessing gifted children. *Roeper Review, 17,* 255–260.

Sternberg, R. J., Conway, B. E., Ketron, J. L., & Bernstein, M. (1981). People's conceptions of intelligence. *Journal of Personality and Social Psychology, 41,* 37–55.

Sternberg, R. J., & Detterman D. K. (Eds.). (1986). *What is intelligence? Contemporary viewpoints on its nature and definition.* Norwood, NJ: Ablex.

Sternberg, R. J., Ferrari, M., Clinkenbeard, P. R., & Grigorenko, E. L. (1996). Identification, instruction, and assessment of gifted children: A construct validation of a triarchic model. *Gifted Child Quarterly, 40,* 129–137.

Sternberg, R. J., & Gardner, M. K. (1982). A componential interpretation of the general factor in human intelligence. In H. J. Eysenck (Ed.), *A model for intelligence* (pp. 231–254). Berlin: Springer-Verlag.

Sternberg, R. J., & Grigorenko, E. L. (1997a). The cognitive costs of physical and mental ill health: Applying the psychology of the developed world to the problems of the developing world. *Eye on Psi Chi, 2,* 20–27.

Sternberg, R. J., & Grigorenko, E. L. (Eds.). (1997b). *Intelligence, heredity and environment.* New York: Cambridge University Press.

Sternberg, R. J., Grigorenko, E. L., & Ferrari, M. (in press). Developing expertise: The respective roles of abilities and deliberate practice. In M. Ferrari (Ed.), *Expertise and its development.* New York: Guilford.

Sternberg, R. J., Grigorenko, E. L., Ferrari, M. & Clinkenbeard, P. (1999). A triarchic analysis of an aptitude-treatment interaction. *European Journal of Psychological Assessment, 15*(1), 1–11.

Sternberg, R. J., Grigorenko, E. L., & Gil, G. (1999). Measuring everyday situational-judgments skills. Unpublished Manuscript.

Sternberg, R. J., Grigorenko, E. L., Ngorosho, D., Tantubuye, E., Mbise, A., Nokes, C., & Bundy, D. A. (1999). Hidden intellectual potential in rural Tanzanian school children. Manuscript submitted for publication.

Sternberg, R. J., & Horvath, J. A. (Eds.). (1999). *Tacit knowledge in professional practice.* Mahwah, NJ: Erlbaum.

Sternberg, R. J., & Kaufman, J. C. (1996). Innovation and intelligence testing: The curious case of the dog that didn't bark. *European Journal of Psychological Assessment, 12,* 175–182.

Sternberg, R. J., & Kaufman, J. C. (1998). Human abilities. *Annual Review of Psychology, 49,* 479–502.

Sternberg, R. J., & Lubart, T. I. (1995). *Defying the crowd: Cultivating creativity in a culture of conformity.* New York: Free Press.

Sternberg, R. J., Nokes, K., Geissler, P. W., Prince, R., Okatcha, F., Bundy, D., & Grigorenko, E. L. (1999). The relationship between academic and practical intelligence: A case study in Kenya. Manuscript submitted for publicaiton.

Sternberg, R. J., Okagaki, L., & Jackson, A. (1990). Practical intelligence for success in school. *Educational Leadership, 48,* 35–39.

Sternberg, R. J., & Powell, J. S. (1983). Comprehending verbal comprehension. *American Psychologist, 38,* 878–893.

Sternberg, R. J., & Smith, C. (1985). Social intelligence and decoding skills in nonverbal communication. *Social Cognition, 3,* 168–192.

Sternberg, R. J., & Wagner, R. K. (Eds.). (1986). *Practical intelligence: Nature and origins of competence in the everyday world.* New York: Cambridge University Press.

Sternberg, R. J., & Wagner, R. K. (1993). The geocentric view of intelligence and job performance is wrong. *Current Directions in Psychological Science, 2,* 1–5.

Sternberg, R. J., & Wagner, R. K. (Eds.). (1994). *Mind in context.* New York: Cambridge University Press.

Sternberg, R. J., Wagner, R. K., & Okagaki, L. (1993). Practical intelligence: The nature and role of tacit knowledge in work and at school. In H. Reese & J. Puckett (Eds.), *Advances in lifespan development* (pp. 205–227). Hillsdale, NJ: Erlbaum.

Sternberg, R. J., Wagner, R. K., Williams, W. M., & Horvath, J. A. (1995). Testing common sense. *American Psychologist, 50,* 912–927.

Stogdill, R. M. (1948). Personal factors associated with leadership: A survey of the literature. *Journal of Psychology, 25,* 35–71.

Strang, R. (1930). Measures of social intelligence. *American Journal of Sociology, 36,* 263–269.

Stricker, L. J., & Rock, D. A. (1990). Interpersonal competence, social intelligence, and general ability. *Personality and Individual Differences, 11,* 833–839.

Strough, J., Berg, C., Sansone, C. (1996). Goals for solving everyday problems across the life span: Age and gender differences in the salience of interpersonal concerns. *Developmental Psychology, 32,* 1106–1115.

Super, C. M., & Harkness, S. (1982). The infants' niche in rural Kenya and metropolitan America. In L. L. Adler (Ed.), *Cross-Cultural Research at Issue.* New York: Academic Press.

Taylor, F. W. (1947). *Scientific management.* New York: Harper & Brothers.

Terman, L. M. (1916). *The measurement of intelligence*. Boston: Houghton Mifflin.

Terman, L. M. (1950). *Concept Mastery Test*. New York: The Psychological Corporation.

Terman, L. M., & Merrill, M. A. (1937). *Measuring intelligence*. Boston: Houghton Mifflin.

Terman, L. M., & Merrill, M. A. (1960). *Stanford-Binet intelligence scale*. Boston: Houghton Mifflin.

Thomson, G. H. (1939). *The factorial analysis of human ability*. London: University of London Press.

Thorndike, E. L. (1920). Intelligence and its use. *Harper's Magazine, 140,* 227–235.

Thorndike, R. L., Hagen, E. P., & Sattler, J. M. (1986). *Technical manual for the Stanford-Binet Intelligence Scale* (4th ed.). Chicago: Riverside.

Thorndike, R. L., & Stein, S. (1937). An evaluation of the attempts to measure social intelligence. *Psychological Bulletin, 34,* 275–285.

Thornton, G. C., & Byham, W. C. (1982). *Assessment centers and managerial performance*. New York: Academic Press.

Thornton, G. C., & Cleveland, J. N. (1990). Developing managerial talent through simulation. *American Psychologist, 45,* 190–199.

Thurstone, L. L. (1938). *Primary mental abilities*. Chicago: University of Chicago Press.

Tornow, W. W. (1993). Perceptions or reality: Is multi-perspective measurement a means or an end? *Human Resource Management, 32,* 221–229.

Tulving, E. (1972). Episodic and semantic memory. In E. Tulving & W. Donaldson (Eds.), *Organization of memory*. New York: Academic Press.

Tulving, E. (1985). Memory and consciousness. *Canadian Psychology, 25,* 1–12.

Tulving, E. (1995). Organization of memory: Quo vadis? In M. S. Gazzaniga (Ed.), *The cognitive neurosciences*. Cambridge, MA: MIT Press.

U.S. Department of the Army. (1987a). *Leadership and Command at Senior Levels (FM 22–103)*. Washington, D. C.

U.S. Department of the Army. (1987b). *Personnel – General Executive Leadership (Pamphlet 600-80)*. Washington, D.C.

U.S. Department of the Army. (1990). *Military leadership (FM 22–100)*. Washington, D.C.

Vallacher, R. R., & Wegner, D. M. (1987). What do people think they're doing? Action identification and human behavior. *Psychological Review, 94,* 3–15.

Valsiner, J., & Leung, M. C. (1994). From intelligence to knowledge construction: A sociogenetic process approach. In R. J. Sternberg & R. K. Wagner (Eds.), *Mind in context* (pp. 202–217). New York: Cambridge University Press.

Vaughan, F. E. (1979). *Awakening intuition*. Garden City, NY: Anchor Press/Doubleday.

Vernon, P. E. (1933). Some characteristics of the good judge of personality. *Journal of Social Psychology, 4,* 42–57.

Vernon, P. E. (1971). *The structure of human abilities*. London: Methuen.

Vernon, P. A., & Mori, M. (1992). Intelligence, reaction times, and peripheral nerve conduction velocity. *Intelligence, 8,* 273–288.

Virga, P. H. (Ed.) (1987). *The National Management Association handbook for managers*. Englewood Cliffs, NJ: Prentice-Hall.

Voss, J. F., Perkins, D. N., & Segal, J. W. (Eds.). (1991). *Informal reasoning and education*. Hillsdale, NJ: Erlbaum.

Vygotsky, L. (1978). *Mind in society: The development of higher order processes*. Cambridge, MA: Harvard University Press.

Wagner, D. A. (1978). Memories of Morocco: The influence of age, schooling and environment on memory. *Cognitive Psychology, 10,* 1–28.

Wagner, R. K. (1987). Tacit knowledge in everyday intelligent behavior. *Journal of Personality and Social Psychology, 52,* 1236–1247.

Wagner, R. K. (1991). Managerial problem-solving. In R. J. Sternberg & P. Frensch (Eds.), *Complex problem solving: Principles and mechanisms* (pp. 159–183). Hillsdale, NJ: Erlbaum.

Wagner, R. K. (1997). Intelligence, training, and employment. *American Psychologist, 52,* 1059–1069.

Wagner, R. K. (in press). Practical intelligence. In R. J. Sternberg (Ed.), *Handbook of intelligence*. New York: Cambridge University Press.

Wagner, R. K., Rashotte, C. A., & Sternberg, R. J. (1994). *Tacit knowledge in sales: Rules of thumb for selling anything to anyone*. Paper presented at the Annual Meeting of the American Educational Research Association, Washington, D.C.

Wagner, R. K., & Sternberg, R. J. (1985). Practical intelligence in real-world pursuits: The role of tacit knowledge. *Journal of Personality and Social Psychology, 49,* 436–458.

Wagner, R. K., & Sternberg, R. J. (1986). Tacit knowledge and intelligence in the everyday world. In R. J. Sternberg & R. K. Wagner (Eds.), *Practical intelligence: Nature and origins of competence in the everyday world* (pp. 51–83). New York: Cambridge University Press.

Wagner, R. K., & Sternberg, R. J. (1989). *Tacit Knowledge Inventory for Sales: Written*. Unpublished test.

Wagner, R. K., & Sternberg, R. J. (1990). Street smarts. In K. E. Clark & M. B. Clark (Eds.), *Measures of leadership* (pp. 493–504). West Orange, NJ: Leadership Library of America.

Wagner, R. K., & Sternberg, R. J. (1991). *Tacit Knowledge Inventory for Managers*. San Antonio: The Psychological Corporation.

Wagner, R. K., Sujan, H., Sujan, M., Rashotte, C. A. & Sternberg, R. J. (1999). Tacit knowledge in sales. In R. J. Sternberg & J. A. Horvath (Eds.), *Tacit knowledge in professional practice* (pp. 155–182). Mahwah, NJ: Erlbaum

Wahlsten, D., & Gottlieb, G. (1997). The invalid separation of effects of nature and nurture: Lessons from animal experimentation. In R. J. Sternberg & E. L. Grigorenko (Eds.), *Intelligence, heredity, and environment* (pp. 42–88). New York: Cambridge University Press.

Wechsler, D. (1958). *The measurement and appraisal of adult intelligence* (4th ed.). Baltimore: Williams & Wilkins.

Wechsler, D. (1981). *Wechsler Adult Intelligence Scale-Revised*. New York: Psychological Corporation.

Wechsler, D. (1989). *Manual for the Wechsler Preschool and Primary Scale of Intelligence* (rev. ed.). San Antonio: Psychological Corporation.

Wechsler, D. (1991). *Manual for the Wechsler Intelligence Scales for Children* (3rd ed.) (WISC III). San Antonio: Psychological Corporation.

Wechsler, D. (1997). *Manual for the Wechsler Adult Intelligence Scales* (WAIS-III). San Antonio: Psychological Corporation.

Wedeck, J. (1947). The relationship between personality and psychological ability. *British Journal of Psychology, 36,* 133–151.

Wertsch, J. V. (1985). *Vygotsky and the social formation of mind.* Cambridge, MA: Harvard University Press.

Wertsch, J., & Kanner, B. G. (1994). A sociocultural approach to intellectual development. In R. J. Sternberg & C. A. Berg (Eds.), *Intellectual development* (pp. 328–349). New York: Cambridge University Press.

Wickett J. C., & Vernon, P. A. (1994). Peripheral nerve conduction velocity, reaction time, and intelligence: An attempt to replicate Vernon and Mori. *Intelligence, 18,* 127–132.

Wigdor, A. K., & Garner, W. R. (Eds.). (1982). *Ability testing: Uses, consequences, and controversies.* Washington, D.C.: National Academy Press.

Williams, S. A., Denney, N. W., & Schadler, M. (1983). Elderly adults' perception of their own cognitive development during the adult years. *International Journal of Aging and Human Development, 16,* 147–158.

Williams, W. M., Blythe, T., White, N., Li, J., Sternberg, R. J., & Gardner, H. I. (1996). *Practical intelligence for school: A handbook for teachers of grades 5–8.* New York: Harper Collins.

Williams, W. M., & Sternberg, R. J. (in press). *Success acts for managers.* Mahwah, NJ: Erlbaum.

Willis, S. L. (1987). Cognitive training and everyday competence. In K. W. Schaie (Ed.), *Annual Review of Gerontology and Geriatrics* (Vol. 7, pp. 159–188). New York: Springer.

Willis, S. L. (1989). Improvement with cognitive training: Which dogs learn what tricks? In L. W. Poon, D. C. Rubin, & B. A. Wilson (Eds.), *Everyday cognition in adulthood and late life* (pp. 300–329). New York: Cambridge University Press.

Willis, S. L. (1990). Contributions of cognitive training research to late life potential. In M. Perlmutter (Ed.), *Late life potential* (pp. 25–42). Washington, DC: Gerontological Society of America.

Willis, S. L., Blieszner, R., & Baltes, P. B. (1981). Training research in aging: Modification of performance on the fluid ability of figural relations. *Journal of Educational Psychology, 73,* 41–50.

Willis, S. L., & Nesselroade, C. S. (1990). Long-term effects of fluid ability training in old-old age. *Developmental Psychology, 26,* 905–910.

Willis, S. L., & Schaie, K. W. (1986). Practical intelligence in later adulthood. In R. J. Sternberg & R. Wagner (Eds.), *Practical Intelligence* (pp. 236–270). New York: Cambridge University Press.

Willis, S. L. & Schaie, K. W. (1994). Cognitive training in the normal elderly. In F. Boller (Ed.), *Cerebral plasticity and cognitive stimulation.* New York: Springer.

Winner, E. (1996a). *Gifted children.* New York: Basic.

Winner, E. (1996b). The rage to master: The decisive role of talent in the visual arts. In K. A. Ericsson (Ed.), *The road to excellence* (pp. 271–301). Hillsdale, NJ: Erlbaum.

Winograd, T. (1972). *Understanding natural language.* New York: Academic Press.

Wissler, C. (1901). The correlation of mental and physical tests. *Psychological Review, Monograph Supplement, 3* (6).

Wong, C. T., Day, J. D., Maxwell, S. E., & Meara, N. M. (1995). A multitrait-multimethod study of academic and social intelligence in college students. *Journal of Educational Psychology, 87,* 117–133.

Woodcock, R. W., & Johnson, M. B. (1989). *Woodcock-Johnson Tests of Cognitive Ability–Revised.* Itasca, IL: Riverside.

Worden, P. E., & Sherman-Brown, S. (1983). A word-frequency cohort effect in young versus elderly adults' memory for words. *Developmental Psychology, 19,* 521–530.

Yang, S., & Sternberg, R. J. (1997). Conceptions of intelligence in ancient Chinese philosophy. *Journal of Theoretical and Philosophical Psychology, 17(2),* 101–119.

Yerkes, R. M. (1921). *The measurement and appraisal of adult intelligence* (4th ed.). Baltimore: Williams & Wilkins.

Yukl, G. (1971). Toward a behavioral theory of leadership. *Organizational Behavior and Human Performance, 6,* 414–440.

Yukl, G. (1989). Managerial leadership: A review of theory and research. *Journal of Management, 15,* 251–289.

Yukl, G. (1998). *Leadership in organizations* (4th ed.). Upper Saddle River, NJ: Prentice-Hall.

Yukl, G., & Van Fleet, D. D. (1992). Theory and research on leadership in organizations. In M. D. Dunnette & L. M. Hough (Eds.), *Handbook of industrial and organizational psychology* (Vol. 3). Palo Alto, CA: Consulting Psychologists Press.

Yukl, G., Wall, S., & Lepsinger, R. (1990). Preliminary report on validation of the Managerial Practices Survey. In K. E. Clark & M. B. Clark (Eds.), *Measures of leadership* (pp. 223–237). West Orange, NJ: Leadership Library of America.

Yussen, S. R., & Kane, P. (1985). Children's concept of intelligence. In S. R. Yussen (Ed.), *The growth of reflection in children.* New York: Academic Press.

Zaleznik, A. (1977). Managers and leaders: Are they different? *Harvard Business Review, 55,* 67–78.

TKIM™

Tacit Knowledge Inventory for Managers

TEST BOOKLET

Richard K. Wagner and Robert J. Sternberg 1989

This task presents work-related situations, each followed by a series of items that are relevant to handling that situation. For each situation, briefly scan all of the items and then rate the quality of each item on the 1 to 7 scale provided. Using a #2 pencil, mark your response on the separate ANSWER SHEET. Try to use the entire scale when you respond, although it is not necessary that you do so for each situation. For example, you may decide that none of the items listed for a particular question is good, or you may decide that they all are. There are, of course, no "correct" answers.

Here is an example:

Your immediate superior has asked for your opinion on a new promotional campaign that she has developed. You think the promotional campaign is terrible and that using it would be a big mistake. You have noticed previously that your superior does not take criticism well, and you suspect she is looking more for reassurance than for an honest opinion.

Given the present situation, rate the quality of each of the following reactions on this 1- to 7-point scale.

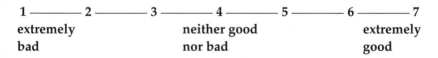

1	2	3	4	5	6	7
extremely bad			neither good nor bad			extremely good

a. Tell her that you think the campaign is great.
b. Tell her that you like the work but have some reservations about whether it is the right campaign for this client.

If the respondent gave the first item a rating of 1, this would indicate that the individual thought this response was extremely bad. A rating of 5 for the second item would indicate that the response is good, although not extremely so.

Please respond to every item, and when you have finished, check to be sure you have not inadvertently omitted a response.

1. You are an executive vice-president in the marketing division of Sherman Electronics, a company that sells audio and video supplies. You have been with Sherman Electronics since finishing college, having spent thirteen years in a managerial role in human resources and two years in your present position.

Sherman Electronics has been losing market share for its products steadily over the past five years. Sherman's strength in the past has been introducing new products before its competition, but now its product line seems to be three steps behind the leaders in a rapidly changing market. A strategy of focusing on more stable segments of the market has been aborted because of fierce competition from large overseas companies.

You believe that your lack of knowledge about the latest audio and video products and technology limits your effectiveness. Your schedule is very busy, but you think it is important to catch up on, and keep up with, innovation that affects your industry.

Rate the quality of the following strategies for becoming more knowledgeable about new products and technology on a 1- to 7-point scale.

1	2	3	4	5	6	7
extremely bad			neither good nor bad			extremely good

1. Ask for a leave of absence to pursue an advanced technical degree.
2. Order a news clipping service (news clipping services provide news from a large number of sources on a given topic).
3. Subscribe to several technical journals relevant to your manufacturing operations.
4. Subscribe to several consumer-oriented magazines that cover your products.
5. Begin attending trade shows of products in your industry.

6. Ask to sit in on weekly discussions of new product ideas held by the Research and Development division.
7. Attend a series of technical presentations by research scientists from outside the company who are brought in by the Manufacturing Operations division.
8. Hire a staff member whose primary responsibility is to keep you abreast of current trends in your industry.
9. Ask the Engineering division to prepare monthly summary reports of innovative products.
10. Ask for weekly presentations for you and your staff on technical issues by staff in the Research and Development and Manufacturing Operations divisions.

2. An employee who reports to one of your subordinates has asked to talk with you about waste, poor management practices, and possible violations of both company policy and the law on the part of your subordinate. You have been in your present position only a year, but in that time you have had no indications of trouble about the subordinate in question. Neither you nor your company has an "open door" policy, so it is expected that employees should take their concerns to their immediate supervisors before bringing a matter to the attention of anyone else. The employee who wishes to meet with you has not discussed this matter with her supervisor because of its delicate nature.

Rate the quality of the following things you are considering doing in this situation on a 1- to 7-point scale:

```
1 ———— 2 ———— 3 ———— 4 ———— 5 ———— 6 ———— 7
extremely              neither good              extremely
bad                    nor bad                   good
```

11. Refuse to meet with the employee unless the individual first discusses the matter with your subordinate.
12. Meet with the employee but only with your subordinate present.
13. Schedule a meeting with the employee and then with your subordinate to get both sides of the story.
14. Meet with the employee and then investigate the allegations if an investigation appears warranted before talking with your subordinate.

15. Find out more information about the employee, if you can, before making any decisions.
16. Refuse to meet with the employee and inform your subordinate that the employee has attempted to sidestep the chain of command.
17. Meet with your subordinate first before deciding whether to meet with the employee.
18. Reprimand the employee for ignoring the chain of command.
19. Ask a senior colleague whom you respect for advice about what to do in this situation.
20. Turn the matter over to an assistant.

3. You have just completed your most important project ever, which involved automating the company's warehouses. You have worked many evenings and weekend days over the last six months on this project. You are pleased with your performance because, despite adversity, the project was completed at the projected cost and on time. Near the project's end, it seemed likely that you were going to need additional time and money. But, through hard work on your part, and by pushing some of your people very hard, you met both time deadlines and cost projections.

In a meeting, your supervisor (having been in his position for six months), brings up the topic of your performance on the project. Expecting lavish praise, and perhaps even discussion of a possible increase in responsibility, you are stunned by his evaluation of your performance, which is entirely negative. He states that some of your subordinates have complained to him directly about their treatment at your hands in the last phase of project completion. He questions your ability to manage others, and wonders aloud about your ability to lead others. He says nothing positive about the fact that you completed the project on time and at cost under adverse circumstances, nor about how hard you worked on the project.

Rate the quality of the following things you might do in this situation on a 1- to 7-point scale.

1	2	3	4	5	6	7
extremely bad			neither good nor bad			extremely good

21. Admit that you perhaps were too hard on your workers, but state that in your judgment, the importance of meeting the deadline and budget projection made your actions necessary.
22. Express disappointment with your performance appraisal, and state that you think it is one-sided.
23. Accept the criticism and explain how you will behave differently in the future.
24. Try to find out if anything else is behind this overly negative evaluation.
25. Begin looking for a new position.
26. Discuss with your supervisor specific examples of where he thinks you went wrong in dealing with the project, and how he would have handled it more effectively.
27. Ask your supervisor to give you a second chance, resolving to yourself to keep him better informed about your activities in the future.
28. Ask your supervisor to help you develop your skills at managing others.
29. Seek the advice of others you trust in the company about what you should do.
30. Admit you might have made some mistakes, but be sure your supervisor is aware of all that you accomplished and the adverse circumstances that you faced.

4. Rate the quality of the following strategies for handling the day-to-day work of a business manager on a 1- to 7-point scale.

1 ———— 2 ———— 3 ———— 4 ———— 5 ———— 6 ———— 7

extremely   neither good   extremely

bad   nor bad   good

31. Think in terms of tasks accomplished rather than hours spent working.
32. Use a daily list of goals arranged according to your priorities.
33. Reward yourself upon completion of important tasks for the day.
34. Be in charge of all phases of every task or project you are involved in.
35. Take frequent but short breaks (i.e., a quick walk to the mail room) throughout the day.

36. Only delegate inconsequential tasks, since you cannot guarantee that the tasks will be done properly and on time unless you do them yourself.
37. Do only what you are in the mood to do to maximize the quality of your work.
38. Take every opportunity to get feedback on early drafts of your work.
39. Set your own deadlines in addition to externally imposed ones.
40. Do not spend much time planning the best way to do something because the best way to do something may not be apparent until after you have begun doing it.

5. You have been asked to give a talk to managers in the company on tips for good business writing.

Rate the quality of the following pieces of advice about business writing that you are considering including in your talk on a 1- to 7-point scale.

1 ———— 2 ———— 3 ———— 4 ———— 5 ———— 6 ———— 7
extremely   **neither good**   **extremely**
bad   **nor bad**   **good**

41. Write reports so that the main points will be understood by a reader who only has time to skim the report.
42. Explain, in the first few paragraphs, how the report is organized.
43. Use everyday language and avoid all business jargon.
44. Work hard to convey your message in the fewest number of words.
45. Consider carefully whom you are writing for.
46. Write carefully the first time around to avoid having to rewrite.
47. Be formal rather than informal in your style.
48. Avoid visual aids, such as figures, charts, and diagrams, because they often oversimplify the message.
49. Use the passive rather than the active voice (e.g., write "30 managers were interviewed" rather than "we interviewed 30 managers").
50. Avoid using the first person (e.g., write "it is recommended" rather than "I recommend").

6. You have been assigned to revise the policy manual for your division of the company. You have six weeks to complete this assignment. The old policy manual was too vague, resulting in several individuals attending to matters only one need handle, and other important matters receiving the attention of no one. Responsibility for the new policy manual is completely yours. The assignment is somewhat of a "hot potato" because of the effects of division policy on the importance of particular management positions in the division. You believe that how this assignment turns out could have important positive or negative consequences for your career.

Rate the quality of the following courses of action you might take in terms of their leading to positive consequences for your career on a 1- to 7-point scale.

1 ———— 2 ———— 3 ———— 4 ———— 5 ———— 6 ———— 7
extremely   **neither good**   **extremely**
bad   **nor bad**   **good**

51. Decide right away if you can come up with a reasonable product that would be satisfactory to most – if not, try to get out of the assignment.
52. Learn as much as possible about your superiors' views on policy covered by the manual.
53. Stick with revisions your superiors favor or probably could be sold on.
54. Get feedback from your superiors on drafts of new policy under consideration.
55. Get feedback from those affected by the policy manual on drafts of new policy under consideration.
56. Form a committee with representation from every department that will share responsibility for the assignment.
57. Find out, if you can, why you, specifically, were chosen for this assignment.
58. Use this opportunity to reduce the power of those in the division who do not support you, as long as you can avoid being obvious about it.
59. Avoid mentioning by name individuals whose poor performance is the cause for a particular policy revision.

60. Don't worry if you miss the deadline for the new policy manual as long as you are making progress.

7. You are responsible for awarding a contract for a new heating system for your plant. As is true for most decisions, the information you have is neither perfectly reliable nor complete.

Rate the importance of the following pieces of information in making your decision to award the contract to the Jackson Heating Company on a 1- to 7-point scale.

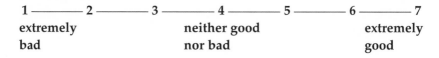

1 ———— 2 ———— 3 ———— 4 ———— 5 ———— 6 ———— 7
extremely   neither good   extremely
bad   nor bad   good

61. The Better Business Bureau reports no major complaints about the company.
62. The bid of the company is $3,000 less than that or any other bid (approximate cost of the system is $65,000).
63. The company advertises their heating system as being the most reliable heating system you can buy for the price.
64. Former customers whom you have contacted personally are favorably impressed with the company and its product.
65. The company's estimate of cost of operation of the heating system was lower than that of competing companies.
66. The company is new.
67. The company promises a very quick installation.
68. The company has provided letters from former customers attesting to the quality of their heating system.
69. The company has done good work for your company in the past.
70. A competitor of your company has recently purchased the same heating system from the same company you are considering awarding the contract to.

8. You are looking for a new project to tackle in the coming year. You have considered a number of possible projects and desire to pick the project that would be best for you.

Rate the importance of the following considerations when selecting new projects on a 1- to 7-point scale.

1 ——— 2 ——— 3 ——— 4 ——— 5 ——— 6 ——— 7
extremely   neither good   extremely
bad   nor bad   good

71. The project is the one my immediate superior most desires to be completed.
72. Doing the project would require my developing skills that may enhance my future career success.
73. The project should attract the attention of the local media.
74. Doing the project should prove to be fun.
75. The risk of making a mistake is virtually nonexistent.
76. The project will require my interacting with senior executives whom I would like to get to know better.
77. The project is valued by my superior even though it is not valued by me.
78. The project will enable me to demonstrate my talents that others may not be aware of.
79. The project is in an area with which I have a lot of experience.
80. The project is the one I most want to do.

9. You and a co-worker jointly are responsible for completing a report on a new product by the end of the week. You are uneasy about this assignment because he has a reputation for not meeting deadlines. The problem does not appear to be lack of effort. Rather, he seems to lack certain organizational skills necessary to meet a deadline and also is quite a perfectionist. As a result, too much time is wasted coming up with the "perfect" idea, product, or report.

Your goal is to produce the best possible report by the deadline at the end of the week. Rate the quality of the following strategies for meeting your goal on a 1- to 7-point scale.

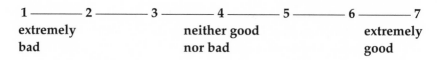

1 ———— 2 ———— 3 ———— 4 ———— 5 ———— 6 ———— 7
extremely   neither good   extremely
bad   nor bad   good

81. Divide the work to be done in half and tell him that if he does not complete his part, you obviously will have to let your immediate superior know it was not your fault.
82. Politely tell him to be less of a perfectionist.
83. Set deadlines for completing each part of the report, and accept what you have accomplished at each deadline as the final version of that part of the report.
84. Ask your superior to check up on your progress on a daily basis (after explaining why).
85. Praise your co-worker verbally for completion of parts of the assignment.
86. Get angry with him at the first sign of getting behind schedule.
87. As soon as he begins to fall behind, take responsibility for doing the report yourself, if need be, to meet the deadline.
88. Point out firmly, but politely, how he is holding up the report.
89. Avoid putting any pressure on him because it will just make him fall even more behind.
90. Offer to buy him dinner at the end of the week if you both meet the deadline.
91. Ignore his organizational problem so you don't give attention to maladaptive behavior.

TACIT KNOWLEDGE INVENTORY FOR SALES: WRITTEN

Richard K. Wagner and Robert J. Sternberg 1989

This task asks you about your views on matters pertaining to the work of a salesperson. There are 8 questions in all. Each question presents you with a sales-related situation and a series of items that are relevant to handling that situation. For each situation, briefly scan all of the items and then rate the quality of each item on the 1 to 9 scale provided by entering the appropriate number in the blanks on the answer sheet. Try to use the entire scale when you respond, although it is not necessary that you do so for each situation. For example, you may decide that none of the items listed for a particular situation is good, or you may decide that they all are. There are, of course, no "correct" answers. Please read every situation and item carefully. You may find some items to be similar at first glance.

Here is an example:

Your immediate superior has asked for your opinion on a sales campaign that she has developed for a new camera. You think the sales campaign is terrible, and that using it would be a big mistake. You have noticed that your superior does not take criticism well and you suspect that she is looking more for reassurance than for an honest opinion.

Given the present situation, rate the quality of each of the following responses on this 1- to 9-point scale.

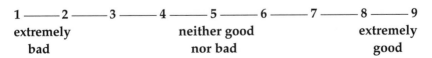

1 ——— 2 ——— 3 ——— 4 ——— 5 ——— 6 ——— 7 ——— 8 ——— 9
extremely   neither good   extremely
  bad   nor bad   good

a. _1_ Tell her that you think the campaign is great.

b. _7_ Tell her that you like the work but wonder whether it is the right sales campaign for that particular product.

The rating of 1 indicates that this response is extremely bad. The rating of 7 indicates that this item is moderately good. Although you may spend as much time as you wish, it will probably take you from 20 to 30 minutes to complete the task. You may turn the page and begin when you are ready. For research purposes, it is vital that you *answer every item.*

1. You have been in sales for four years. Your sales record is better than average, but not outstanding, and you wish to become the top salesperson in your area.

You have decided to set goals for improving your sales performance. Goals you have been considering are listed below. Rate their quality as a means of improving your sales performance, using the following scale. Please remember to read all of the items before responding.

1 —— 2 —— 3 —— 4 —— 5 —— 6 —— 7 —— 8 —— 9
extremely   **neither good**   **extremely**
bad   **nor bad**   **good**

1. Increase my sales volume in units sold by 30 percent per week for the next year.
2. Increase my number of sales presentations to potential customers.
3. Increase my sales volume in dollars by 30 percent per year.
4. Record my goals in writing but do not let others know about them.
5. Increase my sales volume in dollars by 30 percent after seven years.
6. Make 10 more sales presentations to potential customers each month.
7. Increase my sales volume in units sold by 30 percent per year.
8. Commit my goals to memory rather than write them down so that others will not learn of them.
9. Work 10 more hours per month than I currently do.
10. Record my goals in writing and tell others I trust about them.

2. In a recent performance appraisal with your sales manager, you agreed that although your record was good with established accounts, you were not attracting enough new accounts to compensate for normal loss of accounts. Rate the quality of the following ideas for finding new accounts, using the following scale. Please remember to read all of the items before responding.

1 ——— 2 ——— 3 ——— 4 ——— 5 ——— 6 ——— 7 ——— 8 ——— 9
extremely   neither good   extremely
   bad   nor bad   good

11. Send a brochure describing your products to every business in your sales district.
12. Ask your satisfied customers to provide testimonials on their letterhead about your product.
13. Look through the Yellow Pages of the phone directory to discover businesses you do not know about that are potential customers.
14. Test a new sales promotion on a limited number of potential customers.
15. Send a brochure to a limited number of businesses that are most likely to be interested in your product.
16. Let potential customers know of those businesses that are current customers.
17. Get names of potential customers from other salespersons who sell noncompetitive products.
18. Replace your existing sales promotions with new ones.
19. Send personalized brochures (i.e., addressed to individual businesses and geared to their particular business) to those businesses that are most likely to be interested in your product.
20. Tell your sales manager you simply have a bad district and ask for another.
21. At the close of each sale, ask your customer for names of others who might benefit from your products.

3. You sell a line of photocopy machines. One of your machines has relatively few features and is inexpensive ($700), although it is not the least expensive model you carry. The $700 photocopy machine is not selling very well and it is overstocked. There is a shortage of the more elaborate photocopy machines in your line, so you have been asked to do what you can to improve sales of the $700 model. Rate the following strategies for maximizing your sales of the slow-moving photocopy machine, using the following scale. Please remember to read all of the items before responding.

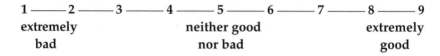

1 —— 2 —— 3 —— 4 —— 5 —— 6 —— 7 —— 8 —— 9

extremely	neither good	extremely
bad	nor bad	good

22. Stress with potential customers that although this model lacks some desirable features, the low price more than makes up for it.
23. Stress that there are relatively few models left at this price.
24. Arrange as many demonstrations of the machine as you are able.
25. Arrange to have several prospects try out the machine in their businesses for 2 months without charge.
26. Stress that the price of $700 is cheap for a copy machine.
27. If a customer wishes to know about other machines you carry, begin by introducing a less inexpensive machine, then introduce the $700 machine you are trying to sell, and finally introduce the more expensive model.
28. If a customer wishes to know about other machines you carry, begin by introducing a more expensive machine, then introduce the $700 machine you are trying to sell, and finally introduce a less expensive model.
29. Stress that you have a large inventory of this machine, so quick delivery is possible.
30. Advertise the current price of $700 as a 50 percent price reduction from the listing price of $1400 when the machine was introduced 5 years ago.
31. Stress simplicity of use, since it lacks confusing controls that other photocopy machines have.

4. As a salesperson, there are a number of strategies for handling one's tasks so as to maximize one's accomplishment. Rate the quality of the following strategies, using the following scale. Please remember to read all the items before responding.

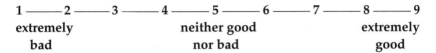

1 ——— 2 ——— 3 ——— 4 ——— 5 ——— 6 ——— 7 ——— 8 ——— 9
extremely   neither good   extremely
bad   nor bad   good

32. When deciding whether you had a productive day, consider how much time and effort you spent, rather than tasks accomplished, because hard work is no guarantee that tasks will be accomplished on a given day.
33. Force yourself to do unpleasant tasks that you would rather not do but eventually must.
34. Take your phone calls as they come in unless you absolutely cannot be disturbed.
35. Begin each day by writing a list of all you intend to accomplish.
36. Do only what you are in the mood to do so as to maximize the quality of your work.
37. Make a practice of returning correspondence and calls all at once at a specific time each day as much as possible.
38. Think in terms of tasks accomplished, rather than hours spent working.
39. Decide at the end of the day what your tasks for the next day should be.
40. Do not attempt to use a detailed plan for your daily activities because sales jobs require flexibility and split-second decision-making.
41. Review a record of your activities weekly as a way of monitoring how you actually are spending your time.

5. You have been working hard to sell your product to a potential customer and believe you are near to completing the sale. The potential customer has been attentive and appreciative during each of your meetings, and has acknowledged that he could use your product. You and the potential customer agree to complete the sale at your next meeting.

In your next meeting the potential customer backs out of the deal for no apparent reason. He claims to be interested in your product, but says that he is not ready to make a buying decision at the present time. Rate the quality of the following responses to this situation, using the following scale. Please remember to read all of the items before responding.

1 ——— 2 ——— 3 ——— 4 ——— 5 ——— 6 ——— 7 ——— 8 ——— 9
extremely   neither good   extremely
  bad   nor bad   good

42. If you suspect that a competitor has entered the picture, ask "Have you been quoted a lower price?"
43. State that you respect the individual's need for time in making the decision, and ask him to call you when he has made up his mind.
44. Point out that by placing an order now, the individual can lock in at the present price even if he does not desire immediate delivery.
45. Ask why the individual is not ready to decide today.
46. Ask what the individual's ideal product would look like, and how this ideal product would complement existing equipment and anticipated needs over the next decade.
47. If you suspect that a competitor has entered the picture, do not let on that you know, but take the information into account when you plan your next move.
48. If you suspect that the problem is concern about possible shipping delays, ask the customer what if you were to guarantee delivery (assuming you could do this) by the end of next week.
49. Ask what it would take to make the sale today.
50. Ask who in the company might be in the position to agree to a sale today.
51. Ask what the individual wants most in the product.

6. You are just finishing your sales presentation to a long-term and valued customer. To your chagrin, the customer says that she is about to order a competitor's product as a replacement for your product line. You have not even heard of the competitor's product. After mentally kicking yourself for not knowing about a competitor's product, you are determined to try your best to salvage the situation. Rate the following strategies for doing so, using the following scale. Please remember to read all of the items before responding.

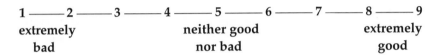

1 —— 2 —— 3 —— 4 —— 5 —— 6 —— 7 —— 8 —— 9
extremely   **neither good**   **extremely**
bad   **nor bad**   **good**

52. Mention that in your opinion, the competitor's product line is shoddy.
53. Ask a series of questions to determine what the customer knows about the competitor's product.
54. Find out what issue, if any, has kept the customer from already placing the order with your competitor, and try to use the issue to your advantage.
55. If your price is higher, point out that higher quality is less expensive in the long run.
56. Point out how not buying from you will hurt both you, your company, and ultimately, competition in the industry.
57. Mention that in your opinion, your company's products are second to none in reliability.
58. If your price is higher, state that the competitor must have left something out, and then try to figure out what that might be.
59. Point out how not buying from you will hurt your customer's company.
60. Ask a set of questions to determine what the customer knows about other potential competitors.
61. If your price is higher, state that you are sure your competitor will raise its prices for subsequent orders.

7. You have just completed a sales presentation to two buyers for a large company. At the conclusion of your presentation, the buyers say that they would like to do business with you, but you will have to cut your price. You believe that your price is both fair and competitive, and if you lower your price significantly there will be little or no margin for profit. However, you are eager to land this account. Rate the quality of the following responses you might make to the buyers, using the following scale. Please remember to read all of the items before responding.

1 ——— 2 ——— 3 ——— 4 ——— 5 ——— 6 ——— 7 ——— 8 ——— 9

extremely	**neither good**	**extremely**
bad	**nor bad**	**good**

62. Stand by your original price, and at the same time stress the quality of your product.
63. After hesitating, propose a very slight price reduction.
64. Disagree with their assessment about the price of your product.
65. Thank them for their time and leave.
66. Drop your price markedly to get the account even though you will not make a profit.
67. Become angry and let them know you are offended by their suggestion to lower your price.
68. Agree that the price may seem high, but then show them how it is in fact quite competitive.
69. Do not lower your price, but make a series of follow-up calls to try to change their minds.

8. You are a local sales representative for a major manufacturer of electric razors. Sales of your razors really explode during the holiday buying season. Due to a shipping delay that resulted when truck drivers unexpectedly went on strike, one of your major customers, a retail chain, received their shipment at the very end of the holiday buying season. As a result, the retail chain has a vast oversupply of razors that it will be unable to sell. To make matters worse, there was a price reduction in the razors after the holidays, so the retail chain paid more for the razors than it would if it bought them now.

A representative from the retail chain has called you angrily about the matter, and demands satisfaction. Rate the quality of the following responses you might make, on the following scale. Please remember to read all of the items before responding.

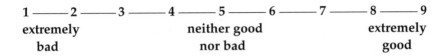

1 ——— 2 ——— 3 ——— 4 ——— 5 ——— 6 ——— 7 ——— 8 ——— 9
extremely   neither good   extremely
bad   nor bad   good

70. Apologize to the representative, explain the source of the problem, and suggest that she take the matter up with the shipping company.
71. Apologize to the representative, explain the source of the problem, and transfer the call to the shipping department in your own company.
72. Offer to take back all of the razors.
73. Ask the representative to accept a price adjustment on the razors that is halfway between the old and new price.
74. Check with your supervisor before making any offers that might fix the problem.
75. Apologize to the representative, explain the source of the problem, and tell the representative that you will see what you can do about the problem.
76. Ask what your company can do to rectify the situation.
77. Offer a special price on future orders if the customer will keep the order they received.

TACIT KNOWLEDGE FOR MILITARY LEADERS

Sample Questions from Platoon, Company, and Battalion Inventories

OVERVIEW AND INSTRUCTIONS

This survey was developed as part of the Tacit Knowledge in Military Leadership project to measure the practical, action-oriented knowledge that Army leaders acquire on the job. The project's main objectives were to identify the important lessons of experience that enable officers to be effective leaders and to use that knowledge to enhance leadership development.

This survey consists of descriptions of typical situations encountered by military leaders. After each situation, there are several options for how to handle the situation. For each option listed, you are to rate the quality of the option on the following 1 to 9 scale:

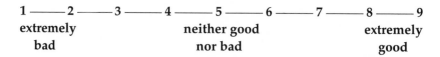

| 1 ——— 2 ——— 3 ——— 4 ——— 5 ——— 6 ——— 7 ——— 8 ——— 9 |
| extremely   neither good   extremely |
| bad   nor bad   good |

Select the number corresponding to your answer, and write it in the blank preceding the option (or on the answer sheet provided). Remember that some or all of the options listed for a particular question may be good, some or all of the options may be bad, or some or all of the options may be neutral (neither bad nor good). There is no one "right answer," and in fact there may be no "right answers." The options are simply things an officer at this level might do in the situa-

Inventories are available on request from the first author or the U.S. Army Research Institute.

tion described. Please rate each individual option for its quality in achieving the goal or solving the problem described in the question. Do not try to "spread out your ratings" just for the sake of doing so. If you think all of the options are good, bad, or whatever, rate them accordingly. DO NOT BE CONCERNED if the numbers are all 9s, all 5s, all 1s, one 9 and the rest 1s, or any other mix. Your answers should reflect your opinions about the quality of the options.

SAMPLE QUESTION FROM PLATOON LEADER INVENTORY

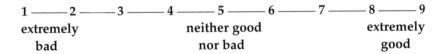

| 1 —— 2 —— 3 —— 4 —— 5 —— 6 —— 7 —— 8 —— 9 |
| extremely bad | neither good nor bad | extremely good |

You are a new platoon leader. The battalion you support is preparing to conduct a night move. You assemble your platoon and tell everyone to start packing equipment in preparation for the move that same night. When you come back to inspect their movement preparation, you find that your soldiers have not packed the equipment and are talking to personnel from other platoons, who are hanging around the area. What should you do?

—— Order the soldiers from other platoons to leave the area.

—— Take charge of the situation, get your unit moving, then talk to the NCOs to bring the chain of command online.

—— Tell the soldiers exactly what you want done and when you will return to reinspect.

—— Assemble your entire platoon and tell them that their work priorities are not on target.

—— Remind soldiers of the time urgency and the need to get many things done quickly in preparation for the night move.

—— Use verbal leadership and commands to influence your soldiers.

—— Wait and see if the soldiers do the task later on their own.

—— Assemble your squad leaders and talk about the situation.

——— Speak to the soldiers in a friendly manner without emphasizing your authority as their leader.
——— Warn the platoon sergeant that you will consider using pun-
ishment (such as an Article 15) if the platoon does not pull
things together immediately.

SAMPLE QUESTION FROM COMPANY COMMANDER
INVENTORY

1 ——— 2 ——— 3 ——— 4 ——— 5 ——— 6 ——— 7 ——— 8 ——— 9
extremely   neither good   extremely
   bad   nor bad   good

You are a new company commander. The previous commander was a
micromanager. This individual was extremely detail-oriented, gave
very little positive feedback, and often tore down the platoon leaders
when even the slightest infraction occurred. For example, the old company commander noted one day that one of the platoon leaders was
wearing a dirty soft-cap, and he called the entire platoon a disgrace.
This behavior on the part of the outgoing company commander was
very hard on the platoon leaders. Several developed nervous conditions such as ulcers and sleep problems. Your goal is to create a more
positive leadership atmosphere in the unit. What should you do?

——— Give all unit members more responsibility than they had
before, and hold them accountable.
——— When you must give negative feedback to your platoon
leaders, do so constructively, pointing out specific areas that
need improvement and explaining how this improvement
can be achieved.
——— Allow the platoon leaders and their soldiers the benefit of
the doubt – don't jump to negative conclusions.
——— Assign work goals with clear milestones to all officers.
——— Involve senior NCOs in the decision-making process.
——— Give the platoon leaders frequent, specific positive feedback.
——— Continue with the micromanagement style since it is common practice in the company, and relieve and/or replace the
lieutenants who cannot handle the stress.

——— Let your subordinates know your intent and then let them develop their own plans.

——— Recognize soldiers' achievements with awards.

——— Have positive expectations: State often that you believe that every member of the unit has the ability to perform well if he or she applies himself or herself and works hard.

SAMPLE QUESTION FROM BATTALION COMMANDER INVENTORY

1 ——— 2 ——— 3 ——— 4 ——— 5 ——— 6 ——— 7 ——— 8 ——— 9
extremely   neither good   extremely
bad   nor bad   good

You are a battalion commander, and you want to make sure that your soldiers and junior officers share your vision for the battalion. Rate the effectiveness of the following strategies for communicating your vision to your unit.

——— Distribute your command philosophy in writing to all soldiers in your battalion.

——— Reinforce your vision in all daily activities and interactions, and do so for the entire term of your command.

——— Do not adhere to a single perspective – be willing to change your vision as necessary to reflect changing needs of the unit.

——— On a daily basis, visit company areas in the garrison and in the field, and highlight shortcomings and the progress that has been made toward achieving your vision.

——— Communicate your vision starting on the first day of your command.

——— Reward those who support your vision, and punish those who don't.

——— Solicit feedback and ideas from your junior officers regarding your vision – be alert for ways to improve it.

Index

Ability model, of emotional
intelligence, 87
Abstract reasoning tests, 1
Academic intelligence, *vs.* practical
intelligence
case examples of, 32–3, 35–7
college students and, tacit
knowledge research on,
155–6
practical intellectual skills and, 32,
221–2
practical problem solving,
defined, 33–4
social intelligence and, 221
behavioral measurement of,
80–2
nonverbal measurement of,
82–7
Academic psychologists, 145–7
Achievement tests, 1
vs. intelligence tests, 123–4
ACT* (A Cognitive Theory), of skill
acquisition, 6–7, 27
Age factors
action space of problem solving
and, 42
cognitive measures and, 40–1
content of practical problem
solving and, 50–1
cross-sectional *vs.* longitudinal
study design and, 39

fluid *vs.* crystallized abilities and,
39, 41–2
goals of practical problem solving
and, 51–2
interindividual variability and,
39–40
management tacit knowledge
and, 154
mechanics *vs.* pragmatics of
intelligence and, 42
in perceiving intelligence, 16
potential plasticity, reserve
capacity and, 44–5
in practical intelligence
development, 36–7, 38–46
primary *vs.* secondary problem
solving strategies and, 52–4
problem interpretation and, 54–6
selection, optimization,
compensation techniques
and, 42–3
strategies of practical problem
solving and, 52–4
tacit knowledge and, 43–4
wisdom and, 60
Appositional information
processing, 22
Apprehension of experience
principle, of cognition, 25
ARI (U.S. Army Research Institute),
xii

279